FACTUAL FICTIONS

FACTUAL FICTIONS

The Origins of the English Novel

LENNARD J. DAVIS

PENN

University of Pennsylvania Press
Philadelphia

Originally published 1983 by Columbia University Press
Copyright © 1983 Columbia University Press
Preface to 1996 edition copyright © 1996 Lennard J. Davis
Printed in the United States of America on acid-free paper

10 9 8 7 6 5 4 3 2 1

Published by
University of Pennsylvania Press
Philadelphia, Pennsylvania 19104-6097

Library of Congress Cataloging-in-Publication Data

Davis, Lennard J., 1949–
    Factual fictions : the origins of the English novel / Lennard J. Davis.
        p.   cm.
    Originally published: New York : Columbia University Press, 1983.
    Includes bibliographical references (p.   ) and index.
    ISBN 0-8122-1610-5 (pbk. : alk. paper)
    1. English fiction—18th century—History and criticism.   2. English fiction—
Early modern, 1500-1700—History and criticism.   3. Literature and history—
England—History.   4. Books and reading—England—History.
5. Journalism—England—History.   6. Fiction—Technique.   I. Title.
PR851.D3   1997
823'.509—dc20   96-38572
                                                                          CIP

To Bella and Carlo

CONTENTS

ACKNOWLEDGMENTS

I WOULD LIKE to thank Edward Said for his continuing advice, inspiration, and encouragement over many years—his help, instruction, and friendship are part of the deep structure of this work. Steven Marcus' careful and demanding reading of the book in its early form was extremely helpful. I am grateful to those others who have commented on the book or discussed ideas with me, among whom are Quentin Anderson, Homer Brown, Richard Ohmann, Brent Harold, Julian Moynihan, Richard McCoy, Allan Mintz, Susan Staves, and Louise Yelin. My thanks to Daniel Casey, Jennifer Crewe, Sue Dapkins, and Gary Stephens, who helped with proofreading and editing. The Andrew W. Mellon Faculty Fellowship at Harvard provided a free year and access to an excellent library system. Finally, I thank Bella Mirabella whose advice, encouragement, and love carried both myself and an unborn child through the best of times and the worst of times.

PREFACE TO THE
PAPERBACK EDITION

W hen *Factual Fictions* appeared in print, it was the first book to apply Michel Foucault's work to the novel and to look at the genre as a discursive practice. While that claim may hardly seem radical now, some of the criticism the book received initially was very much a reaction to the assumption that literary matters were imbricated in a discourse of power, and that the literary could be expanded to include popular fiction, ballads, newspapers, historical accounts, and so on. Tellingly, a critic in *Novel* attacked *Factual Fictions* for having "ignored or slighted much of the important work that has gone before (such as the Defoe studies by Starr and Hunter) and [having] unduly emphasized Foucault's importance" (285). For that reviewer, as for many people at the time, Foucault was simply not important, merely a presumptuous, solipsistic French interloper whose work would never last.

However, my interest in structuralism was fired up by this new way of looking at texts, culture, knowledge. The borders of study expanded away from the analysis of a particular text to an exhilarating if risky attempt to understand an entire paradigm of knowing. Marxism and structuralism initially appeared opposed to one another—the former offering a known political analysis, the latter appearing objective, scientific, and purely interpretative. But Foucault and Althusser both combined structuralism and marxism to create an analysis of power and knowledge. My work on the novel, following this inclusion of structuralism in a marxist analysis, began as a structuralist endeavor and ended up as a materialist one. The work itself bears the traces of that transition—beginning with binary oppositions and ending with ideology. I eventually came to see my project as providing a material analysis for semiotic categories.

In rereading *Factual Fictions* for this new edition, I can see its strengths and weaknesses. The main assertions that the book made strike me as still essentially correct and are ones that have not been seriously disputed in subsequent scholarship. Indeed, many of them have been taken for essential facts about the novel, although when I made them they were hardly so. These are that the novel and journalism are intricately interconnected, perhaps more interconnected than the novel and romance; that cultural attitudes toward fact and fiction shifted during the early modern period; that this shift was influenced by an increasing legal pressure to distinguish levels of proof, veracity, and evidence; that the rise of print culture created new categories of textuality that provoked problems in distinguishing levels of veracity; that there was an interconnection between criminality and fictionality which novels had to try to refute; and finally that the culture enforced this new relation between fact and fiction by isolating narrative forms—news, novels, history—based on their presumed relation to veracity.

My work is not without its flaws. What the work does not do very well is explain why this process happened on a larger scale. Why did capitalist society need to enforce this distinction between the factual and the factitious? By relying heavily on Foucault's work, I found myself facing some of the same problems he did, particularly around the issue of causality in the dispersion of power. If I were to rewrite this book, I would add some of the explanations I provided in *Resisting Novels: Fiction and Ideology* (London and New York: Methuen, 1987), particularly notions about the utility of facts, their cultural capital, as it were, and the development of a consumer society in which a production of fiction could become the thin edge of the wedge of what would eventually make possible the media and entertainment industry.

Feminists will note that this book, while one of the few works on the early novel at this time to include writers like Davys, Haywood, Manley, and Behn, nevertheless lacks a sustained feminist focus. Likewise, there is little mention of the postcolonial, queer theory, or racial and ethnic issues. To these latter points I can only indicate the exigencies and constraints of my historical moment and subject position. Fortunately, so many works are available now that treat the significance of gender roles in eighteenth-century fiction that it is hardly necessary to list them here.

Since *Factual Fictions* was published, several significant books have added to or contended with our knowledge of the beginning of the novel. Nancy Armstrong's *Desire and Domestic Fiction: A Political History of the Novel* (Oxford: Oxford University Press, 1987) remains an important work, having applied Foucault's notion of surveillance and his work on the relation between sexuality and power to the rise of the domestic woman as a character in the novel as well as the deployment of domesticity as an object of construction in the novel and culture at large. Armstrong's linking of gender to Foucault and to the novel produced an important step toward fully understanding the novel as a form of cultural symbolic production.

John Bender's *Imagining the Penitentiary: Fiction and the Architecture of Mind in Eighteenth-Century England* (Chicago: University of Chicago Press, 1987) moves the Foucauldian critique in another direction by focusing on Foucault's work regarding the prison and the gaze. This approach allows Bender to regard the development of the penitentiary, with concomitant notions of individual reform and subjectivity linked to the panoptic gaze of civil and juridical power, as a process linked to the development of the novel. The novel, in turn, is seen as a kind of panopticon that allows readers to observe characters, many of whom in the eighteenth-century novel are indeed criminals who do repent, develop their possessive individualism before our eyes.

Michael McKeon's *The Origins of the Novel, 1600–1740* (Baltimore: Johns Hopkins University Press, 1987) merits discussion, although it is not at all interested in Foucault. Rather, the work brings a dialectical model of development to this discussion through the use of traditional marxist concepts. McKeon sees the novel as arising from a negation of aristocratic values characterized as "romance idealism" by scientific rationality characterized as "naive historicism." The result of this negation is the new discourse of the novel characterized as "extreme skepticism." The plots of various novels are seen in terms of "progressive" and "conservative" re-actions to the uneven development of bourgeois hegemony over aristocratic rule.

Catherine Gallagher's *Nobody's Story: The Vanishing Acts of Women Writers in the Marketplace, 1670–1820* (Berkeley: University of California Press, 1995) brings a leftist, feminist analysis to the issues of fact and fiction, news and novels, textuality and authorship, consumer culture, authorial disavowal, and economics. The work takes up some of the issues raised by *Factual Fictions*, but brings them to quite a different focus, to the benefit of both books.

Spectrally anterior to all these works is *The Rise of the Novel* (Berkeley: University of California Press, 1964), by Ian Watt. While I tried to drive a stake into the heart of that study in the beginning of *Factual Fictions*, Watt's work still lives. I now can acknowledge the anxiety of influence that drove my individualized primal horde at-tack on that work. *The Rise of the Novel* made a serious contribution to the development of novel studies by implying that social and eco-nomic issues had a dramatic impact on the development of the novel. In this sense, Watt was doing for the novel what Raymond Williams was also doing—applying the lessons of sociology and economics to literary forms. That achievement must be recognized.

I hope that this reissue of my book will provoke a new con-sideration of what has become "the origins of the novel discourse." In some sense, all these scholarly accounts have created a collective argument, part of a larger vision of the way society deploys symbolic discourse for the regulation of the body, social class, and produc-tion. Each argues for a slightly different notion of origin, but they also argue together from the vision of a generation of scholars in the last fifty years of the millennium. Whatever confluences are found define a way of seeing and a vision of early modern culture that are different from anything that preceded this analysis. In that sense, I see *Factual Fictions* as part of a shared vision of the novel's relation to power, culture, language, and politics.

Toward a Methodology of Beginnings

S PECULATIONS ON BEGINNINGS tend to take the form of riddles. Some literary genres seem to have had no beginnings. Or at least their beginnings were so buried in human prehistory as to be indiscernible. Thespis was surely no more the originator of drama than Homer was the innovator of the epic or Sappho the mother of the lyric. We have turned to the Greeks out of our need to establish beginnings, to create order and continuity. "Continuous history," writes Michel Foucault, "is the indispensable correlative of the founding function of the subject."[1] That is, the subject, human consciousness, needs to create the notion of continuous history in order to establish itself and its legitimacy. Or, as Edward Said has written in *Beginnings*, the notion of a beginning is "designated in order to indicate, clarify, or define a *later* time, place, or action.[2] Thus we find in the Greeks no true origin, but a mythical template, as it were, through which we trace our desire for an origin.

In contrast to these literary genres without discernible beginnings, there are those that appear to have had quite identifiable beginnings, which we can locate if only we can discover the proper method. The novel, the cinema, and the newspaper are three narrative forms which seem to have begun in some knowable past. The problem is that though these beginnings are within archaeological grasp, they are not clear and luminous; rather they are shrouded in minor details, obscure technological innovations, and problematic chains of causality. As in the case of those genres without discernible beginnings, the particular methodology chosen by those in the present to reveal, to explicate, to exhume these hidden, past moments of origination reveal what Foucault referred to as the "founding function of the subject." For a moment, I would like to look at these various methodologies which try to account for the beginnings of the novel and see what their ideologies reveal.

The first and preeminent notion in any methodology of beginnings is that of the threshold. That is, at what historical moment does narrative, for example, become what we can call novelistic? In investigating such a concept of threshold, we are really asking what are the limits of the novelistic discourse, and attempting to see those limits at their historical moment of establishment. In other words, we are asking what the fundamental elements of the novel are, and how readers would have been able to recognize a particular act of writing as a novel and not as one of a variety of other forms such as romance, history, or tale.

If one looks at the history of novel criticism, there seem to be at least three dominant and, as it were, unconscious methodologies for arriving at the threshold for the novel. I have called these the evolutionary model, the osmotic model, and the convergent model.

The evolutionary model is perhaps the most pervasive one. In literary critical works which search for forerunners, precursors, embryos, and missing links the underlying metaphor is a phylogenetic one. To take an example, Robert Scholes and Robert Kellogg in their book *The Nature of Narrative* avoid, in a sense, the whole question of the novel's beginning by attempting to decenter the novel as the dominant form to which all earlier narrative forms inevitably lead. To do this they broaden their terms so that the novel is only a branch on the evolutionary tree of narrative. However, in the process of displacing the particularity of the novel's beginnings to its roots in general narrative, at the same time they displace the beginning of narrative to some unnameable past point of origin. Scholes and Kellogg give the widest latitude to the term "narrative," defining it in a specifically nonliterary way as simply "the presence of a story and a story teller." Thus, the origin is in effect displaced to "as many as a million years ago [when] man first repeated an utterance which had given pleasure to himself or someone else, and thereby invented literature."[3] Unlike the Greeks, who attributed narrative authority to Homer, Scholes and Kellogg place the origin of their genre almost contemporaneously with the beginning of man. This neolithic, anonymous moment of origination assigns a biological, if not ethological, significance to narrative (and one might add to the genre of literary criticism as well—since that first caveman's auditor grunted what amounted to a meta-textual statement in reply). If narrative can be seen as synonymous with human evolution then, as Scholes and Kellogg say, "the evolution of forms within the narrative tradition is a process analogous in some ways to biological evolution."[4] Their technique here is to see how narrative, as a biological homologue, changed over thousands of years. The novel's arrival on the scene in the seventeenth century then, must be seen in a similar light to the appearance of mammals in the late Mesozoic period.

Ernest Baker in his massive *History of the English Novel* also sees the novel's form as having undergone an "anterior process of evolution." Further, borrowing from the biological dictum which states that *ontogeny recapitulates philogeny*, Baker writes that "the phenomenon of surreptitious growth and gradual mutation that characterised the history of ancient fiction [pre–Anglo-Saxon] will be repeated in the development of the modern novel. . . ."[5] The structuring metaphor for this statement works from the idea that fiction in general underwent an evolutionary process which the English novel in particular repeats during a kind of gestation period. In short, says Baker, "the early history of the novel is the history of something that is not yet the novel."[6] In this paradox of intentionality the truth of the evolutionary model is laid bare—that the protonovel is a nascent, non-thing which waits larvae—like and vaguely formed for its predestined slouch toward Grub Street to be born complete and finished into the world of literature.

One final example: English Showalter in *The Evolution of the*

French Novel is the most specifically Darwinian of the evolutionary critics. He notes that some literary elements in a genre will triumph over others because "certain elements had greater fitness for survival than others." Showalter paints a picture of an antediluvian literary world filled with lumbering "gigantic romances of the 17th century [which] resembled dinosaurs" heading for "extinction. . . . At the same time, the early ancestors of the modern novel were toiling away in obscurity, profiting from their insignificance to adapt better and faster to new conditions."[7] In Showalter, the evolutionary model reaches its most explicit and direct exposition. The genus warfare between dinosaurs and mammals is paralleled precisely by the genre struggle between romance and novel. All that is needed is a literary Watson and Crick to decode the double helix of character and plot.

The obvious flaw in using the evolutionary model for literary analysis is that its metaphor implies a slow, progressive change based on the key biological notion of adaptation. But there is no necessity for literary works to be guided by either slow change or adaptation. In nature, radical mutations usually die, but in literature the radical is frequently the best adapted to survive. Indeed, Dr. Johnson was never so wrong as when he said "Nothing odd will do long" in reference to *Tristram Shandy*, as Sterne's last, sepulchral laugh proves. Moreover, literary forms are not organized by genus and species, and do not share homologous anatomical features. It is not as if we can find the forerunners of the novel by tracing back from horselike narrative to an eohippuslike narrative. The problem, of course, is that in the attempt to find precursors, one must select among a diversity of printed texts and assert that some texts are forebears of the novel, belonging to the same genus but slightly differing species, while other texts are not forebears at all. Such a principle of selection presupposes a recognizable, preeminent consanguity or homology between the novel and its precursors. But the principle of selection used is itself not a neutral one; the criteria for choosing the supposed precursor can stack the deck so that these precursors will seem to lead *inevitably* from primitive narrative structure to the fully realized form of the novel. The myth of the evolutionary critic, as Foucault reveals it, is "to discover already at work in each beginning, a principle of coherence and the line of future unity. . . ."[8] Again, the problem is one of intentionality, seeking an origin to establish a principle of order.

This problem of intentionality is strongly suggested in the title of Ian Watt's classic book *The Rise of the Novel*. There are two notions at work in the title—one of erection, of construction, and the other of triumph, of dominance. In the first, the novel is seen as slowly growing out of some unnamed and unnameable foundation, and taking its place on a site predestined and cleared for it. The conceptual space exists, and the novel only needs to rise and fill it. One is not dealing with evolution here, but with an entirely new structure built on its own foundation. In the second sense of the title—triumph, dominance—there is also a signification of destiny and of power. Both of these concepts imply a hidden, guiding hand directing a confluence of forces toward an inevitable conclusion. And behind the strong intentionality lies the assumption of a necessity—a chain of necessary causes and effects—leading to the origin and hegemony of the novel.

Concealed further within the notion of a rising structure is the idea of the foundation. The use of this metaphor of foundation interferes sharply with or redefines any attempt to talk about origins. Threshold is displaced to foundation. Therefore, Watt does not discuss to any great extent the foundation of the novel—that is to say, the considerable history of early novels in the seventeenth and eighteenth centuries. Instead, he moves rapidly to the Defoes, Richardsons, and Fieldings—those who are prominent participators in the rising of the novel. The question of origin is left somewhat buried in the muck at the bottom of the foundation.

While the methodology of Scholes and Kellogg seems avowedly evolutionary and linear, Watt's general approach is what I would call "osmotic." That is, many of the dominant themes of philosophy and culture are seen as permeating, in rather undefined ways, the structure of narrative and changing it. Consequently, in Watt we

often read lines like "soon the modern sense of time began to per-
meate areas of thought," or "literary change was analogous to the
rejection of universals."[9] Here one finds oneself in the world of
seepages, contaminations, influences, and other unspecified, gen-
eralized causes of change.

The model of osmotic permeability applies particularly to
Watt's use of sociology. The model implies that a profound change
in society should effect an analogous profound change in narrative.
Such a conjecture has the virtue of being basically unprovable and
self-evident. Has capitalism changed narrative? Certainly. But one
wants to know: In what way? By what chain of causality? Although
Watt is hardly reductionist, he ultimately does not supply us with
these micro connections between sociological speculations and literary structural realignments. He often does not show the reader
any necessary connection between, say, a larger, middle-class reading public and a structural change in narrative. Does an expanded
reading public *necessarily* lead to the literary form we call the novel?
To link sociological observation to literary structures in this osmotic
way demands, again, a strong intentionality—a bold yoking of
cause and effect, without necessarily proving the grounds for that
yoking. Again we recall the guiding hand, but in the osmotic model,
the effect is synchronic—whereas in the evolutionary model one
is clearly talking about a diachronic influence. The osmotic model
presents a picture in which a given structural change in society at
a particular historical moment will create a related change in literary
structures.

A third model available to the historian of the novel is best
illustrated by Phillip Stevick in his *The Theory of the Novel* when he
writes that the novel's origins "lie in a dozen different narrative
forms: essay, romance, history, the 'character' biography, comic
and sentimental drama, and so on."[10] The admission here is that
the novel really comes out of *everything* that preceded it. This notion
can be called "convergence" since a variety of forms are seen as
converging into one discrete genre, yet there is no motive given for
this convergence. In this explanation, the novel was not destined

to evolve in a linear fashion, as in the evolutionary model, nor to be affected by social forces, as in the osmotic model, but somehow to happily agglutinate into existence by taking on the best features of disparate forms such as the essay, the history, and so on. This convergence model is clearly nonevolutionary in nature since one could hardly say of the tortoise that it randomly combined the best features of the boulder, the snake, and the fish.

The problem with the convergence model is the absence of any intentionality at all. There is no reason for these disparate types of writing to suddenly clump together. Why should Isaac Bickerstaff suddenly have left the contemplative pages of *The Spectator* and taken to the open road? At what point could Samuel Pepys have turned self-conscious and become a Henry Fielding or, worse, a Laurence Sterne? The absence of an explanatory mechanism for causality or threshold in the convergence model makes it the incomplete and opposite argument from the osmotic model which suggests intentionality without specifying its mode of operation.

Evolution, osmosis, convergence—these three models are by no means the only ones available to literary historians, but they do seem to have been powerfully available ways of conceptualizing the beginning of a genre. If, as I have been suggesting, these models are inadequate because the metaphors upon which they are based are inappropriate, what can replace them? The model I am favoring in this study relies partially on the work of Michel Foucault. The novel, as such, is seen not as a biological entity, nor a convergent phenomenon, but as discourse—that is, in Foucault's usage, the ensemble of written texts that constitute the novel (and in so doing define, limit, and describe it). This ensemble by no means includes only novels and literary criticism, but may include parliamentary statutes, newspapers, advertisements, printer's records, handbills, letters, and so on. In opening the field in this way, it is possible to trace a discourse which may be considerably wider, with different limits and rules than our modern conceptions of fiction and the novel would allow us to apply to the eighteenth century. The evolutionary and osmotic models have for the most part confined their field of study to uniquely fictional works; and the convergent model allowed so many different types of writing that any categorizing itself would seem irrelevant. The aim here is to find the categories and taxonomies that a reader of the seventeenth and eighteenth centuries might have used—even unconsciously—to divide up the whole range of texts we now call narrative.

The grand categories of literary taxonomy—fact/fiction, prose/poetry, printed/unprinted, history/fabrication, fantasy/representation—are not to be taken as simply logical, self-evident ways of classifying narrative, but are to be seen as themselves subjective and highly contextualized. Far from being intrinsic and autochthonous ways of seeing literature, they are part of a general ideological system, a system, one might add, that was by and large unknowable to those within it. As such, these categories themselves are the objects of our study. The aim is to understand the system of order that exists among texts, as well as between texts and society.

In looking at texts, one needs to see not merely what they say, but what they do not say. The unsaid frequently can tell us more than the obviously stated. In this sense, the observer must act like the psychoanalyst who discovers the order of the patient's unconscious in the disorder of free association—in what is repressed, mistakenly said, or denied. Likewise, the literary critic can arrive at the unconscious assumptions, presuppositions, rules, categories, and limits of a discourse by observing what the texts cannot say or are restricted from saying. For example, in the early novel, authors almost always claim to be writing factual accounts rather than fictional ones. Their explanation for doing this is by and large nonexistent since their prefaces preclude any discussion of the subject by the very process of establishing their lie. If we can understand the function of what cannot be said, much can be learned about the early novel's structure.

In using Foucault's notion of discourse, the problem of intentionality is not removed, but at least it is blunted and, to some extent, defined. Since one is not looking for cause and effect, for linear influence, but rather for ruptures and transformations, the question of influence is redefined. Even with a disjunctive history, the problem of change and necessity is still with us. Foucault addresses this problem by saying that changes in discourses need to be analyzed as changes in "tactics or strategies of power."[11] He sounds a socio-political note and, as Edward Said has commented, discourse is not merely a collection of texts that a critic may describe and analyze but is a signifier occupying a strategic place in the structure of power relations. The text or ensemble of texts amounts to, according to Said, "an act of will with ascertainable political and intellectual consequences and an act fulfilling a strategic desire to administer and comprehend a vast and detailed field of material."[12] In this view, the novel is seen as a discourse for reinforcing particular ideologies, and its coming into being must be seen as tied to particular power relations which this book will attempt to explore.

The problem of intentionality is still with us, even in this model. But the question is at least addressed and put into focus. Changes in the order of discourse are a reaction to complex and shifting power relations, as power itself is subject to the weight of the order of discourse. Thus, the ungrounded intentionality of the evolutionary and convergence models are replaced by a rather special kind of historical materialism—special because, it seems to me, the method does not reduce the work of art to a symptom of the age, but rather points out the equality of strategic desires in both the work of art and the act of power. Each makes the other intelligible, and each shares with the other, in some profound and complex sense, the reins of power.

One caution here and throughout this study: when the words "fact" and "fiction" are used, they are not defining two distinct and unimpeachable categories. They are more properly extremes of a continuum. "Truth and falsehood," Northrop Frye writes, "are not literary categories and are only approximately verbal ones. For the literary critic, at all events, everything in words is plasmatic, and truth and falsehood represent the direction or tendencies in which verbal structures go, or are thought to go."[3] To this extent, perceptions, experience, fantasy, and belief are all gradations on the same scale. If humans treat these arbitrary categories as clearly defined, it is because we are habituated to their use. When in the course of this work I do use these terms without qualification, the reader should recall that I am talking about what amounts to our shared conceptions about these categories. Also, the idea that fact and fiction were not significant discriminants of genre during the seventeenth century should not be construed as meaning that the citizen of the Early Modern period was walking around in a permanent state of ontological fuzziness and uncertainty. No judgment is being made about the nature of perception and reality here, rather these observations concerning fact and fiction apply strictly to the limited sphere of printed narrative.

CHAPTER I

Frame, Context, Prestructure

THE GAUNT FIGURE of a man on a horse, out of place and out of time, seems to cast his shadow over any discussion of the European novel. *Don Quixote* has become the habitual point from which to begin the quest. Critics are attracted by the play between illusion and reality, by the boldness and humanity of the characters, the commentary on literature and on the death of the chivalric romance, the beginning of the antihero as an archetype, and so on. Here begins novelistic homelessness and wandering, inaugurated by this errant knight whose only real home was between the pages of romance. Cervantes has come down to us as the seminal novelist from whose line springs the rambunctious Fielding, the iconoclastic Thackery, the prodigious Dickens, and the thousands of others whose life's work it has been to produce novels.

Yet I would like to suggest at the outset that *Don Quixote* should not be considered a novel in the same sense as the novels of Defoe, Richardson, Fielding—perhaps should not even be considered a novel at all. Such a statement is likely to provoke legions of Quixote's followers to take up arms against the windmills of my assertion, and in defense I should add that *Don Quixote* is undoubtedly a work which has its novelistic qualities, as we may call them with the benefit of hindsight. The work is long; it has a continuous, well-defined, central hero or two; it has psychological depth, an episodic plot, and realistic details. The novelistic qualities are impressive, yet it lacks certain crucial elements which would clinch its existence as a novel. This statement is not a literary judgment, but rather it is an historical observation. It will be the burden of the rest of this study to prove the soundness of that observation. At this point, it should suffice to say that the novels of the seventeenth and eighteenth centuries have a unique and characteristic attitude toward fact and fiction, toward external reality and the nature of their own authenticity, and toward previous literary forms which *Don Quixote* does not seem to share. *Don Quixote* is not part of this new and self-conscious genre and was barely referred to as part of that genre by writers of novels until resurrected by Fielding in the mid-eighteenth century. Probably, it is simply a long and unusual piece of storytelling which ultimately may rest genreless, a tribute to uniqueness and individuality, a defiance of discourse.

In order to begin an explanation of the difference, at least superficially, between *Don Quixote* and later novels, it might be instructive to compare Cervantes' work with *Roxana* (1724) by Daniel Defoe. Cervantes wrote his book between 1604 and 1614, and Defoe wrote his some hundred years later. There are obvious differences in the audience for these books—differences of readers, classes, and cultures. But the difference on which I wish to focus is one of expectation. Books come to readers who have specific expectations of what they are going to be reading, what a narrative is or should be, what they will need to have in such a narrative, and so on. This expectation, this totality of elements in the presentation of a book, is itself significant and important to my purpose in determining the total structure of a work. One might conceive of this expectation as a kind of conceptual aura, a presentational context, which surrounds the book as object and which for the sake of convenience I will call the "prestructure" of the work. The term is used to indicate that this presentational context is actually as much a part of the work as the elements of plot, character, development, and so on. A modern equivalent that might illustrate the point is the bestseller which is immediately recognized by its appearing in four separate and different covers, each shiny and electric as it stands before a cardboard display in a bookstore window. Such a vision will bring to a reader a host of associations that are quite different than the associations derived by viewing a jacketless black textbook on accounting. The graphic fanfare of the bestseller—although ultimately unrelated to the actual text—must be said to be part of the general set of impressions that add up to the complete novel.

In the cases of *Don Quixote* and *Roxana*, the prestructure of each work differs profoundly from that of the other. Don Quixote has his head buried in chivalric romances, both literally and figuratively, while Roxana has hers peering somewhat metaphorically from behind a catchpenny ballad or pamphlet about a criminal. Cervantes' readers would be expected to be familiar with romances like *Amadis of Gaul*, whereas readers of Defoe would be more familiar with the tales of criminals that they had read in their daily or weekly newspapers. These differences are not to be treated lightly, and works cannot be compared as if they were equal just because they are able to be placed side-by-side on a bookshelf. Compare for example the prefaces to these two works. Cervantes wrote:

> Idle reader, you can believe without any oath of mine that I would wish this book, as the child of my brain, to be the most beautiful, the liveliest, and the cleverest imaginable. But I have been unable to transgress the order of nature, by which like gives birth to like. And so, what could my sterile and ill-cultivated genius beget but the story of a lean, shriveled, whimsical child, full of varied fancies that no one else has ever imagined. . . .[1]

A comparable passage in the opening pages of *Roxana* reads:

> The history of this beautiful lady, is to speak for itself: if it is not as beautiful as the lady herself is reported to be; if it is not as diverting as the reader can desire, and much more than he can reasonably expect; and if all the most diverting parts of it are not adapted to the instruction and improvement of the reader, the relator says it must be from the defect of his performance; dressing up the story in worse clothes than the lady, whose words he speaks, prepared it for the world.

>   He takes the liberty to say that this story differs from most of
> the modern performances of this kind, though some of them have
> met with a very good reception in the world: I say, it differs from
> them in this great and essential article, namely that the foundation
> of this is laid in truth of fact, and so the work is not a story, but
> a history.[2]

There are several important differences between these works.
The first is that two entirely different kinds and classes of readers
are being invoked by the authors. Cervantes begins his preface with
an address to the "idle reader." The prestructure of *Don Quixote*
presumes that the projected reader has time on his hands, or is idle
precisely because he is reading. The notion that "reading" is an
equivalent to "languishing" comes as a logical consequence of Cervantes' perception that his book is a mere fiction, "the child of my
brain." If the reader can do no more with his time than to occupy
it with reading whimsical tales "full of varied fancies," then he
must indeed be idle.

More can be inferred about the prestructure of *Don Quixote*.
Cervantes, in mocking the overtly pedantic nature of most books
in fact uses Latin to make some of his jokes. Such usage suggests
that readers of *Don Quixote* in Spanish would also be familiar with
Latin, would probably be well educated, and wealthy if not aristocratic. Even Cervantes' ironical references to the fact that his
book lacks scholarly appurtenances "because of my inadequacy and
scanty learning, and because I am too spiritless and lazy by nature
to go about looking for authors to say for me what I can say myself
without them," indicates a joking anticipation of the kind of criticism from monkish scholars that a book like *Don Quixote*, violating
and mocking the expected scholastic prestructure, would be expected to receive.[3]

The reader of *Roxana*, however, is part of an entirely different
prestructure. No longer is reading an idle pastime; it has become
a valuable activity in itself contributing, according to Defoe, to the
"improvement of the reader." While Cervantes has implied that his
work might be flawed by its lack of erudition, Defoe admits his

work might be flawed too; but this time the flaw is found in the fact that the diverting parts may have strayed from the moralistic intention of the work. Scholasticism has given way to moral edification. Defoe makes no apologies for deficient scholarship, and Latin is a dead language for him. Edification is now to be derived from the work itself and the life of the character, and all readers, not only scholars, can derive moral instruction from this novel. Now, the novel is a text close enough to life to serve as a model.

This distinction between types of readers is linked to another difference between these works. Cervantes freely admits that his work is an act of his own imagination. In fact, this point is not an issue for him. Defoe, however, insists that the foundation of his work is "laid in truth of fact: and so the work is not a story, but a history." It is this claim to verity that allows Defoe's readers to feel as though they are not engaging in mere divertissements but are analyzing and learning from the mistakes of others, seeing God's judgments in all that happens to Roxana.[4] "Most of the modern performances of this kind," by which Defoe presumably means novels, are treated as though they were valueless precisely because to read a fiction would be an idle act. By claiming that his work is founded on truth, Defoe, the journalist par excellence of the early eighteenth century, was treating his novel as if it were virtually indistinguishable in genre from his news writings. Cervantes' work, on the other hand, has no relationship to journalism, being much more connected with the chivalric romances of which it was a parody and a negation.

One objection to what I have been saying so far might be that I am taking too seriously the prefatory statements of the author's intentions. Why not just consider these prefaces as playful conventions which do little more than express the author's whimsy? Perhaps readers just took them with a grain of salt. Such an objection wields a kind of Occam's razor by suggesting that the simplest explanation must be the best, and that to call a literary structure a convention ends the problem. It seems to me, though, that to point to the fact that something is a convention is to leave the basic problem unanswered. To understand a convention more thoroughly one would want to know what the significance of the convention was; what myths upheld it, and what myths it upheld—the aim here being to see what aspects of those conventions were, as it were, unconventional.

In Defoe's denial of the fictionality of his work and in Cervantes' claim that his work is the pure product of his brain, one can see a distinction in the way that each author is connected to his text. Cervantes is powerless to "transgress the order of nature" and so produces a work of a like kind "lean, shriveled, whimsical." Even when Cide Hamete is placed in the role of "author" of *Don Quixote*, we never lose the sense that Cervantes is immanent in the text creating these frames and enjoying them. However, Defoe merely claims to be the relator of an overheard or found story; sometimes he allows himself to be the editor of a document provided by someone else. The author displaces himself from the central, creative role, and by so doing denies his connection to the work. This act of disownment shifts the focus of narrative to the being of the protagonist, to the authenticity of the document, to the verisimilar human life itself. Such a shift, and the distance created by the removal of the author, is uniquely novelistic, while Cervantes' approach is more traditional in the canons of tale-telling.

Although both *Don Quixote* and *Roxana* are intricately framed works with fictional authors—Roxana and Cide Hamete—displacing Cervantes and Defoe, these frames work differently in certain crucial ways. If we consider a moment in both books when the maximum number of frames intercedes between author and plot, it may be possible to focus on the difference between novels and other stories. In both cases this moment of maximum enframing occurs as a result of the abrupt intrusion of reality into the fictional constructs of narrative.

In *Don Quixote*, there is a scene in part two during which the knight comes face to face with his typographical self when he meets the bachelor Sampson Carrasco who tells him that a book has appeared in print entitled *The Ingenious Gentleman Don Quixote De*

La Mancha. The book is none other than part one of the novel by Cervantes. However, Carrasco informs us that this book is written by a Moor, Cide Hamete Benengeli, and translated into Spanish by some unnamed Christian, no doubt Cervantes. Here it would seem Cervantes has placed himself in the same role as Defoe, who claimed to be the mere relator or translator of texts. The situation is not, however, entirely analogous. Defoe places himself outside the novel—into the prestructure—by the gesture of authorial disavowal. Cervantes, on the other hand, situates himself in two places simultaneously—within the novel and outside it. He is both author of the novel, and thus on the peripheries of the tale, and at the same time a fictional character (the translator) within the structure of the work. Cervantes has in effect created a kind of perceptual Möbius strip which runs from Cervantes to Don Quixote to Cide Hamete and back to the Christian translator Cervantes. The return of this strip to Cervantes, however, poses few problems to our sense of reality since it is apparent from the beginning of the work that Cervantes is plainly dealing in fictions. Fictionality permits the author to replicate himself within his work.

Cervantes replicates himself not only here but in other places within the book. When Don Quixote sets out on his journey he thinks how wonderful it will be that his actions will be "carved in marble and painted in wood, as a memorial for posterity." And he adds: "And you, sage enchanter you may be, to whose lot it falls to be the chronicler of this strange history, I beg you not to forget my good Rocinante, my constant companion on all my rides and journeys."[5] Without a scribe accompanying the knight and his squire to record their deeds, there must be a sage enchanter who is aware of all words and actions and who can cause the printed book *Don Quixote* to come about. But the sage enchanter goes beyond recording to actually creating events within the story. For example, when Sancho calls his master "The Knight of the Sad Countenance," Quixote replies that "because the sage whose task it is to write the history of my deeds must have thought it right for me to take some title . . . that is why I say that the sage I mentioned has put it into your thoughts and into your mouth to call me now *The Knight of the Sad Countenance*."[6] The sage enchanter here is both recorder of events and shaper of events, illustrator and illusionist, and is clearly performing the function of author. Cervantes is represented within the text in his capacity to record and to create. As the sage enchanter, Cervantes has introjected his authorial function into the very fabric of the story, and can do this only by virtue of the fact that the reader recognizes that an author is at work on a fiction here. Indeed, one could argue that the sage enchanter is also the enemy of Quixote transforming windmills into dragons, as obviously Cervantes does in the process of making the events of his story. In any case, Cervantes' authorial roles are embodied in the double function of sage narrator and sage enemy. As Quixote says, "What a way that scoundrel of an enchanter, my enemy, has of transforming things and making them invisible!"[7]

Because Cervantes' structure is so much based on the premise that the author is freely fictionalizing, the strange moment in which Don Quixote comes across the book of his own adventures can be easily accepted by the reader. In the same way that Cervantes projected himself into the narrative, now the entire first book of *Don Quixote* has been projected into the story itself. Part one is at once a real object in the world (that is, it has sold a certain number of copies, received wide success, etc.) and yet is a fictional construct (it is not really written by Cide Hamete; it exists only as a representation, etc.). As an object in the world, it has had an effect on Spanish society. Carrasco says of the novel that "children finger it; young people read it; grown men know it by heart, and old men praise it. It is so dog-eared, in fact, and so familiar to all sorts of people that whenever they see a lean horse go by, they cry: 'There goes Rocinante'."[8] Through this warp in the fictional construct, we can perceive that the actual book *Don Quixote* has an existence beyond the confines of the narrative. However, there is an irony here since the real world intrudes into the narrative only to the extent that it is represented by the symbol of a fictional book. This is an irony with which we can feel comfortable in *Don Quixote* since the fact that books do represent the world to the knight is a sign of his deranged condition.

Michel Foucault has pointed out about *Don Quixote* that "between the first and second parts of the novel, in the narrow gap between those two volumes, and by their power alone, Don Quixote has achieved his reality—a reality he owes to language alone, and which resides entirely inside the words."9 It is in the disjunction between the written tale of Don Quixote's story and the introjection of the printed version of that story within the second volume that Cervantes most closely approaches being a novelist, if he does at all. It is only by virtue of the use of typography that *Don Quixote's* reality could possibly outstrip and displace the fictional being of the errant knight himself. At this moment, Cervantes is leaving behind the centuries of tale-telling and moving into a special dynamic between fact and fiction that, I am arguing, is the hallmark of the novel.

Defoe uses a frame similar to that of Cervantes, but the implications of Defoe's structures are quite different from those of *Don Quixote*. In *Roxana* there is a scene comparable to the one I have been discussing in which reality intrudes into the fictional narrative. Roxana is introduced to Sir Robert Clayton, an economist who was an actual acquaintance of Defoe's, and Clayton decides to manage Roxana's financial affairs. He actually increases her wealth considerably and also serves as a kind of marriage broker for her.10 In this scene, as in the one in *Don Quixote*, the fictional character is face to face with a representative of the real world. Because of Defoe's prestructure, however, this situation is radically different from the scene in the other book. Since Defoe presents all events in the novel as real ones "in truth of fact," then for Roxana to meet a real person such as Sir Robert is not at all unusual. The framing devices we have seen in Cervantes' work are apparently absent from the structure of *Roxana*. It is only by examining the prestructure that we can see the conceptual machinery that has been brought to bear on the situation.

First, it might be helpful to introduce a few technical terms borrowed from Erving Goffman's *Frame Analysis*.[11] Goffman's book is particularly useful for discussing the novel because it is concerned precisely with the question of how an event is framed or contextualized. Goffman begins by saying that a unit of activity or action (what he calls a "strip," in keeping with his cinematic metaphor, and which we can regard as corresponding to units of plot) can never be seen or understood correctly outside of its context. Two identical strips, for example, will have radically different meanings depending on the frame which surrounds each one. The sum of all the frames surrounding a work, including the social frames, amounts to what I have been calling the prestructure. In this way, strips are transformed—in an almost Chomskian sense of the word—by successive laminations of frames built up around each strip.

All of this terminology might be brought to bear on the following agoraphobic example. The strip I am imagining is of a man on a window ledge of a very tall building who loses his balance and begins to fall; he manages to catch himself by the fingers of one hand and now hangs precariously. The meaning of this strip varies according to the frames applied to it. If the event is framed by our walking along the street and suddenly looking up, our reaction must be fear, horror, or confusion. If the strip is framed by our being in a movie theater watching a film by Hitchcock, responses might range from surprise, curiosity about the outcome, to annoyance at the theatricality of such a hackneyed device for creating suspense. If the film were made by Charlie Chaplin, one might expect an entirely different sort of response. If the movie theater frame is reframed in such a way that a sociologist were watching the reaction of the movie audience to scenes which exploit agoraphobia, then the observer's response might be one of scientific detachment. The first three examples contain only one frame each. The last one is twice-framed. In addition, to introduce another of Goffman's terms, in the last instance a "fabrication" is taking place. That is, a frame is created in such a way that only some people are aware of its existence. If those in the theater believe that they have been invited to watch a movie while the actual purpose of their visit is to provide an occasion for a sociological experiment, then they are the "dupes" of a fabrication.

This is all well and good, but how does this bit of sociological gamesmanship help explain the difference between *Don Quixote* and *Roxana*? In Cervantes' novel, while some characters are involved in fabrications or are the dupes of fabrications, the reader never is. In Defoe's narrative, however, the butt of the major fabrication is the reader him- or herself who is involved in the con game ostensibly perpetrated by the author who maintains that the novel is not fiction but fact. Cervantes' first frame is merely an introduction to his work; it is the rim of the fictional structure resting on a perimeter of reality. Defoe's first frame, however, is different because it implies a hidden frame that actually precedes the overt "first" frame. Defoe's overt "first" frame, proclaiming "This work is true," is masking a more encompassing actual first frame which states, "This work is really not true." This covert frame, by virtue of its precedence, throws all ensuing strips and frames into a mode of deception and ambiguity. In the same way that one term of a mathematical formula can transform the rest of the terms, so too this covert frame transforms all that follows it. Because the reader is never really certain, as shall be seen, whether the covert frame indeed exists, a state of ambivalence is produced in the reader which extends throughout his or her experience of the novel. (I will discuss this type of ambivalence in more detail in chapters 6,7, and 9).

If the overt first frame of each book is a statement about the factuality or fictionality of the work, then the second frame comes to be erected when the author defines his or her role as either writer or editor. In the case of Cervantes, the first frame envelopes the second without inconsistency. If Don Quixote is an imaginative work, then Cervantes is the author of it, and can also project himself within the work. He may also make statements that are true within the book (that is, within the second frame) but untrue in reality. In short, the author admits to dealing in fictions. With Defoe, however, the second frame, depicting the author as editor, must be accepted as fact since the first frame ("this work is true") insists that all succeeding frames are grounded in reality. When the time comes for the third frame to be laminated onto this structure— when the intrusion of genuine reality is depicted in the narrative— very different situations must result from this transformation. When Sir Robert Clayton enters the elaborated structure of *Roxana*, Defoe's readers are constrained to nod their heads and see no discrepancy between the fictionality of Roxana and the factuality of Clayton. When on the other hand Quixote meets the novel *Don Quixote*, Cervantes establishes the confrontation, exercises his imaginative sense, and pulls the reader into yet another artful lamination of literary framing.

The important idea is that the same strip, the same type of event, which is common to a Spanish narrative of the early seventeenth century and an English novel of the early eighteenth century, can be rendered very differently if the structure of the frames and fabrications are examined in some detail. It is precisely this difference which is crucial to the distinction between the novel and previous narratives in prose.

So far in this discussion I have shied away from mentioning a much more problematic frame which envelops the novelistic enterprise—and that is the frame of the reader's belief. There is an extent to which this frame is part of the prestructure as well. With Cervantes the frame of the reader's belief is largely nonexistent— it coincides with the prestructure for the most part. With Defoe, on the other hand, the reader's belief or disbelief in the overt first frame—that the work is fact—is a crucial element in the way the novel will be perceived. One may imagine several types of readers for the Defoean novel: the eighteenth-century reader who naively accepts the work as factual, the reader of the same period who is uncertain whether the work is true or false, and still another who knows that the work is a fabrication. In addition, there is a more modern reader who has biographical and historical material available which suggests that Defoe's novels were fictional.[12] Except for the purely naïve reading of the text, all of these readers will experience a degree of ambivalence toward the interplay of fact and fiction in the novel.

The reader of either century who recognizes Defoe's fabrication will probably experience the least sense of ambivalence. Yet, the phenomenology of reading is such that this reader must split his perception so that there are two readers—the knowing, collusive reader who winks conspiratorially at Defoe's fabrications, and the gullible, belief-suspending reader. However, the process being discussed here is not simply a willing suspension of disbelief. A suspension of disbelief implies that the reader already knows that the work is fictional and allows himself to believe that the events in the novel *could* have happened or could be happening. The process of reading a Defoean novel is that the reader is asked first to believe that the novel is real (the overt first frame) and then to understand that the reality of the novel is bogus (the covert frame). In effect, suspension of disbelief is itself suspended.

Yet the collusive reader of either century must have the succeeding realization that the truth of any frame established by Defoe must be doubted. In this way, Roxana's narrative is read ironically, her conversion to a religious life is doubted, and Defoe's own ethical motives are put into question. Strangely enough, then, an awareness of the process of fabrication will not remove primary ambivalence but will only create an entirely new level or frame in the prestructure onto which this ambivalence is displaced. For the modern reader, this new level of confusion is the locus for the endlessly generated debates on the extent to which Defoe's narratives are ironic or sincere, and how seriously Defoe intended his work to be a moral corrective.[13] Readers in the late seventeenth and early eighteenth century could not routinely assume, as modern critics have done, that the works they were reading were fictions. Defoe muddies the waters frequently by writing about real events in his capacity as journalist. Other works of Defoe, such as *Duncan Campbell*, *Captain Singleton*, and *Jonathan Wild* detail the lives of famous living people, and even *Robinson Crusoe* was "true" to the extent that it was modeled after the adventures of Alexander Selkirk. *Journal of the Plague Year*, too, was an account of a real event based to some extent on actual records and accounts. In view of Defoe's commitment to pseudojournalism, *Roxana* must have been received by the readership with ambivalence.

It was this ambivalent reaction—an uncertainty as to the factual or fictional reality of the work—that I am maintaining was one of the major components in the phenomenology of reading during the early eighteenth century and which was largely absent when Cervantes wrote. The development of a theory of the novel which dealt adequately with the confusion between the factual and fictional role of narrative was one of the central concerns of early novelists, as we will see. The elaborate development of the frame and the concomitant use of authorial disavowal created a mode of literary creation and fabrication which is obsessively bound up with speculations on the capacity of narrative to carry a purely factual or purely fictional message. The importance of the prestructure is to create the boundaries which define, transform, and locate the plot elements of the novel, and in so doing to sharply differentiate the early novel from the types of writing that preceded it.

CHAPTER II

The Romance:
Liminality and Influence

IF DON QUIXOTE'S quest leads us down the wrong road, down the unframed way, in which direction should we turn? Most theories of the novel, whether evolutionary, osmotic, or convergent, have cast glances, however varied, to the romance—particularly the French heroic romance of the seventeenth century. The romance seems a logical place to start if one is intent on finding liminal* or originating moments. Since romances preceded novels as the dominant longish narrations in prose, they must, so the argument goes, be related to novels which are themselves longish narrations in prose. Such reasoning has led to books which discuss "the novel" in the Elizabethan period, or as far back as the Middle Ages, or even classical Greece and Rome.[1] Indeed, any work in prose of a decent length with a single hero falls prey to the definition of "novel." For the time being, I will resist the temptation to define the novel a priori and simply begin to observe what the novel is not.

Rather, I will argue that the romance is not usefully seen as a forebear of, a relative of, or an influence on the novel. The clear fact in the development of narrative during this period is that there was a profound rupture, a discursive chasm between these two forms. We can perhaps learn more about the nature of literary

---

* "Liminal" is being used here to indicate the idea of a threshold, the verging onto a new genre. "Liminality," then, would be that state of being that is on the threshold.

change by focusing on difference rather than similarity. At least, it is possible in this way to treat the idea of a purely literary influence somewhat warily.

One might begin with the assumption that it is impossible to know instinctively the similitude of one literary form to another, particularly when one's judgment is being made so many centuries after the event. One needs to question every term in the definition of the novel as a longish, fictional narrative in prose.[2] Why does the precursor have to be fictional? Why in prose? Why long? Beyond this, the formal and cultural characteristics of the romance must be considered to see whether there is any virtual correspondence between it and the later novel. Do novel and romance share similar functions formally and culturally? Do they address similar audiences? Are their ideological goals alike?

The romance seems so utterly unlike the novel as to be unrelated. This belief does not imply that romances and novels are hermetically sealed in isolated compartments, forever divergent. No doubt readers and writers were exposed to both forms, and echoes of one form might have rebounded off the other. However, because a modern reader might, for example, read both *Newsweek* and *Ulysses* does not mean that we are dealing with homologous narrative forms. There are no easy answers to the question of which forms are actually part of the same discourse as the novel, but the question of influence needs to be treated warily. The origin of the motion picture could not have been treated as cavalierly as that of the novel has been. While the proximity of the historical event of cinema adds to the complexity of the problem, one could not have flatly stated that the cinema was descended from drama, photography, or the novel—nor could it be said that cinema is made up of a little bit of each. The added complexity of the invention and patenting of the technology intercedes between question and answer here in a unique way, but the point is that a casually uncritical answer, such as has been hypothesized for the novel's origin, would never be tolerated. Genres are troublesome creatures and need much more than birth certificates to clear up questions about missing progenitors and problematic origins.

The first thing we should recall about romance is that it was a form which began with a backward glance by associating itself with a classical tradition. The term "romance" is defined by the *Oxford English Dictionary* as "derived from, or representing, the old Roman tongue, descended from Latin. Also composed in, using, etc., a vernacular tongue of Latin origin."* In this sense, the romance was associated, at least linguistically, with Rome. This backward glance was acknowledged and continued through such writers as D'Urfé, Scudéry, and La Calprenède who saw in romance a mythic genealogy and filiation that led directly back to the Greeks by way of the Romans and the medieval bards. The weight of the past lay heavily on these particular works not only in an ideological sense but in a structural one as well. Mlle. de Scudéry writes in the preface to *Ibrahim* (1641) of her debt to the Greeks, her "first masters," and says that she bases her theory of writing on the Greek model for the epic which she calls "famous romances of antiquity."[3] Because of the tendency of romance writers to see themselves as imitating the Greeks, they began their works *in medias res*, had protagonists who were military heroes, preferably who had lived in the distant past, were always noble, whose military and chastely amatory triumphs served to uplift and uphold the society of which they were the highest representatives.[4] The function of such works was, according to Northrop Frye, to celebrate aristocratic rule, idealize power, tradition, and stability.[5]

The readers for these romances, as is clear, were primarily wealthy and aristocratic. One would have had to have a good deal of time and money to buy and read thirty volumes of *Clélie*. A typical frontispiece to a romance might indicate the projected audience for these works. We see a group of aristocrats in all their elegance listening to the story read by a single, seated reader whose

---

* It is also important to point out here that the French word *roman* can be translated as either "romance" or "novel"—a confusing inconvenience given our interest in distinguishing the two. The word *nouvelle* or *histoire* tends to be used in the latter half of the seventeenth century to distinguish a shorter, simpler type of narrative. *Histoire*, of course, can mean either story or history—another linguistic inconvenience that leads us to wonder if these crossovers might reflect some kind of uncertainty in the grand categories of fiction, history, and journalism in France as well as England.

back is turned to the viewer (see Figure 2.1).[6] The picture is interesting not only for its illustration of social class and setting (one notes the juxtaposition of Grecian architecture and pastoral but royal gardens), but because it embodies visually the essence of romance reading. The solitary reader (and here one recalls Cervantes' opening salutation to the "idle reader" or, as Huet puts it, the "*honnetes paresseux*"), with her back to the observer is sealed off in her world of fantasy. Romance is the contrary of the ordinary world, making possible the idealized vision. Yet, even sealed off, the reader still faces the assembled listeners who contextualize the solitary quality of reading by providing the class nexus that ratifies the elite vision of the romance.

If the weight of the past hung heavily on the romance, certain theories and conventions of romance-writing only added to that weight. Because the romance was a form which lacked a classical body of rules (Aristotle never described romance), much activity was devoted to developing theories and speculations about the nature of this form during the seventeenth century in France. Because it was considered an "inexcusable vice" in the neoclassical world to be without Greco-Roman models, the rules of the epic were adopted wholesale to the romance, as we have seen.[7] In addition to these rules, the romancers added or codified a theory of writing that amounted to a set of rules for writing romances, and they explicated these in their prefaces. The first rule may be called that of *vraisemblance* or resemblance. Mlle. Scudéry enunciated this rule in her preface to *Ibrahim:*

> . . . to give a more true resemblance to things, I have made the foundations of my work historical, my principal personages such as are marked out in the true history for illustrious persons, and the battles effective. This is the way doubtless, whereby one may arrive at one's end; for when as falsehood and truth are confounded by a dextrous hand, wit hath much ado to disentangle them, and is not easily carried to destroy that which pleaseth it.[8]

The rule of *vraisemblance* demands that though the work is a fictional one, the actual foundations for the work should be true and the characters should conform to historical reality, though their exploits

FIGURE 2.1

may be made up. As Scudéry wrote in *Artamene* (1649–1653):

> The hero you are about to see is not one of those imaginary heroes
> who are nothing but the beautiful dream of a solitary man who has
> never been in the essence of things. He is an actual hero, but one
> of the most illustrious whose memory has been preserved by
> history.[9]

There is a great emphasis placed on telling the story in a quasi-
historical way so as to arrive at a kind of narration which carries
some of the authority of history but none of the factuality. We are
in a grey area of verity which one writer called "that historical way
of poeticizing or poetical way of historicizing, or displaying in the
feigned seeming, unfeigned adventures and actions."[10] This bit of
double-talk actually reflects the massive confusion that was beginning as writers attempted to create a discourse that could bear the
weight of verity. It is clear that here the historicizing comes in
second to the poeticizing. La Calprenède implied as much when
he wrote that his writings were 'unassailable historically as long as
not contradicted by history.'"[11]

This theory of *vraisemblance*, it is important to note, is hardly
a theory of formal realism, and is simply a way of saying that for
actions to appear credible they cannot be totally invented. The
purely fictional had not attained at this point any legitimacy and
was generally seen as nothing more than mere lies. Charles Sorel
in *De la connaissance des bons livres* (1671) expressed his scorn for
purely invented works in a discussion comparing the purely fictional with the quasi-historical:

> Is it not like comparing a monkey with a man? What satisfaction
> can we hope from a tale that being purely fictional gives us no
> assurance at all that the events that it reports accord with the laws
> of sovereign prudence . . . because that which is imaginary and
> contrived for pleasure has absolutely no force in discourse.[12]

I am interested by the fact that Sorel finds the idea of a pure fiction
rather bizarre. One might conjecture that the normal state of affairs
for writers was to write something that was neither firmly one or

the other. The state of ambivalence I have been suggesting seems to have constituted a kind of norm in reading narrative, and narrative as such seems to have been indifferent in some way to the extremes of fact and fiction, preferring to rest in the grey area between. This distinction holds true for English prose narratives, as will be seen. Mlle. de Scudéry follows this line of reasoning when she characterizes her work as more than "a fable but not a history, and it is enough that he who wrote it allies the work to *vraisemblance* without always linking it to truth."[13] Scudéry's notion of history is heavily influenced by that of the Greeks, but she also recognizes that such historians themselves have problematic conceptualizations of history. She notes that Herodotus mentions historical events that Xenophon does not and vice versa, that they contradict each other, and so she has decided to follow "sometimes one and sometimes the other according to who is more or less appropriate to my design . . . [and several times following their example]. I say that which neither of them has said, because, after all, I am inventing a fable and not writing a history."[14] There are several things one might note about this series of statements. First, Scudéry never denies that she is writing fiction. She begins with the understanding that her work is fable—not history. Thus, in terms of the prestructure of the work, the document she presents is not framed in any sense of the word. She is not creating a fabrication when she says that her hero is real—since the actual person Cyrus did in fact live, even though Scudéry invents much of his life and thoughts. The main function of the historical underpinning is to defictionalize the work to an acceptable threshold of credibility. Second, Scudéry's model for historicity is itself a highly fictionalized one based on the eclectic and eccentric methods of Herodotus, Xenophon, Thucydides, and other classical historians. It was not until Bayle's insistence on documentation and the use of primary sources in the latter part of the seventeenth century that French historians could be said to be strictly factual in their writings.[15] With such models, Scudéry feels free simply to fill in all the blank spaces left by what the historians did not say. Third,

Scudéry places her characters in the distant past because that is where there is the greatest room for invention. One should not choose a century "so distant that almost nothing in particular is known about it, nor so close that all that has happened is too well-known; enough to suppose events that an historian could have likely been ignorant of and should not even have told."[16] So the classical past can be said to be the ideal place to set the action of a romance. Ironically, to set a work in the present or recent past would be *invraisemblable* since, given the assumptions of the romance writers, it would be unrealistic to suppose that a hero of the present would have been unknown or that his or her every deed should have remained unrecorded except by the romancers.

Obviously, this variety of *vraisemblance* is totally unlike the realism of Defoe, Richardson, or Fielding. The romancers defined their verisimilitude as limited to the just placement of protagonists in the dim past of classical history—after which, within the limits of plausibility, the protagonist could go off winning hearts and slaying enemies in the most unrealistic of ways. The author's commitment was to pseudohistorical accuracy, but not to accuracy of action, thought, and so on.

The other central rule of romance—that of *bienseance*—adds further to the distance between novels and romances. The demand for *bienseance*, or decorum, is one that insists no vulgar manners be depicted in the narrative, that virtue always be rewarded, and that in general the mores and customs of the period in which the story takes place be changed and adapted to the current conventions of good manners. In the case of stories set in Rome, Persia, or Greece, this would mean that various forms of excess, particularly sexual ones, could not be allowed to appear in romance.[17] Though the rules of *vraisemblance* and *bienseance* seem at first to oppose each other—on the one hand a demand for historical foundations and on the other for ahistorical moral censorship—in reality they go hand in hand within the limits of the romance. *Vraisemblance* really implies not historical fidelity or realism, but actually what one might call "moral verisimilitude"; that is to say, an author should depict the world not as it is (or was) but as it should have been. Thus a *vraisemblable* depiction of Cyrus would have him behave the way a chaste, ideal romance hero should, whether or not he ever did so.

In France, the writers who felt constricted by the *vraisemblance/ bienseance* rule wrote works called, among other things, *nouvelles*. For example, Donneau de Visé wrote in 1669:

> I have no doubt that some unbelievable things will be found in my *Nouvelles*; but the reader will please notice that I am not a poet in this work, but an historian. The poet must stick to vraisemblance, and correct truth that is not believable. The historian, on the contrary, must write nothing that is not true; and provided that he is sure of telling the truth, he need not have a concern for vraisemblance.[18]

The theoretical difference between this new point of view and that of the older romancer's is very important. The writer of *nouvelles* saw himself as primarily an historian and not a poet. While the poet was bound to *vraisemblance*, the historian was bound to facts, and so *vraisemblance* was seen not as a technique of realism but as a censoring device which stands in opposition to factuality and truthfulness. The romancer's view of the world is thus based on the effacing of the offending or nonconforming fact or event and the creation of the ideal, the paradigmatic, the traditional. The writer of novels, on the other hand, sees narrative as more oriented to the specific, the particular, the eccentric, the factual. In this sense, we must say that the form of representation in the romance was qualitatively different from that of the novel, and as such can hardly be said to be homologous.

One could say that writers of *nouvelles* in France saw themselves as embarking on an entirely new form of writing in the last quarter of the seventeenth century.[19] The word *nouvelle* at this time served as a signifier of this rupture. There is, as usual, a problem in terminology here: the word *nouvelle* does not simply translate as "novel" since a *roman* could be a novel as well. English Showalter, for example, maintains that the "*romans*, the *nouvelles*, the *histoires*, the *mémoires*, whether *historique*, *galantes*, or *veritable*, were virtually indistinguishable from each other."[20] However, it is remarkable that though the content of the novels themselves may have differed little from romances, the prestructures of these works make rather strong distinctions between novels and romances. For example, Jean Regnould de Segrais writes in *Les Nouvelles Françoises* (1656):

> . . . we have tried to recount things as they are and not as they should be: moreover it seems to me the difference between the romance and the novel is that the romance writes these things as *bienseance* requires and in the manner of the poet, whereas the novel must partake more of history and strives more to give images of things as we ordinarily see them than as our imagination might picture them.[21]

Segrais reinforces the earlier statement of Visé, and one has a sense of a consensus among these new writers which becomes apparent in certain repeated and reinforced phrases that seem to add up to a consensual, collective manifesto against the romance. Indeed, the very existence of the antiromance as a form, as early as *Don Quixote* in Spain and *Le Berger Extravagant* (1628) by Sorel in France should indicate that many readers and writers were actively sounding the death knell for the romance as a form. In France, the works of Furetière, Scarron, Subligny, and others in the mid-century actively rode the wave of antiromance sentiment, as did many writers in England.

Another important discriminant between genres is that the novel takes place in a more recent time setting than the distant past of the romance. One study points out that after 1660, writers began to set their stories in more and more recent epochs so that around 1670 works generally were placed during the Italian wars; by 1690 in the epoch of Louis XIII and the Fronde; and after 1670 one began to see action in the immediate past.[22] As we have seen, the theory of romance demands the distant setting, but the word *nouvelle* (to be discussed further in chapter 3) points to a kind of recentness or familiarity. Charles Sorel in 1664 distinguished between the two forms saying that novels recount "things recently occurred, otherwise there would be no reason for calling them novels."[23] This emphasis on recentness is one of the characteristics of the novel which tends more toward a report on the world as it is than a reflection on the way things were.

Perhaps we can say that one of the primary distinctions between romance and novel is that romances insist on the actual existence of their protagonists in history while admitting that their story is invented, while novels assert that their stories are factual, although in reality their protagonists have no historical existence. Because novelists deny that they are creating an illusion, they are frequently forced into the position of claiming that they are only editor to some found document. This act of authorial disavowal helps establish the rim of the prestructure which makes the novel a framed narrative, as opposed to the romance. Mlle. de Scudéry, aware of this convention of the novel, mocks the reader who will not accept her pseudohistorical romance, saying: "If this reason does not fully satisfy the scrupulous, they have only to imagine— to put their minds at rest—that my work is taken from an old Greek manuscript in the Vatican Library—but one so precious and rare that it has never been printed and never will be."[24] What Scudéry uses as a joke, however, becomes over the next hundred years the insistent convention of the novel. Isaac Claude, for example, writes in his preface to a novel, "Here is a true story [histoire] that I give you under the guise of a novel." And by 1731, the Abbé Terrasson could rewrite the joke of Scudéry's without the pretense of humor in his title page of Sethos which read "History of life taken from private memoirs of ancient Egypt translated from a Greek manuscript."[25] And in the same year, Abbé Prevost wrote of his novel Cleveland that it was not fictional:

> The history of M. Cleveland came to me from a good source. I received it from his son. . . . He had read my memoires, and that was the strongest reason that he brought it to me to speak of his father. . . . He permitted me to take a copy of his manuscript, and having brought it to France on my return, I made it one of the most important occupations of my spare time in order to give it the form under which it is able to appear today.[26]

After 1710 there was a general tendency for French novelists to claim that their works were true.[27] The insistence that their works were true tended to separate and draw generic lines between the romancers and the novelists, especially in the minds of the latter. While romance was presented as unframed invention founded on quasi-historical material, the novel was presented as an ambiguous form—a factual fiction which denied its fictionality and produced in its readers a characteristic uncertainty or ambivalence as to whether they were reading something true or false.

This ambivalence or confusion certainly marked the reactions of many French readers. Bayle in his *Dictionary* noted that it was because of this confusion between fact and fiction in narrative "one does not dare believe that which is at base believable." Bayle goes on to say that "one has no other way of discerning between fiction and true facts except by knowing from other books whether that which is narrated is true."[28] Bayle seems to be expressing a general cultural problem—how to create a veracious narrative when the very conditions of narrative were put into jeopardy. The helplessness of Bayle's solution—to look in another book—is founded on tautology, since faked histories tend to destroy any credibility print may have had in the first place (see chapter 9). Sorel makes precisely the same point: ". . . the feigned action which one introduces [into the work] along with the true ones will cause the others to be suspected of duplicity, just as when one finds a false part in important business, all the rest is put in doubt."[29] For this reason, Sorel was opposed to having the uneducated read novels since they might mistake fiction for history.

What seemed to be significant for French society at the end of the seventeenth century was that readers were experiencing considerable difficulty and frustration in trying to tell whether the narratives that they were reading were true or not. Bayle notes that this "inconvenience" grows more frequent with the appearance of "les amours secrettes, l'histoire secrete," and so he suggests that the authorities actually pass a law requiring writers to narrate either pure history or pure fiction, "or that at least they [these laws] can serve as a hook to separate one from the other, truth from false-hood."[30] Bayle's call for an intervention by the state in the affairs of fiction foreshadows the censorship of novels during the eighteenth century in France, as well as the use of the libel laws in England to inhibit what could be printed. The desire expressed by Bayle to have the definitions of factual and fictional narratives neatened up a bit was not, it would seem, atypical of the wishes of the age. Boursault in his introduction to the *Prince de Condé* (1675) enforces Bayle's call by warning in advance that he will deal truthfully with the events of war described in his book but will be inventing his story at those moments when he describes matters of love.[31] Boursault's solution to the problem is a programatic one, artificially labeling that part of the story which is true and that which is false, yet it serves its purpose.

At stake was the capability of narrative to carry the burden of factuality and reliability. Readers were confronted by, in effect, a species of uncertainty over the conventions of narrative. One result of this confusion was that new definitions of genres such as history, journalism, and fiction would have to be drawn. It was Bayle himself at this time who was one of the originators in France of the idea that history would have to confine itself to strict documentation, and so his interest in the problems of factual and fictional narratives in literature is consonant with his concerns for historical accuracy. Even Abbé Prevost, whose *Cleveland*, as we have seen, attempted to pass off fiction as fact, is not exempt from the very confusion he is helping to foster:

> One sees appearing these days many works that one does not know in which rank to place them, and which have become problems from the first moment of their birth. Is it clearly decided, for example, that *The Turkish Spy*, the *Memoires of Rochefort*, those of Pontis, etc. must be ranked in the class of novels or in that of books of some authority?[32]

Prevost expresses the dilemma for the reader—intelligent, educated, or not—that there was no final way of knowing whether a particular memoir, life, or history was true or false. Prevost's confusion is not strictly one of an inability to say what constitutes truth—one is not speaking of epistemology here—but rather of an inability to label discourse, to identify genre. I would not doubt that this problem is with us today to some degree, but what seems apparent is that for the seventeenth and eighteenth centuries the issue was a new and pointed one. Discourse, during this period, as I will demonstrate, was shifting, rearranging itself, and reaccommodating the lines of difference. Consequently, old models and paradigms failed to apply, and Bayle as well as others were clutching straws in the wind by asking for a power that would demand writers create only stories of pure invention or, on the other hand, stories only of pure fact.

In this context, novels, with their framed prestructures, were perceived as distinctly unlike the romances that preceded them. "One is as far as one can be from the air of the romance in these new novels [*romans*]" is the way that Bayle put it.[33] The recurrent code embedded in the novelistic prestructure is one of rupture with the past, with the romance tradition, with stories about the distant past. The writers of romance, however, and theorists of romance like Bishop Pierre Daniel Huet spent much of their time trying to forge a connection and a legitimacy between traditional writings and the romance forms. Huet, in his work *Traité de l'origine des romans* (1670), links the romance to Greek and Roman models as well as showing how these classical forms passed through the hands of the Moors and pagans to arrive safely in Christian lands.[34] Such a difference in orientation, in underlying assumptions, and in results must point to the fact that romance and novel cannot be said to be part of the same discourse.

In arguing for a sharp distinction between romance and novel, I do not wish to imply that all literature will then neatly fall on either side of these two poles. Some works will be easily defined as romances, others as novels, and others will resist definition. This state of affairs should not surprise us since literary study is hardly a science and, even within the scientific community, taxonomy often fails to fit certain ambiguous organisms and elementary particles. Works like those of Madame de Lafayette in *La Princesse de Montpensier* (1662) and *La Princesse de Cleves* (1678) are great defiers of genre, usually thrown up to the faces of literary systematizers in defiance of theory. These two narratives are not as overblown and tendentious as the heroic romances. Although the story is "romantic," Madame de Lafayette claims openly to writing fictions, yet these are also certainly historically based. If pressed for a definition of genre, I would argue for these works being novels, although one could also say that her novel was not "a lineal descendant of the mid-seventeenth century romance, but the product of a parallel and separate form of fiction," as one writer has put it.[35] Charles Sorel in 1664 listed the *Princesse de Montpensier* as a novel along with the works of Segrais, Scarron, Boisrobert, Cervantes, and Voiture, and I see no reason to deny his perception.[36] Sorel's criteria seem to have been that the events recounted had recently happened, that the whole story is rather short, and that the stories are true to some particular human experience.

One of the reasons Madame de Lafayette's works were seen as novels despite their romantic content is that they are, their claims to fictionality not withstanding, framed narratives, although the framing is of a different type than we have seen thus far. It is true that Madame de Lafayette wrote in the preface to *La Princesse de Montpensier* that she was merely presenting "an adventure invented at will" and not making any attempt to foist fiction as fact.[37] Yet because her work passed for a *roman à clef* depicting the amatory adventures of herself and her lover, its admission of fictionality served actually the opposite purpose.[38] In a quasi-allegorical work of this nature, as for example in the case of *Gulliver's Travels*, the author's insistence on the fictionality of the work is only a covert instruction to the reader to regard the work as being actually factual. A *roman à clef* is by definition framed; at the level of narrative the characters may be fictional, but on the allegorical level their actions must conform to some kind of truth. Thus based on the criteria of brevity of length, recentness, and framing, the works of Madame de Lafayette seem to fit into the schematics of the novel.

One could list certain characteristic differences between the novel and romance:

1. The romance is set in the distant, idealized past; the novel is set in a more recent, less heroic, setting.
2. The romance is based on the epic; the novel is modeled on history and journalism.
3. The romance is usually not set in the country of the author but in a remote and exotic location; the novel tends to be set in the locale of the author, that is, the novel tends to be a national form of literature.
4. The romance depicts the life of the aristocracy and is designed for an upper-class reader; the novel tends to be more middle class in scope and is geared to a slightly less aristocratic readership, although this statement is less true in France of the seventeenth century than in England.[39]
5. Romances tend to be long and episodic; novels are shorter and more compact of plot.
6. Romances value the preservation of virtue and chastity; novels tend to focus on illegal doings and forbidden passions.
7. Novels of the eighteenth century tend to be written in the first person or in letter form; romances are never written in these forms.[40]
8. Romances make clear that they are mixing fact and fiction to create an essentially fictional plot; novels tend to deny that they are fictional.
9. Romances follow the rules of *bienseance* and *vraisemblance*; novelists openly reject these rules since they claim to be writing history or recording life as it is.

While this list is arbitrary and simplified, can we not say that, based on the rough cut of these observations, we are confronting two rather different forms of narrative—forms with antithetical structures, readers, prestructures, characters, plots, and traditions? Even a hundred years after the demise of the heroic romance, Clara

Reeve in England could write with authority that "no writings are more different than the ancient romances and the modern novel."[41]

The problem that faces us in discussing the origin of a genre is one of influence. If we confine ourselves to literary evidence or literary precursors, we must inevitably wind up with evolutionary theories—theories which then must rely on the totalitarian logic that the novel is either descended *from* romance or is a deliberate revolt *against* romance. This are-you-still-beating-your-wife construction forbids any deviation from a shared set of assumptions about the nature of literary change.[42] Indeed, it is difficult to steer clear of this kind of logical necessity, and yet it is the aim of this book to try and avoid the problems of influence, or at least to mitigate the most outrageous ones, by referring questions of influence back to a social, cultural, and technological ground—that is, to a more material base. This goal can hardly be called unique. Nevertheless, one would hope that such a project might shed some light on this phase of cultural development. While I have argued here that there was a profound rupture between novel and romance, I do not think we can usefully see this discontinuity simply as a reaction against romance. Rather, to understand the complexity of this shift we are forced to move to an explanation outside the purely literary, as the following chapters will attempt to do.

CHAPTER III

News/Novels:
The Undifferentiated Matrix

IF THE ROMANCE and the novel can be seen as two quite different entities, then where can one look to find an anterior discourse related to the novel? Did the novel merely spring from the head of its earliest practitioners? Is there any continuity to literary genres or is there only difference? Do we rely on Michel Foucault's notion that the history of discourse is based on the concepts of discontinuities and transformations or must we look at ideas like continuity, influence, and evolution?

We begin here with two specific problems. First is the question of the national individuality of literary genres. Is the history of the *nouvelle* in France parallel to the development of the novel in England? This is primarily a historical question but its theoretical ramifications are significant. Usually, in discussions about the beginning of genres, there can be a universalist tendency to attribute a monolithic development to a particular aesthetic form. Hence, the rise-of-the-novel phenomenon which sees England, France, and Spain as reacting together to some exterior propulsion to create the universal form of the novel despite national backgrounds and traditions. The argument for this transnational development is not to be discounted, and of course there is much credibility to the idea that the rise of the middle class brought into being a universal reaction of European cultures to this economic restructuring. One does feel somewhat sorry for the rising middle classes having to bear the burden of so many cultural changes since it would seem

that the rise of the middle class and industrialization are the processes (along with sublimation and repression) that have been used
as prime movers of almost all change. The weakness of the middle-
class hypothesis is not that it is incorrect but only that it is incomplete. Why should a rising middle class *necessarily* lead to a 250-
page book about a man on an island or a young girl who resists the
seduction of her master? Tracing the microdevelopment of this
cultural transformation in its particular national context is crucial
to any explanation of the novel's origins. One needs to know why
increased leisure time necessarily leads to novel-reading particularly
and not billiard-playing or taking excessively long walks? Moreover,
the predilections of a rising middle class in one country do not
preclude the development of differing predilections in another
country.

  In the previous chapter, for example, I have attempted to show
that the romance as it developed in France seems to have had a
rather different tradition than that of England. In fact, in England
there seem to be few if any D'Urfé's or Scudéry's, except in
imitation or translation. Although romances were popular among
some segments of the upper classes and wealthier middle classes,
the vogue for long romances was by and large absent among most
Early Modern English readers. I hope to show in this chapter that,
far from emerging from the shell of romance, for the most part the
novel in England had an entirely different origin. In this sense, I
am treating the development of the novel in England in relative
isolation from continental developments. I am not denying the
transnational phenomenon, but I am suggesting a more particular,
circumstantial approach. My own research has indicated that the
novel in England seems to come from an internal development
relatively unaffected by continental influence and interchanges.
While I do not rule out such influence, interchanges, parallel developments, and so on, it is the limitation of this work to concentrate
on contextualization and cultural developments within England.
The task rests with those more familiar with the discourses of
France, Germany, Spain, and other countries to see whether the

course I am tracing has its parallels in Europe. My suspicion is that the novel's development in Europe may not be far from the circumstances I will be describing in England, although there are sure to be crucial national differences. For example, in the middle of the eighteenth century it seems quite likely that the English novel came to be a model for the French novel far more than the French novel did for the English.[1]

A second problem of any study of the novel's origins is that we lack the language or even theoretical framework to talk about the concept of continuity. As we have seen, the notion that all continuities are either a *reaction to* or an *influence of* another form is simplistic and all-encompassing, though much of literary history relies on this paradigm. Yet in rejecting this approach, we are still faced with the problem of trying to talk about the mechanism of origination. The problem of causality does not disappear because we reject the operative mechanism of causality. Thus, for conceptual purposes, I would like to at least posit another system of causality as we move through the course of this study. I suggest that rather than a series of genres displacing each other, we are looking at a discourse that is forced to subdivide. Exactly what the discourse is, and what causes it to subdivide will have to await the accumulation of evidence.

The discourse can be partially named: it is prose narrative in print. The field will remain quite vaguely defined at this point. What constitutes the nature of this field of inquiry and of the unit of study itself? Does narrative itself constitute a discourse? Despite the existence of critical books on the subject of "narrative," for our purposes it must be considered too broad a term to define a specific field of study with its own rules and limits. Clearly, the existence of narrative must have been coterminous with language itself and can include anything from folk tale to reminiscence to story, fragment, recounting, or myth. As such, it is too global to constitute a discourse. If one adds "prose" to modify narrative, the situation is qualified somewhat. Narratives which predate the sixteenth century have been mostly written in poetic form, as indeed have the earliest narratives of the Greeks and the medieval epics. Prose narratives are somewhat rare in the European tradition, particularly if one excludes histories and hagiographies. Thus, "prose" seems to act as an effective limiter or definer of discourse, at least in reducing the field of inquiry. When one adds the further modifier of "print" to prose narrative, have we added an effective term or are we creating an artificial signifier? If we add "quadrophonic" to the phrase "classical music on magnetic tape," is this an effective or an artificial distinction? I would argue that print has to be seen as an essential definer of discourse automatically ruling out oral narrative, which, like narrative in general, is so undefined a category that it probably cannot be considered a discrete discourse. Print raises another problem as well, since we need to wonder if this technological advance itself changed the nature of prose narrative in any significant way. The technology of print does seem to have been crucial to the existence of prose narrative, if only by changing the audience somewhat it changed the form and content. All of this remains to be proven. At this point, however, the case for the theory that printed prose narrative itself constituted a discourse needs at least to be presented. The addition of the word "print," to return to the analogy, is quite unlike the addition "quadrophonic" but not unlike the addition of "on magnetic tape," since it would appear that certain kinds of music are now performed differently with the advent of electronic recording, and that certain types of performances would be impossible without this kind of transcription.[2]

If we move forward along the historical continuum from prose narrative of the Greek, Roman, or medieval periods to the first connection between narrative and print; or if we move backward, on the other hand, from the full-blown narratives of the eighteenth and nineteenth centuries to the earlier printed prose narratives, we arrive at a common point, what the sixteenth century called "novels"—that is, printed news ballads and tales. The first intersection of print and narrative that was a genuine product of the technology of moveable type (and not simply the printed version of earlier nonprinted forms) was the news ballad of the sixteenth century which was called, among other things, a "novel." The early prose narratives of the sixteenth century—the tales of criminals, brief accounts of jokes and jests, Boccaccio-like love intrigues—were also called "novels." The point of intersection here may only be linguistic, but it bears examination. Why were these diverse forms of literature—the news ballad, the criminal tale, the early newsbooks, the tales, short stories, jests, and so on called by the same name? What did they have in common? What is the significance of this nexus?

Let us start first with typography and its intersection with narrative. It would seem, for the most part, that after Caxton printed the first books in England people read substantially the same type of narratives in print as they might have read in manuscript. The kind of literature written changed very little if at all as a result of printing. Chivalric romances, grammars, religious books, legal treatises, fables, histories, and so on were unchanged in structure or content by typography. Initially, even the price of printed books was not significantly lower than that of those in manuscript. It was, however, the reduction in the price of using paper over parchment that brought down the price of books—the difference in the price paid to a scrivener as opposed to a printer hardly being significant.[3] Although printing may have made books more numerous and therefore more available, the process seems to have had little major effect on the nature of what was printed.

However, what print did make possible was the introduction of a technology that permitted the rapid and relatively instantaneous publication of matters of public interest—that is, printing made possible news or journalism, or as the sixteenth century called such works—novels. The main form of journalism in the sixteenth century was the printed ballad. To be sure, ballads existed before the advent of moveable type, but the printed form was meant to be read as well as sung. As such, the printed ballad was not conceived of as an oral form, and its layout, woodcuts, and typeface are consciously assembled to add to its graphic and typographic

presence. Also, the printed ballad was basically journalistic—
which is to say, more likely to be read immediately after the event
reported than the ballad of a wandering minstrel, which might
recount exploits of the more distant past, and be sung months or
years after its composition. As Hyder Rollins has written, somewhat incorrectly, ballads were "the equivalent of modern newspapers."[4] Equivalence aside, the main function of ballads was to
act as newspapers to inform primarily the literate and illiterate
lower classes of public events such as earthquakes, wars, murders,
freaks of nature, and supernatural happenings, as well as to preach
religious homilies to those considered most likely to commit violent
acts. Some ballads did focus on love, history, and other non-news
events, but the journalistic ballad far outnumbered all other types.[5]
For example, in the year 1569, three-quarters of all licensed ballads
in England dealt with the Northern Rebellion.[6]

The title of a ballad from the seventeenth century gives us a
clue about the relationship between the nonjournalistic ballads and
the journalistic ones; a love story is called "Private News From
Chatham,"[7] and is clearly seen as a variety of news. That ballads
were primarily seen as journalistic is also suggested in a dialogue
from Thomas Middleton's *The World Tost at Tennis* (1620):

> SCHOLAR: I could make ballads for a need.
> SOLDIER: Very well, sir, and I'll warrant thee thou shalt never
>   want subject to write of: one hangs himself today, an-
>   other drowns himself tomorrow, a sargeant stabbed next
>   day, here a cart's nose, and a pander in the tail; *hic mulier
>   hoec vir*, fashions, fictions, felonies, fooleries:—a hundred
>   havens has the balladmonger to traffic at, and new ones
>   still daily discovered.[8]

In speaking of ballads, one is not talking about a minor production of the printing trade which lay in the shadow of the real
production of printing—great literature, religious works, histories,
and so forth. Ballads made up from one-quarter to one-third of all
publications listed in the records of the Stationers' Company from
1560 to 1650. That is to say, ballads were the dominant type of

publication printed during these hundred or so years, and as such they constitute a radically new discourse in the European information system.[9] Ballads themselves were printed in the same form as the royal proclamation—each page printed on only one side—and as such acted as a usurper in more ways than one of the royal prerogative on information dissemination, since before ballads the only preexisting information dispersal systems were the royal and the ecclesiastical ones.

The new and unusual thing about these ballads was their capability to report almost instantly on the immediately past event—a feat made possible by the technology of printing. Since the ballad was printed on only one side of a sheet, the sixteenth-century printer could produce about 1,000 sheets in eight hours.[10] This meant that a good portion of the literate population of London, as well as the illiterates who heard the ballad being sung, could be informed of an event almost overnight—a feat of information dispersal unheard of before print. As Rollins writes, "If an earthquake frightened London one day, the next morning saw the publication of at least one ballad mournfully describing that calamity. . . ."[11] With this invention, narrative was given the ability to embody recentness, hence to record that which was novel—that is, to be a "novel."

In looking at ballads, one sees quite frequently the words *novel*, *newes*, and *new* being used interchangeably. Ballads always claim to be new, as if that word were at once a guarantee and a disclaimer. What the ballads had to sell, as we have seen, were their newness, their recentness. Titles for ballads abound in claims for newness, such as "A most excellent godly new ballad: Showing the manifold abuses of this wicked world," or "New newes of two most famous seafights."[12] Another ballad emphasizes its recentness:

> Come buy my new ballet, I have't in my wallet . . .
> 'Tis newly printed, and newly come forth.[13]

Autolycus, in Shakespeare's *The Winter's Tale* sells ballads and stresses that the particular virtue of the one he is selling is that it is "but a month old" (IV. iv. 262). Ballad singers were reported to

have cried out "Ballads, my masters, ballads! Will ye ha' any ballads
o' the newest and truest matter in all London?"[14] Rollins' *Index* lists
at least 179 ballads beginning with *new* or *news*, and Rollins notes
that "all ballads were made to insist upon their newness . . . [be-
cause] people were so well aware of the printer's habit of re-issuing
old ballads that the first question they asked the singer was usually,
"Is it new?"[15] This questioning of the balladeer is striking not only
because people were leery of getting stale material, but because,
almost by definition, the discourse of *newes* was one which demanded recentness.* Without that signifier, a ballad was not really
part of the discourse. It is in this sense that I would like to assign
the title "news/novels" to describe the discourse now being examined, since the discourse is clearly one in which these two terms
intersect in crucial ways.

   However, in the same breath it must be pointed out that
although ballads claimed to be new, and *newes* claimed to be new,
these forms frequently were not. As will be seen, each element of
this news/novels discourse is characterized by a contradictory or
double quality. To be more specific, I'd like to examine the idea
of the newness of *newes* or the novelty of novels as it was used in
the sixteenth century. *Tarlton's News Out of Purgatory* (1589) is not
a ballad or a news-sheet but a collection of eight tales, most of
which are lifted directly from Boccaccio, hardly a recent source.
Quite frequently ballads which may have originally been printed
as news were reprinted enough times, sometimes over decades,
until they passed into the material of folk tales. The paradox of
this insistence on recentness in patently old material is captured
in the title of a ballad "New, new and never old, a good tale cannot
be too often told."[16] The ballad, then, claimed to be new and often
was, although it often was not. Such a contradiction was the rule
rather than the exception in the news/novels discourse. The reason
for this state of affairs will have to remain unexplained for the
moment.

* I have retained the spelling *newes* for those works which would fit the sixteenth and
seventeenth centuries' definition of that word, as opposed to *news* which I use for our own
concept of journalism.

We have been looking at the idea of recentness as a signifier of genre; let us look at the general sense of the word *newes* itself. *Newes* does not denote what the modern reader would assume to be news—an essentially factual, though perhaps ideological, account of the details of current public affairs, yellow journalism notwithstanding. Fact and *newes*, however, for the sixteenth century could be mutually exclusive categories. The word *newes* was applied freely to writings which described either true or fictional events, quotidian or supernatural occurrences, and affairs that may have been recent or several decades old. It is not unusual, in looking through the *Register of the Stationers' Company* to find ballads listed side by side with such different titles as "Newes out of Kent," "Newes from the Tower Hill," "Newes out of Heaven and Hell," and "Newes from Pluto's Court." The variety of uses of the word *newes* in these examples is considerable.

If one leaves the realm of ballads, the word *newes* crops up in the unlikely category of prose fiction. *The Sack Full of Newes* (1557) seems to have been both a jestbook and a play. Thomas Nashe's *Strange Newes* (1592) was a reply to his critics written partially in verse, partially in prose, burlesquing, among other things, news accounts of the day. In 1606 Thomas Dekker produced a satire called *Newes from Hell*. One wonders what *newes* could mean—or could not mean—if it was applied to such diverse types of literature as ballads, prose tales, and jestbooks. Another author calls his collection of tales from Greek, Italian, and French sources "these newes or novelles."[17]

The word *newes* was also used to describe books written in prose which reported on foreign wars and noteworthy occurrences abroad, such as *Newes Out of Antwerp*, a newsbook from 1580.[18] This use of the word *newes* turns up in a play published in 1591, in which an upper-class gentleman indicates his scorn of the lower-class nature of news when he says, "Prognostications, newes, devices, and letters from foreign countries . . . are but used as confections to feed the common people withal."[19] Here, *newes* clearly has a journalistic sense.

If we look at the various words used to describe these books of news reports, we see here too an ambiguity concerning the categories of fact and fiction. These newsbooks were called *corantos*, *nouvelles*, *novels*, and *newes*, all of which carry the connotation of recentness or newness. Yet all of these terms, excepting *coranto*, were also equally used for books of fictional tales. Since English foreign news in the latter half of the sixteenth century was almost exclusively produced by translating Dutch, French, Spanish, or German newsbooks and publishing them, the use of foreign titles makes sense.[20] *Coranto* is an English borrowing of a Spanish word, which in turn was taken from the French *courant* meaning current, or up-to-date, according to the *Oxford English Dictionary*. The word *novela* is also a Spanish word associated with the French *nouvelle* which likewise meant new, current, and later in the seventeenth century came to be identified with the purely literary form which replaced the romance. *Nouvelle* is taken from the Latin *novellus*—a diminutive of *novus* which meant new or extraordinary. Naturally, the word *newes* would be expected to share the same origin, meaning also that which was new, as it did.

However, *nouvelles*, in addition to being newsbooks, could also be applied in the fifteenth century to collections of tales and jests. For example, *Cent Nouvelles Nouvelles* (1486) was a collection of folk tales and stories. The title clearly plays on both senses of the word. The Spanish *novela* too had its journalistic referent, but it could also refer to a tale or short story. The word "novel" began to be used in this latter sense in England around 1566, according to the *Oxford English Dictionary*. The range of the word *newes* was extremely broad at this time in history, as we have seen. And what is quite significant is that the news/novels discourse seems to make no real distinction between what we would call fact and fiction. That is, fictional tales seem to be considered *newes* as readily as would an account of a sea battle or a foreign war.

If the news/novels discourse is characterized by a disinclination to distinguish between fact and fiction as a signifier of genre, why then do ballads and newsbooks, for example, spend so much time

claiming to be "trewe?"* The use of this word is as highly contradictory and ambiguous as the use of the word *newes*. *Trewe*
frequently appears in the title of works which clearly could not
have been true—such as this ballad printed in 1597 entitled
"Truewe and Dreadful new tydinges of bloode and brimstone
which God hathe caused to rayne from heaven within and without
the cytie of Strale Sonet, with a wonderful apparition seen by a
citizen of the same cytie named Hans Germer which met him in
the field as he was travaylinge on the waie."[21] Another ballad that
appeared about the same time was equally unbelievable: "A most
miraculous, strange, and trewe Ballad, of a younge man of the age
of 19 years, who was wrongfully hanged at . . . Bon . . . since
Christmas last . . . and how God preserved him alive, and brought
his false accuser to deserved destruction."[22] Other, even less credible events are listed in a ballad, "A Lamentable List of certain
Hideous, frightfull and Prodigious signes . . . ," which includes
water being turned to blood, armies fighting in the air, three suns
in the sky, rains of gore, blood oozing from bread, worms in the
shape of men and so on.[23] While it is obvious that supernatural
events might be believed by many to be true, it is also clear that
the gullibility of ballad readers was well-known. Even those who
believed in miracles and supernatural interventions might still have
grounds for doubting the reliability of such events when recorded
in ballads.

A frequent practice of printers which indicates something
about their lack of concern as to the distinction between fact and
fiction was the use and reuse of the same woodcut in ballads re-
gardless of whether the picture really illustrated the printed material. In a ballad of the execution of Francis Throckmorton, for
example, a woodcut shows a man being beheaded. Throckmorton,
however, was hanged, and this cut was clearly used for any account
that might vaguely fit.[24] Or again, less explicably, a ballad called
"A mournful Dittie on the death of certain Judges and Justices of

* I am using *trewe* to define the concept available during this period for things that may or
may not have been *true*.

the Peace," shows a woodcut representing two men exclaiming over a baby in a dish being placed before them by a servant, a detail which, however interesting, is not even vaguely mentioned in the ballad.[25]

Ballad writers spent a good deal of effort trying to document and prove that their stories were indeed verifiably true. In "Nature's Wonder or a True Account of how the Wife of one John Waterman . . . was delivered of a strange monster" (1664), the attending physician attaches an affidavit saying that he "saw them all three alive." And in "Newes From Hereford or a Wonderful and Terrible Earthquake" (1661) a list of nine witnesses, including two church wardens and two constables, is attached for the benefit of the dubious.[26] Another ballad, about a murder in which the victim reappears seven years later after having been conveyed to Turkey by a spirit, swears and adjures that

> . . . such as unto Cambden do resort
> Have surely found this is not false report,
> Though many lies are dayly now invented,
> This is as true a song as ere was printed.
>
> . . . Let not this seem incredible to any,
> Because it is a thing affirmed by many,
> This is no feigned story, though 'tis new,
> But as 'tis very strange 'tis very true.[27]

One notices the characteristic marks of the news/novels discourse here. First is the affirmation that the work is *trewe* (and also affirmed by many, thus legally true), and also the insistence that the work is new. There is even the contradictory suggestion that because the work is new some might consider it feigned. Another ballad called "News good and new, too good to be true," contained the same ambivalence. Its chorus reads "I never will believe it, 'tis too good to be true," and the verse follows:

> This newes doth much amaze me,
>   the which you have me told.
> And truly to believe it,
>   I dare not be too bold,

> I would that true it were,
>   as it to me is new.
> But I will not believe it,
>   'tis too good to be true.[28]

We see here as well all the hallmarks of the news/novels discourse:
the insistence on truth, and at the same time, since we are dealing
with an inherently contradictory discourse, the refutation of truthfulness, and finally, the notion of recentness.

A final way of securing belief by ballad writers was to register
the work in the *Registers of the Stationers' Company* with the notation
that, for example, the story was "recommended for matter of truth
by master Judge Fenner under his handwrytinge shewed in a Court
or assemblie holden this Daye."[29]

This insistence that ballads were true is more complex a phenomenon than can simply be explained by saying that cagey writers
were attempting to put something over on a gullible readership.
No doubt that motive was present, but, as we will see, it is also
clear that many of the readers knew that their *newes* was not *trewe*
and did not think that fact very significant. To say simply that
readers were gullible fails to explain the obsession with *treweness*
or *neweness* and fails to answer the question of why these qualities
became desirable ones for balladeers to boast about. What can be
said about the nature and significance of such a convention? To be
sure, there are Mopsas and Dorcases in every crowd, as Shakespeare
shows us in the following interchange from *The Winter's Tale* (IV.
iv. 254–79), but if we look at Shakespeare's treatment of the ballad
we can learn more.

CLOWN What hast here? Ballads?
MOPSA Pray now, buy some. I love a ballad in print, a life, for
       then we are sure they are true.
AUTOLYCUS Here's one to a very doleful tune, how a usurer's wife
           was brought to bed of twenty money-bags at a bur-
           then, and how she longed to eat adders' heads and
           toads carbonadoed.
MOPSA Is it true, think you?
AUTOLYCUS Very true, and but a month old.

DORCAS   Bless me from marrying a usurer!
AUTOLYCUS   Here's the midwife's name to't, one Mistress Tale-
porter, and five or six honest wives were present. Why
should I carry lies abroad?
MOPSA   Pray you now, buy it.
CLOWN   Come on, lay it by. And let's first see moe ballads; we'll
buy the other things anon.
AUTOLYCUS   Here's another ballad of a fish that appeared upon the
coast on Wednesday the fourscore of April, forty thou-
sand fathom above water, and sung this ballad against
the hard hearts of maids. It was thought she was a
woman and was turned into a cold fish for she would
not exchange flesh with one that loved her. The ballad
is very pitiful and as true.
DORCAS   Is it true too, think you?
AUTOLYCUS   Five justices' hands at it and witnesses more than my
pack will hold.

The credulity of the country women in this scene was certainly a
target for Shakespeare's ridicule. But we also observe here the
suggestion that print might be seen as a guarantor of truth (albeit
frequently a dubious one). Even the tradition of affixing affirmations, affidavits, and judges' testimonies to ballads, a practice that
was in full swing by the end of the sixteenth century, it would
appear, is a remarkable tribute to the fact that the news/novels
discourse was reaching toward the possibility that printed narrative
could perhaps carry the burden of truth. The contradictory nature
of *newes* is born out by Rollins who writes that there is hardly a
play written during the sixteenth and seventeenth centuries that
does not mention the ballad and always with ridicule. Yet at the
same time the playwrights who ridiculed ballads frequently also
wrote them themselves.[30]

Perhaps more than anything, it is the quality of ambivalence
that characterizes the reaction to ballads as a form and also to
the news/novels discourse. The works themselves insist on their
newe and *trewe* qualities, but these insistences seem to be fighting
an inherently fictional and antique tradition. At the same time, the
inherent doubleness of the discourse, its contradictory stance, only

strengthens the contradictions within it. The news/novels discourse is both old, new, false, and true; it is ultimately unconcerned, paradoxically, with the very terms of its existence; and by affirming that it is new and true, it denies those qualities at the same moment.

We come to even greater contradictions if we look at the criminal biographical ballads (see chapter 7). These were accounts of the lives of criminals, their subsequent execution, and their last dying speech. Of all the ballads in general listed in Rollins' *Analytic Index to the Ballad Entries in the Stationers' Register*, the most popular single subject, according to my count, was criminal behavior. There were 50 ballads about murders (more than on any other topic), 45 on hangings, 15 on public burnings, 3 on pressing to death, and 2 on beheading—all these add up to 115 ballads on criminality. The next most popular topic was Queen Elizabeth with 54 ballads; the Spanish Armada comes in third. Criminal ballads tend to be not only journalistic, recent, and so on, but they are usually alleged to be written by the criminals themselves. Titles often include phrases such as "which he wrote the day before his death," or "made with his owne hand in the Marshalsye, after his condemnation."[31] In the ballad "The Life and Death of Mr. George Sandys . . . " (1626) a third-person narrative of the rogue's life is followed by a short poem which one of Sandys' accomplices, who was also executed, wrote "with his owne hand, a little before his death."[32] These claims to the actual composition of the ballad by the criminal, along with the first-person narrative, would seem to have rendered the ballads even more *trewe* since people were not only getting an account of an event, but were in some metonymic contiguity with the work of the criminal. The fact that the ballads were sold at the execution itself and immediately after to those who were not there created the illusion not only of immediacy and recentness but of contiguity. This illusion is fostered, for example, in one ballad by a felon asking to have the ballad of another famous criminal sung at his own execution.[33]

Of course there are certain problems with this kind of narration, since if the criminal speaks in the first person, he can hardly describe the complete details of his own execution. Such implausibilities do occasionally occur in ballads, as in the following case:

> Upon the twelfth of July now,
> I on a Hurdle plac't,
> Unto my execution drawne,
>   by weeping eyes I past;
> And there in Smith-field at a Stake,
> My latest breath I there did take. . . .[34]

Interestingly, the literary takes priority over the possible in this situation, and one is reminded of Pamela recording events at the most impossible moments. One other approach to solving the problem of the execution of the first-person narrator is found in a ballad called "A Warning For All Desperate Women" (1633) in which a wife laments her own execution for the murder of her husband. The ballad continues consistently in the first person until the penultimate verse when a third-person narrative intervenes at the crucial moment that the wife is consumed by flames:

> God and the world forgive my sinnes
>   which are so vile and foule,
> Sweet Jesus now I come to thee,
>   O Lord receive my soule.
> Then to the Reedes the fire did put,
>   which flamed up to the skye,
> And then she shriek'd most pittifully,
>   before that she did dye.[35]

The awkwardness of this narrative solution underlines the contradiction within this type of ballad between the need for the greatest authority of truth, expressed in the first-person narrative and the claim that the work was written by the criminal's own hand, and the difficulties inherent in trying to sustain such a narration within the constraints of imminently losing the narrator. This conflict will emerge again later when the first-person epistolary novel comes into force, and when such writers are Richardson will have great difficulty in balancing out the demands for authenticity and narrative logic. However, in the criminal ballad, the insistence on truth is based again on the contradictory quality of the news/novels discourse since the ballad could never actually have been written by the criminal. Criminals, we presume, were too busy with other affairs to learn rhyming and scanning along with their basic skills of culling and canting. In maintaining that the authors were actual criminals, writers of these ballads reveal the inherent contradiction of the news/novels discourse—that affirmation of veracity is tantamount to denial.

One other major aspect of the news/novels discourse is the emphasis on forcibly decreasing the distance between the reader and the text. Although the oral tradition implies a kind of physical proximity between listener and speaker, there is no guarantee that the stories told were in any way immediate. Print and written narrative, it is true, have usually implied a separation of reader from event and from the record of that event. However, with the advent of journalism, the temporal distance between reader and event is bridged by the technology of instantaneous dispersal of news—which makes possible a relatively small temporal gap between reader and event. Moreover, the perceptual or narrative distance is decreased as well by such devices as claiming that the work was "writ by his own hand" or by furnishing a wealth of reportorial detail. For example, the description of the following execution, read in the privacy of one's own home, brought the external details of the event closer to the reader than other kinds of writing might have:

> His Belly ripped open wide, his Bowel all he gat.
> And to the fire he [the executioner] straight
>   them threwe which ready there was made:
> And there consumed all to dust, as is the fire's trade.
> His head cut off, the Hangman then, did take it up
>   in hand:
> And up alofte he did it showe, to all that there did stand.
> And then his body in four parts was quartered in that
>   place:
> More pity that his traitorous heart, could take no
>   better grace.[36]

Even if we assume that the event reported is stylized, and granting that Dante had surely done the same kind of reportage earlier, there is something new about the reader's being able to follow this account of an event that may have happened only last week. Now events are brought perceptually closer to the ballad reader than to his ancestors.

One can observe the proximity of the reader to the text in the woodcuts which accompanied ballads. As a contrast to this proximity recall the illustration depicting the French readers of romance (figure 2.1). The upper-class nature of the group is apparent, as is the removal implied by the reader whose back is to the observer. There is a lack of immediacy and a strong sense of closure. Compare this with the illustration from a ballad entitled "A Fool's Bolt is Soon Shot" (1629) (figure 3.1). The Fool in the picture faces the reader who is present by virtue of being the implied target of the Fool's arrow. The gaze of the Fool constitutes a rather new graphic form of conceptualizing the role of the reader in which a direct relationship is implied between subject and object. On either side of the Fool, outside a border which clearly represents the border of the page, stands the reader's substitutes, dressed in nonaristocratic clothing. These two are reduced in size, as if they were on a different plane than the Fool; one looks out at the reader and the other looks at the Fool, thus establishing the entire dynamic of the reading process. Even the text emphasizes this new and double relationship:

> Good friends beware, I'm like to hit yee,
> What ere you be here's that will fit yee,
> Which way soever that you goe,
> At you I ayme my bolt and bow.
>
> Stand wide my masters, and take heed,
> For fear the Foole doth hit yee,
> If that you thinke you shall be shot,
> I'd wish you hence to get yee.[37]

That the reader is about to be hit by the satiric barbs of the Fool and cannot escape criticism is the overt message of the ballad,

A FOOL'S BOLT IS SOON SHOT

𝔄 𝔉ooles 𝔅olt is soone shot.
𝔊ood 𝔉riends beware, 𝔍'me like to hit yee,
𝔚hat ere you be heer's that will fit yee;
𝔚hich way soeuer that you goe,
𝔄t you 𝔍 ayme my 𝔅olt and 𝔅owe.

To the Tune of, *Oh no no no not yet.*

1 STand wide my Masters, and take heed,
  for feare the Foole doth hit yee,
If that you thinke you shall be shot,
  I'de[1] wish you hence to get yee;
My Bowe you see stands ready bent,
  to giue each one their lot,
Then haue amongst you with my Bolts,
  for now I make a shot.

2 He that doth take delight in Lawe,
  and euer to be brangling,
Would be[2] like to the Bells were hang'd,
  that loues still to be iangling;

  [1] *Text* Id'e.   [2] *Text* he.

FIGURE 3.1

which then goes on to lambast various professions. One is clearly dealing with a graphic presentation and a formal content specifically tailored to print and to reading, in which the dynamic of the reader's role is deeply involved. The significant fact is that the reader is seen both as a primary subject within the ballad as well as the voyeur outside the frame of the ballad. Given the assumptions of the news/novels discourse, journalism demands that the reader be actively or passively part of the ongoing story, since newspapers tell the story of the daily world in which the observer lives. In this sense, the reader's functions are split in a way I would think was unique to this discourse—that is, the reader is at once subject and object. The effect of this duality is that ballads can preach at readers to obey various religous and moral precepts and at the same time permit those same readers to voyeuristically watch these transgressions as they are described.

Perhaps the most interesting visual representation of the dual role of readers is found in the well-known bawdy ballad "The Crost Couple, or a Good Misfortune" (see figure 3.2).[38] The story is about a narrator who stumbles upon a man and a woman making love on the grass. The narrator climbs the nearest tree and spies on the partial successes of the man in his wooing. At the penultimate moment to consummation, the narrator, vicariously experiencing the couple's excitement, twists to get a better look and falls out of the tree:

> I turn'd and scrued my body round,
> To see my gallant scale the Town
> But his getting up made me tumble down. . . .

The lovers flee and the moral is given:

> And now I hope a warning 'twill be
> How they in such sinful pleasures agree
> For fear of this Devil that fell from the tree. . . .

The woodcut for the ballad reveals the narrator as a disembodied face hidden in the tree. The bodilessness of the narrator expresses, perhaps, a notion of the disembodiment of reading, an emphases

The crost Couple, OR
A good Misfortune.

Which in a pleasant Ditty discovers,   The fortunate cross of a couple of Lovers.
To a New NORTHERN Tune, much in fashion.

ILle tell you a tale no stranger than true,
  of a fa la la la la la la
The sport on't is old, but the Sonnet is new
  'tis a fa la la la &c
The story sprung from under a Bush
From a tongue & a tune as sweet as a thrush
But I fear it will make a fair Lady to blush
  with a fa &c.
Nay do not turn your faces away
  with a fa &c.
Here's nothing that can your Vertue betray
  with a fa &c.
Let not your fancies look a squint,
The Author would never have put it in Print
If there had been any uncivil word in't
  but a fa &c.
I tell you no tales of Battels & fights
  with a fa &c.
Of wonders of Monsters of Goblins or sprights,
  with a fa &c.
Nor yet of a Thief that got a reprieve
I do not intend your spirits to grieve

.   .   .   .

I went to walk one Evening-tide
  with a fa &c.
My fancy did lead me by a Wood side
  with a fa &c.
'Twas in the prime of all the spring
Which giveth delight to every thing,
I saw a Maid listen to hear a man sing
  to her fa &c.
The tempting dressings that she was in
  with a fa &c.

Would almost seduce a new Saint to the sin
  with a fa &c.
She was a fair & lovely maid
About her wast his Arm he laid
The beautiful'st baggage is soonest betrai'd
  to a fa &c.
I got me strait up into a tree
  with a fa &c.
Where I might see all, and no man see me
  with a fa &c.
The tree was thick and full of growth
The top on't did hover so over them both
  [That if I had fall . . .]
There many amorous glances they cast
  with a fa &c.
But that was not all, the best is at last
  with a fa &c.
Something it seems the youth would do
Which she would not consent unto
Have patience, & you shall know e're you go
  with a fa &c.
When laid on her side, she turn'd to the tree
  with her fa &c.
I durst have sworn she had look'd upon me
  with her fa &c.
He many points of division did run
But she cry'd out no, I shall be undone
He tun'd up his pipes though, & thus he begun
  to her fa &c.
Oh come my own dear let's dally a while
  with a fa &c.
Thou hast quicken'd my spirits now with a smile
  and thy fa &c.

FIGURE 3.2

on the voyeuristic nature of the process, and the ultimate in what Freud would call a "displacement upward." The narrator takes the place of the reader as a vicarious participant in the story and voyeur to the incident. Cupid, too, looks on.

The theme of this illustration was quite popular, it would seem, and it recurs in other ballads. In "John Robinson's Park, Or a Merry Fit of Wooing" we see the same picture (see figure 3.3), although the story is somewhat different. The narrator here too stumbles upon a young couple talking:

> But what they did else
>   It must stay behind . . .
> Their sport being ended
>   away they did go
> This gallant brave Keeper
>   and his Fallow Doe.
> For sporting and courting
>   he had pleased her mind. . . .[39]

The illustration for this ballad again depicts the overseen sexual encounter, and the woodcut appears to have been a tracing from the previous one or vice versa. In yet another ballad "The Knight and the Beggar Wench" we see again another derivative woodcut from this series (figure 3.4). In all of these depictions, the narrator is smaller than the main subjects and bracketed into the corner of the picture, touching and being cut off by the frame. Without investing too much significance in these details, I think we can say that the narrator's double role as subject and voyeur is expressed by the graphically ancillary position in which he is placed. The repetition of this image—which almost amounts to a primal scene fantasy—should show us the interest this configuration had to ballad readers. I would argue that this scene seemed so apt because it embodied the essence of ballad-reading—a voyeurism which decreased the perceptual distance between the reader/narrator and the event, including the reader as a subject within the text. The fact that the ballad "The Knight and the Beggar Wench" is narrated by the knight himself creates the displaced location of nar-

Iohn Robinsons Park, Or a merry fit of Wooing.

Within a Park a young Man met a Maid
With courting and sporting the Damsel with him staid
In pastime and pleasure she uttered her mind
Saying pray thee sweet hony be loving and kind.

AS I went through
  John Robinsons Park,
I heard a Bird singing
  which pleased my heart:
It pleased my heart
  and contented my mind,
Saying pray thee sweet hony
  be loving and kind.

Be loving and kind Love
  and take my advice,
And be no more cheated
  at Cards or at Dice,
For the Cards and the Dice
  Love, will do the much harm,
Then stay at home Honey
  to keep thy love warm.

Sweet hony make much
  of thy Fallow Deer,
To hunt them and chase them
  thou needst not to fear;
Take pleasure at home
  to content thy mind,
And I pray thee sweet hony
  be loving and kind.

To take my advice,
  it will do thee good,
To encrease thy health
  and nourish thy blood,
It will be to thy pleasure
  and content thy mind.
Then pray thee sweet hony
  be loving and kind.

Within thy own Park, Love
  thou hast a pure Doe,
To hunt at thy pleasure
  full well thou dost know,
Then take thy fill
  to content thy mind,
Then I pray thee sweet hony
  be loving &c,

Uncouple your Dogs
  and sound up thy horn,
And lay them on closely
  thy Doe for to chase,
For better thou may hunt her
  from Evening till Morn,
While I in my arms love
  Thy body imbrace.

FIGURE 3.3

The Knight and the Beggar-Wench.

Which doth a wanton prank unfold,
In as merry a story as ever was told.

The Tune is, The Kings delight, or Turn-Coat.

I Met with a jovial Beggar
And into the Fields I led her,
   and I laid her upon the ground;
Her face did not invite mee,
Nor her smock did much delight mee
   but I think the young whore was sound;
With Ladies both fresh and gay
I often did sport and play,
     yet a Beggar I'le take
     for varieties sake,
She'l please mee as well as they.

I have a good Wife, as fair
As ever drew English aire
   her pleasure is past compare,
Her cherry lips, cheeks, and eyes,
Her belly, her breast, and thighs,
   might any but I suffice,
With her I so often play
And weary my time away
     That a fouler to mee,
     Would be fairer than shee,
Variety wins the day.

This Beggar I shall describe,
Without any hope of bribe,
   was one of the maunding tribe
Shee had a fine foot and leg,
As nimble as Doe or Stag,
   and then she began to begg;
So soon as my Horse shee sees
She fell down upon her knees,
     The whore had a sack
     That hung at her back
Well furnish'd with Bread and Cheese.

She struck mee into a dump
The jade was both young and plump,
   with a round, and a ranting Rump;
Her feature had so much force,
It raised in mee remorse
   and drew mee quite off my Horse,
But when I began to wooe
She told mee she would not doo,
     Quoth *I* pretty Mort,
     Let mee shew thee some sport
Shee kist mee, and answered no.

FIGURE 3.4

rator-in-tree to the reader, who is looking over the shoulder of the knight as he performs his deeds. The illustration implies that the overseer is the reader.

In another ballad, "Fourpence Halfpenny Farthing, or A Woman Will Have the Oddes," the narrator is again a concealed witness to a sexual transaction which is negotiated and consummated for the sum of fourpence halfpenny farthing. Later, the narrator again runs into the woman in question and reveals that he had overseen her mercenary/erotic encounter:

> How now sweet lasse, can you thus passe
> By me without regarding.
> Though you have forgot
> yet I have not
> the fourpence halfpenny farthing.[40]

The narrator is not only the subject and voyeur, but he then goes on to proposition the reader saying that he will record all that had passed and sell it for the price of fourpence halfpenny farthing. Aside from the light this ballad casts on Early Modern price equivalents, the ballad also implies an alliance between the narrator as erotic voyeur and the reader who pays the same price for his vicarious pleasure as the original client did for his recreation. The erotic/mercenary relationship is passed along with prostitute to voyeur/narrator to reader, and certainly emphasizes the vicarious quality of reading I have been describing.

All this has to do with journalism and the news/novels discourse in the sense that the ballad as a form and news/novels as a discourse seem to be characterized by the new role of the reader as someone closer to the events being described than earlier readers and auditors might have been. The possibility of the interaction between reader and text was increased by having a serialized or intermittently produced text, like the ballad, which wrote about immediately past events. The phenomenon of pamphlet wars, in which one writer answers another in print, began during this period and it certainly is a consequence of this feeling that one could answer a text and respond to the printed word. Pamphlets, newspapers, and ballads initiated a kind of reader involvement that reached culmination in the late seventeenth century with *The Athenian Mercury*, published by John Dunton, which spent most of its time answering readers' letters on love, philosophy, mathematics, and religion. And, in the same way, the later novel of the eighteenth century would participate in this intimate relationship with the reader; one thinks of Fielding cajoling his reader, Richardson giving the impression that we are voyeuristically reading a lady's letters, or Defoe preaching to his typographically gathered congregation.

The characteristics that have emerged so far in this consideration of the news/novels discourse are an insistence on recentness as well as on factuality (despite the fact that the works might be neither new nor true), and a decreasing of the perceptual distance between reader and text. In addition, the news/novels discourse is characterized as one which historically has answered the needs of the lower classes to be informed about public events. The tensions at work in the ballad—claims to truth and recentness and the simultaneous inability of the narrative to support factuality—point in the direction of the later use of "news" and "novel" as two words which define fairly clearly their respective allegiance to fiction and fact. This line of thinking leads also to the tentative theory that the news/novels discourse is a kind of undifferentiated matrix out of which journalism and history will be distinguished from novels— that is factual narratives will be clearly differentiated from fictional ones. We have seen up to this point that there is no commonly agreed upon narrative capable of sustaining factuality in print since fact and fiction were not significant discriminants of genre during this time. Of course this does not mean, as I have said, that there was no criteria for fact or fiction during this period, but rather that genres were not defined by their allegiance to truth-telling or invention.

In order to explain this state of affairs, we need to realize that the distinction we now make between fact and fiction was not the same distinction made before the eighteenth century. William Nelson in *Fact or Fiction: The Dilemma of the Renaissance Storyteller* points out that history and fiction blur into one another from Greek and Roman times until the end of the sixteenth century. Cicero, he notes, classified *fabula*, *historia*, and *argumentum* into a single species of *narratio*, even though we now catalogue these genres (fantasy, actual history, and comedy) into separate and fairly exclusive groupings. Written histories, Nelson remarks, carried no assurance of truthfulness until the end of the sixteenth and the beginning of the seventeenth century.[41]

Even an historian such as Sir Walter Raleigh refused to give up the convention used by the Greeks of inventing speeches to fit the particular historical event, and Raleigh maintained the right of inventing an historical occurrence, like the French romancers, if no contradictory records were available: "But in filling up the blanks of old histories, we need not be so scrupulous. For it is not to be feared, that time should run backward, and by restoring the things themselves to knowledge, make our conjectures appear ridiculous."[42] Raleigh's criterion of truth—absence of controversion—was a governing one. By the same token, writers of ballads, newsbooks, and novels might claim their work was *trewe* since no one could prove them false. According to Raleigh's definition, if one wrote tales about people who never existed, that is if one wrote complete fabrications with no relation to reality, imaginative fiction, allegories on current events, or simply told the stories of actual events changing only the names of the people and places—one would still be writing a *trewe* account. Fiction could be *trewer* than truth. Of course, it should be pointed out that even while Raleigh was writing, a movement toward empiricism and documentation had begun under the aegis of the Society of Antiquaries with such historians as William Camden, Sir Robert Cotton, and Ben Jonson. However, documentation of history did not genuinely take hold until the late seventeenth and early eighteenth centuries, and certainly there was no movement in this direction on the part of journalism until much later.

Sir Philip Sidney, responding to the Puritan Stephen Gosson's assertion in his *School of Abuse* that poetry was the mother of lies, wrote in his well-known *An Apology for Poetry* (1583) that virtual truth is often less veracious than moral truth. For Sidney, as for the ballad writers, it was the moral or example drawn from the event, rather than the detailed description of the event itself, that represented truth. While Gosson cited Plato's authority in banning the poets from his republic, Sidney argued that the historian "is bound to tell things as things were," but the poet can "frame his example to that which is most reasonable, be it warlike, politic, or private matters," and in so doing yield from the historical event the truth that eludes the historian of facts.[43] Sidney maintains "that a feigned example hath as much force to teach as a true example." Here he relies on Aristotle, who says in the *Poetics* that "poetry deals with general truths, history with specific events."[44]

Truth does not necessarily walk at the side of fact in the sixteenth century as we have seen. Michel Foucault notes that during this period, the primary operation of the intellect was to search for the sign beneath the event, just as the birth of a monstrous child was an important occurrence not for the event itself but as a sign of God's intention: "The function proper to knowledge is not seeing or demonstrating; it is interpreting."[45] This attitude toward reality diminishes the value of the literal train of events, and only requires these events in order to plumb their depths and find the genuine stratum of moral truth by interpretation.

Histories, stories, and news accounts, then, were important to the sixteenth century only insofar as they clearly taught lessons and offered interpretations. If they were not new, if they were not accurate, or even if they were completely fabricated, they could still serve this purpose. In fact, the more the event was worked over, the more readily it would yield its moral example. As Sidney had indicated, far from being the mother of lies, poetry, though opposed to the language of detail and accuracy, was the father of historical truth. This view might also help to explain why verse, rather than prose, was so frequently used to write news reports in ballads. Although prose could better carry the consecutive, linear arrangement of events, these details do not in themselves amount to anything, and may even confuse the reader. Verse, however, can better extract the moral truth from the carcass of the quotidian.

My point in this chapter is that during the late sixteenth and early seventeenth centuries it was an extremely unusual, if not impossible thing, for a reader to consider a narrative as being purely factual or actually recent. The news/novels discourse had been inaugurated as a result of a technology which permitted, but did not guarantee, a text of recentness. Likewise, with the beginning of the report of recent events came the problem of proving the truth of that report. The readers of these novels, ballads, *newes*, and so on clearly valued the idea that a narrative *might* have been true, but they bought the narratives whether true or false. The large collection of ballads which Samuel Pepys kept should illustrate that even a fairly well-educated man could be a consumer of this type of journalism and not, one presumes, because he was wonderfully gullible. Rather he collected such works because they were news and because they represented access to an information dispersal system never before open to the lower and middle classes. Although the news/novels discourse is built on a series of contradictions, as we have seen, those contradictions, far from discrediting the genre, do precisely define that genre. That is, the news/novels discourse is marked by an inherent doubleness or reflexivity; it is by definition exactly *not* what it says it is. Its claims to recentness and veracity are not only falsely made, but they are also unprovable. Readers of such works would be literally unable to say whether what they were reading was true or not. This ambivalence is also a characteristic of the news/novels discourse, as will be demonstrated. As long as the fiction was factual, or as long as the facts were fictional, balladeers, news writers, and novelists were well within the limits of their discourse.

CHAPTER IV

Prose News: Continuity, Seriality, and Ideology

IN THE SEVENTEENTH century, the ballad was replaced by the newsbook or news pamphlet as the major form of journalism, and, in the process, prose replaced poetry as the adequate language for describing the ongoing events of the world. When news began to be defined ideologically, it became more significantly dangerous to the government. As that happened, there grew a more pressing need to define legally the nature of "factual" news, which then might be banned, as opposed to fictional narrative, which was not specifically dangerous, at least not obviously so, and might be allowed to circulate. The history of that process of defining fact and fiction in a cultural sense, is also the history of the splitting of the undifferentiated matrix of news/novels into novels on the one hand, and journalism and history on the other. To understand this development, we need to turn to the history of prose news during the seventeenth century.

For our purposes the first significant development was the creation of a notion of continuity and seriality—two characteristics necessarily associated with journalistic publication. News would come to develop an existence that was more permanent than the ephemerality of the occasionally occurring ballad or flying sheet, and it would develop an audience whose reflex was to turn to a printed page to find out what was happening outside the window, as it were. In this sense, journalism would develop the capacity to comment on the world in a regular, continuous manner instead of the spotty, eccentric, and discontinuous way it had appropriated from the flying sheet.

The first serially printed, that is, published at some regularly scheduled interval, newsbook is reputed to be Nathaniel Butter's *The Courant, or Weekly News from Foreign Parts* (1621) which was translated from the Dutch. Formally, newsbooks very much resembled pamplets except that they contained journalistic reports. Foreign newsbooks and news-sheets had provided most of the prose news in the early seventeenth century. However, when James I banned the importation of these foreign newsbooks in 1621, Nathaniel Butter rushed in to republish them in England where they could not be considered foreign, and hence were allowed to be sold.

The earlier news forms—ballads and flying sheets—continued to be read in the first quarter of the seventeenth century, as were occasional broadsides and pamphlets. However, all these varieties were published irregularly. The sense that public events of the world could be transcribed as they happened in some kind of regular serial format seems to have been largely absent from the culture before the advent of *The Courant*. Printed news, rather than being part of an ongoing journalistic account of the world's story, was much closer to the tale or short story with which it shared its name etymologically. These accounts were "novels"—they were written on the occasion of the unusual, the quirky, the puzzling. They did not provide continuing reportage but only a view of the isolated event as it occurred. News-sheets and ballads, like short stories and tales, related sensational events or interesting anecdotes, but as yet a distinct journalistic sense of time had not arisen nor had the regularly occurring newspaper with a fixed title and regular readership.

Journalism is not, after all, history, and it requires a special sense of time that does not cast events in the powerful retrospect of narrative's past tense. Narrative, it would seem, had carried with it a signification that the events it described were distantly past. Journalism made possible, as we have said, the capacity for narrative to describe the quite recent past. However, it was not until the appearance of the regularly occurring serial newspaper that printed narrative could literally keep up with the passage of time. A regularly printed newspaper could take advantage of what amounted to a "median past tense" mediating between the past (reserved for narratives and history) and the present (which was most likely confined to spoken language, poetry, drama)—and this tense would be uniquely a journalistic one implying that what one was reading had only a slightly deferred immediacy. The development of such a sense of time was the extension of the capacity of print to contain recentness. Recentness was made possible by the technology of print, as we have seen, but the median past tense of journalism was only made possible by combining continuity with recentness.

This journalistic past tense should not be considered a strictly grammatical tense but rather a semantic one, if such a notion is permissible, or it might be seen as a linguistic signal that alerts the reader to interpret the nature of "past" as being more immediate. An example of this mediating journalistic past tense is found in one of Butter's early newsbooks. The headline read: "The State of Tillies and Brunswicks Armies since the last encounter."[1] The word "last" implies a mediation of the past. The reader is given a sense of the continuity of events, and is informed that the journalistic past extends only back to the last newsbook and no further. Even the title of this newsbook, *The Continuation*, stresses the sense of continuity, and readers would buy such works for a continuous relay of information rather than reports of discrete, isolated events. Only when there is a sense of suspense in readers as they watch the world's history unfold can printers like Butter sell news.

Further, just as we have seen with ballads, the news depends on the fact that the newsbook buyer is both object and subject, both reader of events and participant in those events. The story related in newsbooks is about the external events of the world. But, at the same time, the idea of continuity and recentness implies the reader's involvement in that externality. The reader becomes, through the process of reading news, a participant in that external reality. Paradoxically, the reading of these kinds of narrative does not remove readers from the world but rather makes them more a part of that world. A merchant cannot simply dismiss an account of ships being attacked by foreign sailors as a fiction since he may be affected by that information. The voyeuristic quality of ballads is carried along the news/novels discourse to the actual possibility of being involved in the scene one reads about. The news/novels discourse, as it develops, draws the reader within it in a way that is quite new to Western culture. The reader is brought within the frame of the discourse both spatially and temporally since his life is brought within the compass of print and his perception of the passage of time is taken on by the median past tense.

When a reader during the seventeenth century thought of buying a news-sheet or newsbook, the notions of recentness, continuity, and seriality must have been key signifiers for this discourse. Such signifiers, I might emphasize, were violently dissimilar to those of the romance developing in France during this same period, and it would take quite an imaginative leap to try to equate the development of the novel, with its emphasis on continuity, seriality, and recentness, with the romance.

With the shift toward prose and regularly printed news in the seventeenth century, the news/novels discourse remained as ambivalent toward fact and fiction as it had been in the previous century. Just as ballads had been characterized by their mixing of an insistence on truth with a lack of concern about the actual veracity of a news story, so too prose news was seen as an inherently double or reflexive discourse. In Ben Jonson's *The Staple of News* (1625) the new trade of journalist was ridiculed as being dishonest. In the preface to the reader, Jonson wrote that the author

> prays you . . . to consider the newes here vented, to
> be none of this newes, or any reasonable mans, but
> newes made like the times newes (a weekly cheat to
> draw money) and could not be fitter reprehended,

> than in raising this ridiculous office of the staple,
> wherein the age may see her owne folly, or hunger
> and thirst after published pamphlets of newes, set
> out every Saturday, but made all at home, and no
> syllable of truth in them.[2]

The standard attacks on news, as we have seen before, focused on the fact that news was made up, fictional, and only published to cheat people of their money. One notices, here, a new accusation— it seem to have been a particularly galling fact that these reports were published regularly ("a weekly cheat," "set out every Satur- day"). Continuity seems to be identified as a fault of the discourse. In the same year as Jonson's play, Abraham Holland similarly attacked Butter in a poem called "A Continu'd Just Inquisition of Paper Persecutors":

> . . . But to behold the wals
> Butter'd with Weekly News compos'd in Pauls,
> By some decaied Captaine, or those Rooks,
> Whose hungry braines compile prodigious books . . .
> To see such Butter everie weeke besmeare
> Each publike post, and Church dore, and to heare
> These shamefull lies, would make a man, in spight
> of Nature, turne Satyrist and write
> Revenging lines, against these shameless men
> Who thus torment both Paper, Presse, and Pen.[3]

The malice directed at the weekly news in this poem, including the punning reference to Nathaniel Butter in the first lines, suggests that printed news seemed to those who derived their news from other sources a kind of debasement of information by a new tech- nology which befouled the idea of news, as the scatological im- precations here suggest. One notes the repetition here too of the words "weekly" and "everie week" as if to imply that the very regularity of the news had something new and irritating about it. The idea of serial publication seems something that the poet finds objectionable; and the idea of continuity, which serial publication requires, must have represented enough of a cultural innovation to be taken note of in this way. Perhaps the threat of an omnipresent weekly expression of the lower class's presence, compounded by what must have been more than occasional barefaced lies on the part of news writers, gave pause to many of the literati and upper classes.

By 1626, only five years after Butter began his journalistic enterprise, the news writer had become an easily identifiable type or character, and he is always depicted as lying. In John Fletcher's play *The Fair Maid of the Inn* he appears as "a lying stationer . . . a new Mercurius Gallo-Belgicus" (IV. ii.).[4] In 1631, a book of characters, includes among the other stock figures a "coronto-coiner":

> His mint goes weekly, and he coines money by it. Howsoever, the more intelligent merchants do jeer him, the vulgar do admire him, holding his Novels oracular. . . . Whisperings, mutterings, and bare suppositions are sufficient grounds for the authoritie of his relations. . . . He is all ayre, his eare always open to all reports, which, how incredible soever, must pass for currant, and find vent, purposely to get him currant money, and delude the vulgar.[5]

Here "novels" are clearly identified with the vulgar as opposed to the "more intelligent merchants." News publications are also clearly identified as fictions created to make money for the writer. The tone is one of class-derived scorn, and in this genre the news writer was so discredited that one author could say that the journalists "have used this trade so long that now everyone can say it's true as a Currantoe, meaning that it's all false."[6]

Surely, most readers of printed news, unless they were extremely credulous, must have recognized that the news they were reading was not accurate or truthful, and perhaps this distinction did not bother them. Although a willingness to read in newspapers what may not be true is certainly a mark even today of readers of mass-circulation papers, the seventeenth-century reader's perception is qualitatively different. Today's reader is aware that journalism is a discourse which is supposed to report on facts and events in the real world, even if it does not always do so. The seventeenth-century reader, as we have seen, probably had no such expectations.

If ballads carried little assurance of verity and made small distinction between fact and fiction, why should it disturb the same reader that news in general should do the same?

By and large the attacks on the news that we have seen have been by those members of the upper class or of the writers who were dependent on that class. The class distinction is significant here because the upper classes and wealthier merchants had available to them an alternate and preexisting news information system based on exclusive oral channels, letter-writing, and private communication. Therefore, these groups did not need journalism of the kind we are looking at. Merchants, artisans, journeymen, and others—were the prime consumers of the news/novels discourse, and as such the discourse was seen as constitutively vulgar, untrue, and potentially dangerous to the interests of the aristocracy. However, it was only during the turbulence preceding and during the civil war that news began to be seriously considered by all parties as politically troublesome. As it became increasingly important to mobilize public opinion and the support of all kinds of people, news began to be an important tool of political ideology.

In this sense, the crucial change in the news/novels discourse came during the middle of the seventeenth century, when news became ideological, and in so doing also became one of the powerful creators of ideology. The existence of a serially printed newsbook which could cover domestic events helped to create a revolution in the way that government would now have to function. The newfound continuity of journalism, its ability to create an ongoing, coterminous account of public events became associated with another cultural development—a regularly subscribing group of readers who were also defined by their political interests. The development of such a group, well-represented by the lower classes, bound together by political interests, and now reading a regularly printed journal must have constituted a serious social force with which to reckon. It is clear that pamphlets, for example, while they had an extremely wide readership and were printed in greater profusion than newsbooks, were only occasional in nature, peaking in production during the time of greatest political unrest in 1642 and then dropping off.[7] Pamphlet production rose and fell, but newsbooks and news-sheets remained steadily, serially, present on the scene, though individual papers might survive or fail.

Whereas earlier the news was not particularly political and had a readership that might range through all segments of the lower classes, now intense partisanship began to flourish at the same time as domestic news was permitted to be printed. Clearly both of these developments were part of a larger social convulsion. The newsbook began to develop into an instrument to effect social change by forging a connection between writing, political interests, and political events. Whereas earlier interest in news had come largely from a curious and credulous readership, now it became more pragmatic. The Parliament in its struggle against the King had to turn to the citizens for support, and its main avenue of appeal was the press. G. M. Trevelyan noted that "former Parliaments had spoken for the people, but never called upon the people to protect them."[8] Who exactly the "people" were is perhaps difficult to define with clarity, but what is clear is that in previous eras kings had seen the citizenry as a force to keep tightly reigned, but that now the King had to appeal for their support. Samuel Hartlib predicted in a pamphlet that "the art of printing will so spread knowledge that the common people, knowing their own rights and liberties, will not be governed by a way of oppression."[9]

Both the Royalists and the Roundheads quickly developed their own regular newsbooks, each employed for the purpose of calling up the assistance of the populace. News, born in disgust and apparently repudiated by the entirety of the aristocratic class, finally gained a certain legitimacy in being one of the few means available for political parties or the government to address the populace. In the past the populace, mute and homogenous, could only murmur individually and inarticulately in the face of the monolithic power of the royal proclamation or respond collectively by rioting. But now the populace could respond to governmental language, could speak through the mechanism of the press, in an articulated voice. With the beginning of the partisan newsbook, diversity of opinion within the populace could find expression.

Whereas printed news as a whole had been considered false before, now the word "false" begins to be used to signify ideological position. False news is the news printed by the opposition party. In this sense, news may be factually true, yet for political purposes the opposition must see it as false. Instead of attacks on the news coming from those in power, now abuse is carried on by and within the press itself. Each political side claimed their newsbooks were the only authentic ones. Such titles as *Mercurius Civicus, London's Intelligencer or Truth impartially related from thence to the whole Kingdom to prevent misinformation* now become common.

The battle of abuse between *Mercurius Britanicus*, a proparliamentary newsbook, and *Mercurius Aulicus*, a Royalist publication, is illustrative of this kind of mutual accusation. These two publications seem to have been specifically conceived to hurl opprobrium at one another. This mudflinging was performed with such energy that each paper was filled almost exclusively with denunciations and refutations of the other. For example, in the following excerpt *Britanicus* rakes *Aulicus* over the coals:

> Now Reader though Aulicus be the licenst liar, yet this one [*Aulicus*] too ex officio, and indeed lying is the chiefe engine whereby they support their credits both with forraigne States and at home, but if men were not willfully blinded and hardened, even to their owne destructions, they would come out from their darkness and falsehoods into the apparent light and truth.[10]

This apparent monopoly on light and truth is the claim of each mercury which, because of its ideological commitment, sees itself within a parenthesis apart from the general definition of news as "lies." *Britanicus* continues, saying that *Aulicus* had taken upon itself to correct some "mistakes" which *Britanicus* had made in a past issue. In turn, *Aulicus* is accused of making "many mistakes": "Sometimes thou mistakest the Parliament for pretended houses; and sometimes the new Assembly for young Levites; and Losse, for Victories; and Irish Rebells, for good subjects, these are all thy mistakes. . . ." Clearly, the mistakes being spoken of by *Britanicus* are actually errors colored by political beliefs and are not simple misrepresentations of facts. The Parliament is composed of "pretended houses" only if one has sided with the Royalists, and one party's "losse" is another's "victorie."

To be in error had dimensions that went beyond politics alone. Concurrent with the political upheaval of the time was a significantly related linguistic upheaval. A revolution in writing was advocated by Puritans in the use of "the plain style"—that is, the use of everyday language in writing and preaching, avoiding elaborate tropes, metaphors, and figurative language.[11] We are talking here mainly about sermons on the one hand and printed discourse on the other. When one newsbook accused the other of being in error regarding the use of words, it could simultaneously be accusing that publication of being in error regarding religion. When Puritans attacked the elaborate style of the Anglican clergy, they were attacking the Laudian's Royalist proclivities as well as their preference for the "beauty of holiness."[12] The plain style claimed for itself a closer kinship with the Word of God than with the ornate words of man; thus for Puritans it became a religious obligation to use language in an unambiguous way. One's choice of words was thus ideologically determined and ideologically significant. Hence, to be a liar—as *Britanicus* accuses *Aulicus* of being—is to go against the designs of God. Indeed, one newspaper made this equation specific by saying that all pro-Royalists were witches.[13] One has the sense here of a powerful triangulation on language, religion, and politics which would give the act of lying or of not telling the truth a powerful significance.

Indeed, Thomas Hobbes conceived of language as central to the political ordering of society in a similar way. In *Leviathan* (1651) Hobbes grounded his political observations in a linguistic and epistemological analysis which began with the role of the senses and imagination, and then quickly moved to human speech—assuming that these fundamentals of human perception constituted the underlying structure of any political theory. For Hobbes, reason must be based on accurately perceiving objects in the material world and correctly naming them: "Seeing then that truth consists in the right ordering of names in our affirmations, man that seeks precise truth had need to remember what every name he uses stands for and to place it accordingly. . . ."[14]

This insistence on the correct use of language does not come from a desire for rhetorical niceties but rather is directly related to political matters. Religious and political errors result from errors in perceiving and naming things, and language perpetuates these errors by fixing the incorrect concept to a word. When words move away from the world of things and begin to represent abstract concepts, then language becomes imprecise and dangerous. Hobbes calls this notion the doctrine of "separated essences," by which he means that the essence of a thing is separated out from its corporality, with the result that such signification means "nothing." Words ought to be the embodiment, as it were, of things: "For the circumscription of a thing is nothing else but the determination or defining of its place, and so both the terms of the distinction are the same."[15] And the cause for much religious and political error results from the use of words that do not signify. Hobbes singles out "names that signify nothing but are taken and learned by rote from schools such as hypostatical, transubstantiate, consubstantiate, eternal-now, and the like of canting schoolmen."[16] The distinctly ideological nature of the words chosen by Hobbes indicates the very inseparability of the issue of language from that of ideology and religion for those involved in this controversy.

Though Hobbes himself seemingly defied the conventional triangulation of religious beliefs, language, and politics—by being at once politically allied with the Puritans and linguistically with the plain style, while remaining independent and secretly taking communion—he mirrored to some degree certain Puritan writers and philosophers in his perception that language had deteriorated from an earlier purity and therefore needed correction. Hobbes wrote that "the first author of speech was God himself, that instructed Adam how to name such creatures as he presented to his sight." While this original language was based on the correct naming of things, all of it "was again lost at the Tower of Babel." The lexical golden age, having been destroyed, was succeeded by a period of decadent and defective language in which the England of Hobbes' time still found itself. Abstract words, "separated essences," and even metaphoric language were signs of an opacity in language that was a result of post-Babel existence. Thus, words are used in senses other than that for which they were "ordained" and so they "openly profess to deceit."[17] In this sense, for Hobbes, man must free himself from error—both religious and political—by transforming language so that it accurately describes the world of objects.

The categories of truth and falsity modify their definition, to some extent, under this new critique of language. According to the demands of the plain style, language should embody in itself the object it names or describes. Unlike the language used in writing ballads, which asks us to read through the surface of details to the essence of truth, the Puritan's attempt was to arrive at a language that represents things, that embodies those things in itself. According to Michel Foucault, who describes the process of linguistic change during this period, the desire for representation leads to language's abandonment of the notion of a "Primary Text open to interpretation and polysemousness, and with it the entire, inexhaustible foundation of the words whose mute being was inscribed in things; all that remains is representation, unfolding in the verbal signs that manifest it, and hence becoming discourse." Foucault says that as polysemousness or metaphorical thinking is abandoned, commentary or interpretation yields to criticism of "the discursivity of representation."[18] Before, the true meaning of the kind of language used in the ballad was to be found by a hermeneutic delving beneath the details of the news, which might be false, to the essence of truth and morality beneath the surface. Now truth would lie much closer to the surface; true-speaking had much more to do with language and politics in news, in a growing concern about the

accuracy of detail, and a growing legal mechanism to define, analyze, and contain the nature of the representation.

To be in error, to tell lies, to create falsehoods now all pointed
in the direction of an ideological and political act, at least insofar
as the news/novels discourse is concerned. It is possible to say that
this conceptual and linguistic state of affairs might have arisen
independently of printed news, but one scholar, at least, points to
a "profound interconnection . . . between the new Age of Ideology
. . . and the 'communications revolution' grounded in the development of printing. . . ."[19] Alvin Gouldner demonstrates that the
development of news was a major cause of social movements and
ideologies, saying that "the men and women who wrote and read
ideologies differed from earlier, literate persons in that they were
a *news-reading public*." In fact, Gouldner goes so far as to say that
ideologies are "defined as symbol systems generated by, and intelligible to, persons whose relationship to everyday life is mediated
by their reading—of newspapers, journals, or books—and by the
developing concept of 'news'. . . ."[20] Gouldner's analysis of news
is more complex than my presentation of it here suggests, but one
has the sense from what he says that the development of the news/
novels discourse is intimately linked to the growth of ideologies,
that language became more centrally the focus of questions about
truth and falsehood. Fact and fiction, as categories themselves,
while not defined, became in some sense more problematical in
their relation to the news/novels discourse.

With the development of the news/novels discourse's ability
to create an ongoing, coterminous account of reality through the
use of seriality, continuity, and recentness, came the possibility for
the growth of a regular readership with shared values, politics, and
ideologies. The ideologizing of language, in turn, created the conditions for legal intervention into the realm of the discourse to
diffuse the politicizing of news/novels, which then created the conditions for a definition of fact and fiction in which the former could
be repressed and the latter more or less ignored. The ensuing

history of the intervention of government control in the seeming innocence of the discourse that brought readers ballads about women giving birth to frogs is one which also gives us insights into the splitting up of the news/novels discourse into news on the one hand and novels on the other.

CHAPTER V

The Law and the Press: Splitting the Discourse

ONE OF THE central questions about the origins of genres is—what causes change? Is there a necessary cause, a force, or an aim to changes in literary genres, or are we consigned to a realm of impenetrable forces, complex and shifting uncertainties, and vague speculations on taste, style, and so on? In the case of the novel, can we say that there is an element of destiny? Was the Western world destined to head toward the goal of the novel? Could anything else have happened along that headlong rush, or is the path of history also the path of destiny?

It is possible to talk about the necessity for change on a formal level. One could say that the tale was too short to develop a character or a plot adequately, or that romance was too episodic for psychological realism. But buried in such discussions is the unexplained core of necessity. Why should one particular change and not another occur? Are there only formal solutions to formal problems? Switching to the social context does not eliminate the problems of causality. If there is a cause-and-effect relationship between political and cultural events, and few would deny that there is, the actual microtechnique of that relationship is frequently avoided or obscured. It is quite common to say that the relationship between literature and society is "complex," "subtle," or "overdetermined" and to avoid trying to create causalities at all. In effect, this approach amounts to a kind of smoke screen used to avoid the very fact that we actually lack any rigorous methodology to account for the relationship between literary genres and historical change. While no one would deny that this relationship is indeed complex, subtle, and overdetermined, unless we can pinpoint fairly concrete interactions, are we not deluding ourselves about the nature of the knowledge we are producing?

In an attempt to confront those problems that seem to appear automatically when any discussion of causality is raised, I will try in this chapter to anchor myself in some cause which could be said to bear directly, or fairly directly, on the actual physical appearance of the novel. Going beyond the general assertion of causality, it is possible, I would argue, to say that certain social forces manifest themselves fairly directly on literary works. The laws which define and limit the cognitive space of a work, genre, or ensemble of texts are frequently not only literary laws but legal ones as well. That is why I have chosen here to examine the tangible effects of legal interventions in the sphere of printed prose narrative. As Michel Foucault has pointed out frequently and persuasively, discourse is a manifestation of power, and can be used to control thought as well as be controlled by institutions of power.[1] The full extent of legal intervention in the discourse of novel-writing can tell us much about the function of that discourse as it came to be defined in certain crucial ways by the laws.

My method could be labeled materialist, since I am searching for ways of talking about the intersection of the material world with the aesthetic world. Therefore I have focused on the intro-duction of the technology of print into narrative, and now on the effect of actual legal restrictions on the limits of narration. How-ever, I am not claiming that laws—even the most effectively en-forced ones—are free from nonmaterialistic consideration. No law can prevent artists, reformers, or revolutionaries from writing and printing what they will. But laws can do two things: they can reflect the will and the assumptions of the people who make them, and they can control to some extent the production of printed matter and the archival record of that production. To the extent that the law can do the latter, it can be said to be a direct influence on what would be submitted or even written for publication; to the extent that it does the former, law can provide a relevant clue to general and class attitudes. Of course the legal viewpoint is not, in and of itself, even remotely a complete explanation for the beginning of the novel. I do not claim that the novel came into being because certain laws were passed and others were clarified and refined. Yet I do think it is possible to say that legal causality is a legitimate, fairly direct, and powerful explanation of how certain aspects of the novel developed.

A contemporary example may help us understand the fairly direct implications of legal tampering with a discourse. In December 1979 the U.S. Supreme Court refused to review the $75,000 award won in a suit brought by Paul Bindrim, a California psychologist, against Doubleday and Company for publishing a work of fiction by Gwen Davis called *Touching*. Bindrim maintained that he was the, real-life model for a fictional character in *Touching* who was a bearded leader of a nude encounter therapy session. Ms. Davis was obviously engaged in writing fiction, although she may have had some notion that her fiction was a *roman à clef* or even that she was merely writing from experience. In any case, the Supreme Court in effect created a new definition of fiction which insists that a work is fictional only if there is no resemblance between literature and life. The power of the libel law and the sanctions it contains may now be brought to bear against all authors who claim to be writing fiction, making sure that their works remain comfortably distant from recognizable experience, the author's claims to fictionality notwithstanding. Doubleday and Company made this law even more effective by bringing its own charges against Ms. Davis, suing her for $138,000 to cover the $75,000 award plus interest, legal, and other expenses. One could argue that such legal decisions have little effect on what various novelists write, but one must consider the considerable personal loss that would come now once the discourse has been defined legally in this narrow sense of fiction as fiction only. As I will demonstrate in this chapter, such redefining of fiction and fact by the law has had some considerable effect on the news/novels discourse.

If we do look to English law, we will see that just as we have seen a massive confusion between the nature of fact and fiction in ballads and newsbooks, so too will we see this confusion in laws passed to control the spread of those pieces of journalism which were antigovernmental or heretical. The earliest laws that deal with criminal libel are the common laws, and they reflect an attitude toward libel which disregards whether the libels themselves were true or false. The only significant factor was that the libel had the malicious intent of causing a breach of the peace. If a statement caused damage to the reputation of another, whether or not it was true, then it was considered a libel.[2] These definitions were part of the common law which applied to all the property-holding citizens of England. But it was with the statutes *Scandalum Magnatum* that the aristocracy was separated from the common law and special libel laws were applied.

The first of these statutes was enacted in 1275 and declared that "from henceforth no one be so hardy as to tell or publish any false news or tales whereby discord, or occasion of discord or slander, may grow between the King and his people or the great men of the realm."[3] In the next century, this statute was modified to include an enumeration of these great men, namely "prelates, dukes, earls and barrons, and other nobles."[4] These laws created the category of seditious libel, libel against the state, and consequently the prosecution of these cases was assigned to the King's Council rather than the common law courts. It was from the King's Council that future control of the press would emanate. However, what is significant about these laws of *Scandalum Magnatum* was that, unlike common law libel, seditious libel had to be a false accusation. Simply defaming a member of the nobility could not be considered libelous if the accusation was true.

With this set of decrees, there was at least a criterion of truth about a libelous statement, a distinction between a factual accusation and a fictional one, at least within the King's Council. At the same time, the common law made no such distinction. This double attitude toward the criterion for truth in the legal sense is fascinating since it is exactly the opposite of what one would imagine—it was more difficult, at least in principle, to convict the libeler of a king than a libeler of a citizen since the accusation against the king had to be proven to have been false. This state of affairs would shift the burden of defense to the prosecutor, who had to prove that the nobleman did not or could not have done what he was accused of doing. Given the realities of power this approach should not have been difficult, but as time went on it became cumbersome to enforce the seditious libel law since so many potential libelers claimed to have been speaking the truth.[5]

These laws provided the base for future state prosecutions of printers and writers. However, as the news/novels discourse developed through the sixteenth and early seventeenth centuries, the whole notion of true and false libels became problematic. First of all, as we have seen, ballads and newsbooks as well as fictional tales all intersected and interpenetrated each other so that it would be difficult to isolate what was a mere story from what was something more than a story. Further, since many writers tried to avoid prosecution, they might deliberately cloak their attack on the government in the form of a satire, an allegory, or a fiction. Therefore, a narrative which on the surface was fictional, could at the same time constitute a veiled attack on the government. For example, the policy of enclosure and conversion of arable land to pasture, which resulted in the eviction of a considerable portion of the English peasantry so that sheep could graze, is attacked in a ballad written during the reign of Edward VI. Rather than attacking the King, the balladeer attacks the sheep for reasons of judicious metonymy:

> The sheep he is a wicked wight;
> Man, woman, and child he devoureth quite . . .
> Men were wont off sheep to feed;
> Sheep now eat men on doubtful deed.
> CHORUS: The black sheep is a perilous beast;
>   *cujus, contrarium falsum est.*[6]

For legal purposes would this ballad constitute a libel? Is it even to be considered a factual statement? Can such a work be considered libelous since it does not defame anyone, although it asks the reader to see through a relatively thin veil of signification to the hidden libel?

To deal with this new category, the judicial system would need a machinery to force potentially libelous material out of the protective embrace of the allegorical, the satirical, the imaginative. In order to establish such a machinery, distinct categories of indictable and nonindictable (that is to say, news and fiction) would have to be defined and established. The law would either have to become more subtle, to anticipate the maneuvers of writers and printers trying to slip through the loopholes, or would have to become more blunt and heavy-handed by simply restricting all manner of printing. Both approaches were tried.

During the reign of Henry VIII numerous laws were enacted against the printing trade which would fall under the category of blunt measures. Henry attempted to stop the importation of foreign books since most of these advocated heretical Lutheranism. The book trade in England in the beginning of the sixteenth century was largely dominated by foreigners, and they were seen as potential agents in the cause of Luther. In 1523 there were thirty-three printers and booksellers in England and more than two-thirds were aliens.[7] In view of this state of affairs, Henry saw the entire publishing industry, such as it was, as filled with heretical, plotting foreigners, and so he passed a variety of laws to restrict that trade and its productions.[8] Licensing began for the first time in 1524 under the purview of the church and was then moved to the King's Council in 1538. This shift corresponded to a realization that the press was not just dangerous because of its Lutheran leanings but because the press, as a new invention, was inherently dangerous to royal power. In this sense, the royal monopoly of information was being usurped by the printing press.

Succeeding monarchies also crudely tried to curb the press. In 1557 Queen Mary established the Stationers' Company with the express aim of stamping out "scandalous, malicious, schizmatical and heretical" printing by creating an organization which could search and seize illegal presses.[9] Queen Elizabeth devised a more efficient licensing system, and it was under her reign that the Star Chamber came into being as a functioning judiciary body separate from the King's Council, of which, it may be recalled, it had been a part earlier. The Star Chamber met in secret and could use torture—both practices violated the common law. It was the Star Chamber that became the truly heavy-handed agency of the law used to bludgeon printers into submission. All of these actions were part of a not very subtle frustration on the part of the government with its inability to control the press as unlicensed antigovernment publications continued to appear with great frequency. This frustration must be seen as a result of the legal system's inability to define in clear, formal terms both legal and illegal prose narrative. Licensing avoided this difficulty somewhat by allowing the state to restrain printers prior to the printing of a work without having to explain precisely what was offensive or libelous in the work.

Perhaps in an attempt to begin a more subtle approach, the Archbishop of Canterbury and the Bishop of London, who were the licensers designated by the Star Chamber Decree of 1586, issued an order in 1599 banning all satires and epigrams. Rather than banning illegal works en masse, the decree is remarkable in barring only the offending genre. Though the approach is still rather blitzkrieg-like, the ruling is significant since it is the first time I am aware of that a *style* of writing, as opposed to a proscribed *content*, was prohibited. The legal establishment was clearly trying to define what form—not what content—of narrative was libelous by nature.

However, it was the more heavy-handed approach to libels that continued in the courts. Having difficulty in proving libels against the state as false, the Star Chamber in *De Libellis Famosis* (1606) ruled that it was irrelevant whether the libel was true or false, what was crucial was that the very existence of the libel caused others to think less of the person who was attacked.[10] The judges decided to amend the earlier *Scandalum Magnatum* statutes because they reasoned that if an ordinary citizen under common law did not have to establish the falsity of a libel, why should kings and great men have to? This ruling plunged the English law back into a disregard for the factuality or fictionality of a statement, and seems to reflect an inability to establish criteria for truth or falsity in treatment of libels. Without such definitions, the legal system could have little effect on shaping the news/novels discourse. The discourse could be banned, but it could not be modified. Only when the legal system moved toward a definition of fact and fiction during the eighteenth century would the news/novels discourse have to move toward a definition as well.

It was during the first quarter of the eighteenth century that there was concrete and rapid movement toward defining, for legal purposes, factual and fictional narratives. The combination of the lapsing of the licensing laws at the end of the seventeenth century and the passing of the Stamp Act of 1712, as well as the revision of that act in 1724, provided the legal mechanism for the creation of such distinctions.

The lapsing of the Licensing Act in 1695 is generally heralded as the end of censorship in England. Indeed, some critics have cited this new-found freedom of the press as one of the causes of the rise of the novel. However, quite the opposite effect was generated—freedom of the press was restrained rather than expanded. Although the right to censorship prior to printing was relinquished by Parliament when it gave up licensing, the most stringent common laws against libel and seditious libel were still in effect. While the Licensing Act was troublesome for printers, the common law courts were worse since a printer could not be forewarned of the illegality of his book and so would run the risk of having his entire printed edition confiscated after he had produced it. The printer, too, could be fined, imprisoned, and physically punished, whereas under the Licensing Act printers would suffer at worst a returned book and a slight financial loss. The licensing law was allowed to lapse not out of compassion for the press or freedom of speech but because the law was ineffective.[11] John Locke, in *Letters of Toleration*, argued against licensing when he said that the common law would cover the transgressions of printers more effectively, as the legislators recognized in the language of the bill itself which noted that "there is no penalty appointed for the offender therein [in the old Licensing Act], they being left to be punished at common law [as they may be] without the Act."[12] Since all the previous legislation and statutes that dealt with prior censorship had been so ineffective in stopping the printing of antigovernment works, the common law had to be relied on. But the common law, too, was indifferent in its definition of the truth or falsity of a libel.

Nonetheless, the use of the courts was not ineffective in stifling the nature of what could be printed. According to one historian of the law, "no single method of restricting the press was as effective as the law of seditious libel as it was developed by the common-law courts in the later part of the seventeenth century."[13] Certain modifications of the definition of libel in the eighteenth century strengthened these laws. One such decision was made in *Rex* v *Tutchin* when Chief Justice Holt ruled in 1704 that any criticism of the government was libelous. He wrote: "To say that corrupt officers are appointed to administer affairs is certainly a reflection on the government. If people should not be called to account for possessing the people with an ill opinion of the government, no government can subsist."[14]

This ruling continued the concept that any "reflection" or criticism, whether true or false, was libelous and as such could be prosecuted. In effect, any allegation of governmental abuse or wrongdoing that was printed in a newspaper would be illegal. Further, according to an act of Parliament, it was considered a breach of parliamentary privilege for a newspaper to mention even the names of the members of Parliament.[15] The actual proceedings of the Houses of Parliament were forbidden to be recorded in the press, as well. For the lawmakers, the issue was not that some statements were true and some false, but that any statement about the workings of the government was patently illegal. The limits of what could be printed were being set so rigidly that print was becoming an arena in which only the most guarded discourse could appear. In print, one could not criticize the government, relate the proceedings of Parliament, mention the name of a specific government official, write a satire on a known public or private person, and so on. The truth or falsity, the accuracy or inaccuracy of any of the above narrations was still, at least legally, irrelevant.

Enforcement of these laws was fairly ruthless in the early eighteenth century. The prosecutor did not have to persuade the jury that a printer had maliciously intended to inflame sedition. Rather the jury merely had to decide whether the defendant had been the printer of the publication in question. The judge alone ruled on the question of malicious intent.[16] In effect, this procedure meant that for all practical purposes the jury had no say in the question of the defendant's guilt; it could only establish the facts of the evidence. Although juries began to revolt as the century went on, convictions for seditious libel ran into the hundreds in the seventeenth and eighteenth centuries.[17] However, these were only convictions, and many more printers were harassed by having "informations" filed against them for which they were called into court, intimidated, and charged with court costs. In this sense, convictions were really not necessary in order for the law of seditious libel to function oppressively.[18] This oppression was furthered by the use of general warrants—that is, warrants which do not have to name specifically the premises or individuals. These warrants had been banned for all other felonies by the beginning of the eighteenth century, but were still permitted in the case of seditious libel.

It had long been a way to escape prosecution by writing allegories or by using false names and abbreviations. As Jonathan Swift explained:

> First, we are careful never to print a man's name out at length; but as I do that of Mr. St––le: so that although everybody alive knows who I mean, the plaintiff can have no redress to any court of justice. Secondly, by putting cases; Thirdly, by insinuations; Fourthly, by celebrating the actions of others who acted directly contrary to the persons we would reflect on; Fifthly, by nicknames either commonly known or stamped for the purpose which everybody can tell how to apply.[19]

The sole purpose of this circuitousness was to create a coded language which on the surface would not be libelous, although without much trouble a reader could penetrate the code and understand the attack. To limit the nature of what could be printed and to try to define the nature of these factually fictional writings, the government began to insist that such encoded language constituted a libel nonetheless. In *Queen* v *Hurt* (1711) it was decided that defamatory writing using only one or two letters of a name so that it necessarily referred to one person in particular was libelous. Even the use of irony and sarcasm, which cannot actually be said to be part of the direct content of a work, could constitute libel if such use maliciously attempted to encourage scandal.[20]

Richard Steele, accused of libeling a member of Parliament while Steele himself was in the House of Commons, argued in his own defense that if a piece of writing had an innocent meaning on the surface, although it could be interpreted to be defamatory, then the innocent interpretation should be the one accepted. He wrote, "If an author's words in the obvious and natural interpretation of them have a meaning which is innocent, they cannot without great injustice be condemned of another meaning which is criminal."[21] Steele's view of things, however, was not that of the legal system's and even veiled or allegorized attacks on the government were subject to prosecution.

Thus by developing a powerful system within the courts to tighten the limits of narrative, the government was able to use a preexisting set of rulings to define the limits of the news/novels discourse. In essence, these legal decisions made it more difficult for narratives to rest in some grey area between fact and fiction. These narratives that bore too close a resemblence to the world, that were too factual, ran the risk of being legally actionable; those narratives that clearly asserted their fictionality and that bore little resemblence to the world were unharmed.

In 1712, the government tried a new approach and decided to tax news. However, the problem for the government was that they had never defined what constituted news, nor had the printers of news. The Stamp Act of 1712 was an attempt to ban most newspapers by specifying that publications of half-sheet size be printed on paper that had a half-penny stamp affixed to it, and those of a whole-sheet size be taxed with a one-penny stamp.[22] Larger publications were taxed at a lower rate. What is significant in these numbers is that the law really does not contain a definition of news, and that publications are only defined in terms of their physical format. The Act does make a distinction between "all books and papers commonly called pamphlets" and "all newspapers or papers concerning public news, intelligence, or occurrences." However, this distinction is largely based on format alone as the law demonstrates by taxing newspaper-sized publications and allowing pamphlet-sized publications to be taxed at a lower rate. Here the government is assuming that form equals function. It was precisely this format-oriented approach that was the downfall of the Stamp Act of 1712. Printers were quick to discover this loophole since what was being penalized was not really news but the printed format. The Stamp Act stated that papers of less than one sheet had to pay a tax on "every printed copy," while editions longer than one sheet had to pay the tax "in one printed copy." This distinction in wording was obviously accidental, yet printers interpreted the distinction to mean that newspapers of a single sheet had to affix one stamp *per copy* while longer publications had to affix one stamp *per edition*.[23] Making use of this interpretation, printers simply expanded their single-sheet publications (which in quarto were four pages) to one-and-one-half sheets (six pages), thus falling under the second category specified in the Act and only having to pay three shillings for each edition.

It was not until 1724 that the Stamp Act was revised to counter this maneuver. The revision specified that there would still be a tax at the same rate as the Act of 1712

on all pamphlets and on all printed newspapers or papers containing publick news, intelligence or occurrences (that is to say) for every pamphlet or paper contained in half-sheet or in any lesser piece of paper printed, the sum of one half-penny; and for every pamphlet or paper, being longer than half a sheet. . . .

Here the law no longer bases its definition of what is taxable on the format of the publication. Rather, pamphlets and newspapers are grouped together if they happen to contain news. The law notes that

> authors or printers of several journals, mercuries and other news-papers do, with intent to defeat the aforesaid payments, and in defraud of the crown, so continue as to print their said journals and newspapers on one sheet and a half-sheet of paper each, and by that means they neither pay the aforesaid duties . . . but enter them as pamphlets, and pay only three shillings for each impression thereof. . . .[24]

This law will eliminate such loopholes by defining or specifying news rather than simply banning a particular format.

This law is a turning point in the history of the press and consequently of the novel. Its implications may seem innocuous, but its significance lies in the fact that it is the first law governing print which based its definition of printed matter not on *format* of publication but on the *content* of what was printed. News, it said, was what defined the category of that which is taxable. The details of the typographical layout did not. Hereafter, the legal system would have to grapple with defining what separated news from other kinds of narrative. The government would have to define and delineate what constituted news, which was taxable, from novels, histories, and biographies, which were not.

The printers, not to be daunted by the law, used their un-flagging cunning to circumvent even this revision to the Stamp Act by printing the news segment of their papers on only one sheet, for which they paid the penny tax per sheet, and then adding a literary section which would not be taxable since it contained no news.[25] Forced by the specifications of the law, printers were compelled to divide up a previously intact discourse—narrative—into the taxable (news) and the untaxable (fiction, history). While one cannot claim that this revision of the Stamp Act was the unique cause of the subdivision of the news/novels discourse, it seems possible that the decision both reflected and initiated such a splitting.

Although printers seemed to know what news was, since they put only news on the stamped segment of their publication, the legal definition of news still needed to be hammered out. A controversy concerning *The Bee: or Weekly Pamphlet* helped to establish, at least legally, the limits between news, pamphlets, and history. These limits had been in the process of formation since news began appearing regularly in the 1620s. Until this point, news had developed an ongoing narrative and with this a special journalistic time-sense that mediated between past and present. Now a more precise definition of news had to be established. The owner of *The Bee*, Eustace Budgell, displaying a printer's canniness when faced with laws that inhibited his profits, tried to avoid the Stamp Tax by claiming that his publication was a pamphlet and not a newspaper because it was printed on three sheets rather than one-half or a single sheet. Budgell was clearly appealing to the older legal distinction based on format rather than content. In 1733 the Register of the Stamp Office refused, according to *London Magazine*, to give *The Bee* this classification because "he looked upon it as a weekly collection of news, and therefore ought to be printed in a half sheet, and bear the half-penny stamp, as all other weekly collections of news do."[26] The inherent confusion of the Register's decision, which at once refused to allow the distinction based on format, noting that the content of the paper—news—is the important criterion, and yet still insists on the definition by format saying that *The Bee ought* to be printed in half-sheets like the other collections of news, is informing. The Register seems to be caught in the cross fire between the two ways of defining news, and his confusion would seem to be typical of the time.

Budgell, who in his tenacity helped differentiate the category of news from that of history, protested the Register's decision and changed tactics somewhat by claiming that his was not a newspaper at all but rather a miscellany like the *London Magazine*, which contained an untaxed monthly news summary. The *London Magazine* gave this definition of news in response to Budgell's claim:

> The true import and meaning of the word news is the return of intelligence, of any kind, by the posts foreign or domestick. But all

transactions of a month's standing, are, long within that time, recorded in the Secretary of State's Office, then, by the law of nations
becomes memorials, and all future recitals of them fall under the
proper and only denomination of history. All monthly collections
are bound up annually with proper indexes; and any attempt to
bring such collections within the stamp revenues, might as well
include Josephus, Rapin's History, and Baker's Chronicle.[27]

While recognizing that the *London Magazine* had a definite self-
interest in protecting its right to print untaxed monthly news sum-
maries, we can still see that a fairly distinct formulation separating
news and history had been arrived at. News becomes history after
it has been entered in the Secretary of State's Office, or after about
one month. Thus, the farthest mediations of the journalistic median
past tense would be understood to be limited to this period. That
is, any accounts of events further back than one month would not
be considered part of the journalistic discourse. At the same time,
history now begins to be defined as dealing with more recent events
than the older concept of history had allowed.

In another case relating to defining "news," Abel Boyer had
been able to print *The Political State of Great Britain* which recorded
the proceedings of Parliament despite the standing orders of Parliament against such practices; Boyer did this by postponing publication of his reports until after each session had adjourned. He
claimed that by following this procedure he was writing history
and not reporting current events.[28] Of course, Boyer was politic
enough to report mainly news favoring the party in power, and
this circumspection might have helped keep his periodical in business. Robert Dodsley, who published a sixteen-page miscellany
that did not pay the Stamp Tax called *The Public Register: or The
Weekly Magazine*, was fined for printing a news summary that was
only a week old. Thus, through the abrasive honing of the legal
system, a definition of news was achieved—news was a narrative
of public events supplied by the posts and under one month old.
This definition, however crude, does begin to provide a clarification
of the word *new*, which as may be recalled, was used in ballads
without any clear reference to time. This definition of news re-

maimed seemingly unchanged through the nineteenth century. The
Newspaper Libel and Registration Act of 1881 comfortably defines
a newspaper as "any paper containing public news, intelligence,
or occurrences, or any remarks or observations therein printed for
sale, and published in England or Ireland periodically, or in parts
or numbers at intervals not exceeding twenty-six days. . . ."[29]

At this point, we are indeed quite far from the cultural indif-
ference to fact and fiction in narrative that was characteristic of the
sixteenth and seventeenth centuries. Now, at least in this legal
sense, there was an attempt to define what constituted news and
consequently what constituted history and the novel. Now novels
seem to have been assigned the responsibility for carrying fictional
discourse, and news had the responsibility for carrying factual
discourse. The wedge has been driven, as it were, and the old
undifferentiated matrix has subdivided, as we will see. Even the
custom of having novels appear in serial form in the newspapers,
a custom which reflected the undifferentiated origins of the discourse and the mutual similarities of news and novels, went largely
out of fashion by 1744.[30] Despite the return of novels to newspapers
in the late nineteenth century, fiction by and large would be printed
in specialized, nonjournalistic periodicals such as those Robert
Mayo describes in *The English Novel in the Magazines, 1740-1815*.

As we have seen, the effect of the battery of laws used against
the press was to force a distinction between potentially libelous
and nonlibelous material, that is, between journalism and literature.
But the law also had the effect of forcing writers who wished to
write about the world away from such overtly political modes as
the one offered by the newspaper and toward a more protected
form of writing. That form might take many shapes—more overtly
allegorical or satirical, for example—and the novel was a less overt
form that was, in effect, an ideological description of the state of
life in a particular country. The novel's view was not strictly journalistic, although the novelist did become a kind of reporter of
events, but of events sufficiently removed from the real world to
be safely protected from legal action or reaction. As will become

evident in the ensuing chapters, it was not a coincidence that so many authors during the eighteenth century in England were directly associated with journalism. One could say, as I hope to show, that in a sense these writers saw themselves as inheritors of the news/novels discourse, and consequently they saw themselves as writing about the events of the world as a reporter might see them.

CHAPTER VI

Theories of Fiction in Early English Novels

IF ROBINSON CRUSOE wound up on an island, historians of the novel were partially responsible for putting him there. Until fairly recently, it had generally been the practice of literary histories of the novel, to regard Defoe as the first English novelist, and most treatments of the novel tend to move quickly from *Don Quixote* to English *Robinson Crusoe*, from one gaunt touchstone to the other, with the assumption that this was the most direct way along the road to the great tradition. *Crusoe*, however, was far from being an isolated novel in a sea of romances. Quite a few other English writers had been creating what we might call, without fear of abusing the term, novels.[1] These early novels have been relegated to the category of "popular fiction" and allowed to moulder there. Charlotte Morgan noted, for example, that "popular fiction, generally speaking, had no literary merit; and as it had no other aim than immediate success, it rarely possessed more than ephemeral interest, so that on the whole it may be regarded as a negligible factor."[2] Even Ian Watt, whose *Rise of the Novel* had done much to place novels in their proper class perspective, begins his book with *Robinson Crusoe* and dismisses the earlier forms of popular fiction as irrelevant. Watt glides over serialized fiction, which, as we will see, was the predominant reading material for a good deal of the literate public, saying that "the poorer public is not very important; the novelists with whom we are concerned did not have this [serial] form of publication in mind. . . ."[3] Watt is wrong on this score, and his decision to begin at the moment when novels began to be more widely accepted by the middle-class reader creates the impression that before Defoe there was not much in the way of prose fiction. Watt barely mentions the novels of Aphra Behn, Mrs. Manley, Mary Davys, Ned Ward, Eliza Haywood, and others.

While it may be true that many of these works are inferior to those of Defoe, Richardson, or Fielding, there is much in them that is essential to understanding the history of the novel. Certainly, Defoe at his worst is not as good as Manley at her best, and the *History of Rivella* is as inventive and creative as two-thirds of Defoe's hack exercises.

These early English writers, like some of their French counterparts, took particular pains to distinguish their works from the romance. Even such a remote viewer as Samuel Johnson, writing well after the formative period of the novel, said of romance, "Why this wild strain of imagination found reception so long, in polite and learned ages, it is not easy to conceive."[4] Johnson sounds the characteristic English call against the French romance. Although most British novelists took pains, as we will see, to divorce themselves from heroic romance, there was a vogue in certain English social circles for the French romances. These were translated into English during the mid-seventeenth century. However, quite quickly the antiromances of Furetière, Sorel, Scarron, Le Sage, and Subligny were also translated between 1654 and 1678, a fact which indicates the strength of antiromance sentiments in England as well. The appeal for romances came mainly from the English upper classes who frequently assumed classical names and read these works in groups.[5] English romances tended to be pale imitations of French works—see, for example, Roger Boyle's *Parthenissa* (1654) and Sir George MacKenzie's *Aretina or the Serious Romano* (1660).

While there was no doubt interest in romance, that interest came from a small, elite part of the potential reading public. Congreve, in 1692, clearly reveals the taste of the majority of readers in his definition of the novel and the romance. In contrast to the "lofty language, miraculous contingencies and impossible performances" of the romance, "novels are of a more familiar nature" and "delight us with accidents and odd events, such which not being so distant from our belief bring also the pleasure nearer us."[6] This distinction was also obvious to Lord Chesterfield in the mid-eighteenth century who wrote that a romance was "twelve volumes, all filled with insipid love, nonsense, and the most incredible adventures."[7] And thirty years later, Clara Reeve could again make the same division between lofty, heroic romances which were remote and cold, and the novel which "gives a familiar relation of such things, as pass everyday before our eyes, such as may happen to our friend, or to ourselves and we are affected by the joys or distresses of the person in the story, as if they were our own."[8]

Early English novelists developed, to a far lesser degree than their French counterparts, a theory of fiction that makes clear that English writing is meant to be seen as distinctly English, as opposed to the French romance. Like French novelists, the English distinguished between novel and romance by noting that novels were not made up or based on remote history, but were true. Thus, the English novel begins on an inherently framed assumption. There seems to have been in England a far greater sanction against fictions than there was in France, and this state of affairs was no doubt due in part to the Puritan condemnation of fiction as being only lies.

Puritan writers like John Bunyan had to take great care to avoid writing lies when they had recourse to narrative. Bunyan manages to steer his way around the problem of fictionality in his work by falling back on the older tradition that poetical truths might be truer than real ones. In his introduction to *Pilgrim's Progress* (1678), Bunyan defends himself against the charge that his work is "feigned" by saying

> . . . What of that? I trow
> Some men, by feigned words, as dark as mine,
> Make truth to spangle and its rays to shine.[9]

Of course, Bunyan can refer to the biblical example of Christ who spoke in parables "by types, shadows, and metaphors,"[10] and in fact the epigraph on the title page of *Pilgrim's Progress* is taken from *Hosea* 12:10 "I have used similitudes." So armed with biblical justification, Bunyan journeys through the thickets of the fact-and-fiction controversy, and camouflages his backsliding into invention by claiming that his story is really "delivered under the similitude of a dream." Thus the work is framed doubly by its open demand for interpretation and yet its deliberate inclusion into the shadowy world of sleep and dreams.

Though *Pilgrim's Progress* is caught between its existence as a "feigned" work and its aim to make truth "spangle and shine," its story is about the quest for the ultimate truth. Novels, it would seem, have taken on the burden of trying to give us reports on the world, and this virtue seems to have been conferred paradoxically by the fact that the very existence of novels is bound up in the illusory creation of the appearance of truth. Bunyan's *Life and Death of Mr. Badman* (1680) is also an allegory, but this time instead of being a dream, it is structured as a dialogue between Mr. Wiseman and Mr. Attentive. The dramatic form permits an air of credibility to enter the story, and of course frames the work. Bunyan claims this time that "all things that I here discourse of, I mean as to matter of fact, have been acted upon the state of this world, even many times before mine eyes."[11] By this we can presume that Bunyan means that Badman, while not a real person, is a composite character and the particulars of his life are "true" in the sense that they have happened to other people at other times. However, Bunyan takes this notion one step further and says that he will include in the work true stories "which are things known by me, as being eye and earwitness thereto, or that I have received from such hands, whose relations as to this, I am bound to believe."[12] He will indicate these true stories by inserting in the margins a small printed hand (☞) to point to the special paragraphs that are in fact interpolated tales not all unlike the brief lives of criminals newspapers usually carried. For example:

> I know one that dwelt not far off from our town, that got himself
> a wife as Mr. Badman got his, but he did not enjoy her long: for

one night as he was riding home . . . his horse threw him to the
ground, where he was found dead at break of day; frightfully and
lamentably mangled with his fall, and besmeared with his own
blood.[13]

One does not have to read many of these specially marked stories
to realize that their "truth" is based on the same criteria as the
truths of the early newsbooks. Such stories are plentiful. For example, there is the one about a woman who used to swear by using
the expression "I would I might sink into the earth if it be not so,"
and who met a strange but not at all unpredictable end.

Bunyan's crude method of segregating fact and fiction by confining the former to a semiologically identifiable section of the page
is an attempt to resolve the troublesome intermixing of fact and
fiction which seems to be characteristic of these early prose narratives. Bunyan's solution lacks subtlety, however, because it fails
to see how deeply enmeshed in the dialectic of fact and fiction is
the very structure of such works as his. Perhaps Bunyan realized
intuitively his complicity in the sin of fictionalizing when he
stressed that Mr. Badman's worst trait was in fact the telling of
lies: "When he was but a child, he was so addicted to lying that
his parents scarce knew when to believe he spake true, yea, he
would invent, tell, and stand to the lies that he invented and
told. . . ."[14]

Badman's parents might be likened, allegorically speaking, to
the reader of prose narrative of his time. In fact, Bunyan seems to
make a specific reference to the news/novels discourse when he
says that people tell lies in "their news, their jests, and their tales
must needs be adorned with lies; or else they seem to bear no good
sound to the ear, nor shew much fancy to him to whom they are
told."[15] The linking of news, tales, and jests here seems to be far
from fortuitous, and the implication that such modes of narrative
are necessarily contaminated with fictions is also worth noting. It
was Bunyan's accomplishment to step lightly around this contam-
ination of fiction and carry forth his message to the world.

Aphra Behn was among the first novelists in England to claim her work was true. Of course, ballads, newsbooks, and criminal tales had made such claims, so it does not seem unusual to have Behn make the same assertion. As early as 1688, when *Oroonoko* was written, Behn inaugurated, it would seem, the now familiar disclaimer:

> I do not pretend, in giving you the history of this royal slave, to entertain my reader with adventures of a feigned hero, whose life and fortunes Fancy may manage at the poet's pleasure; nor in relating the truth, design to adorn it with any accidents, but such as arrived in earnest to him: And it shall come simply into the world, recommended by its own proper merits, and natural intrigues; there being enough of reality to support it, and to render it diverting, without the addition of invention.[16]

The tone one instantly perceives is a sort of general scorn for invention, entertainment, and feigned heroes. Works of imagination, which may be manipulated at the writer's discretion, are not really worth one's time. The hidden reference seems to be against the French romance's predeliction to add to history, to invent upon historical foundations. Behn has discarded Bishop Huet's justification of fiction by its elegance of style or by its moral instruction. She can do this because, according to the framing device she has established, she is not writing fiction. That there is "enough reality to support" the novel and that such facts as there are will divert the reader are sufficient justifications for the work.

Behn instinctively places herself in the news/novels discourse by inaugurating an inherently reflexive or double discourse based on contradictory assertions. For example, she places a sanction on the use of "accidents" and "intrigues." An "accident," as the word was used in the seventeenth century according to the *Oxford English Dictionary*, was "anything that happens without foresight or expectation, an unusual event, which proceeds from some unknown cause"; an intrigue was "a complicated state of affairs . . . plotting or scheming." In other words, Behn is saying that novelists should avoid coincidences, unexpected turns of event, plotting, scheming, reversals of plot—in short, a novel should avoid being a novel.

Behn is here practicing the essence of reflexive discourse—affirmation by denial. When she says her work is truth, she means that it must shun fictional devices such as coincidence. However, coincidence in a novel is a structuring device that aligns parallel plots, unites formally disparate elements, and allows metaphoric and moral meaning to be drawn from the work. Outside of the realm of literature, however, coincidence was seen during the seventeenth century as an act of Providence, the hand of God at work in the world. So if a novelist denied writing a fiction, thus attributing all coincidences to the hand of Providence, then that novelist would put him or herself in the bad faith position of claiming to know how Providence *would have* acted in a particular situation. The author pretends, in effect, to be God—an action not generally smiled upon in religious circles.

Aphra Behn is very clear in claiming not to be writing a fiction: "I was myself an eye-witness to a great part of what you will find here set down; and what I could not be witness of I received from the mouth of the chief actor in this history, the hero himself, who gave us the whole transaction of his youth."[17] This proof by physical contiguity is typical of the news/novels discourse, as we have seen in ballads and newsbooks, and we should recall that such personal testimonial is impossible given the limits of romance. In another work by Behn, *The Fair Jilt* (1688), the dedication is to one Henry Pain, Esq. However, we are not simply presented with a laudatory puff; Behn takes the occasion to ask Pain to authenticate the truthfulness of the text, a ploy which ballad writers had used as well. The work, writes Behn, is recommended by the fact that "it is truth: truth, which you so much admire. But 'tis a truth that entertains you with so many accidents diverting and moving, that they will need both a patron, and an assertor in this incredulous world."[18] With a little help from her legal friend, Behn can claim to have backing for the assertion that her work is true. In this sense, patronage becomes attestation as well.

It seems fitting, in view of Behn's attitude toward fact and fiction that so much of *Oroonoko* should have to do with fabrications, deceit, and lying in one form or another. In Oroonoko's tribe, lies are unknown. Lying is seen by Behn as a natural consequence of civilization and does not exist in a natural state. She writes of Oroonoko's tribe that "these people represented to me an absolute idea of the first state of innocence, before man knew how to sin."[19] The tribe is so oblivious to false statements that, for example, they begin to mourn an English governor who had sworn to come on a certain day and failed to show up or to send word that he could not come. The tribe believed that "when a man's word was past, nothing but death could or should prevent his keeping it." When the governor actually did arrive, ". . . they asked him what name they had for a man who promised a thing he did not do? The governor told them, such a man was a liar, which was a word of infamy to a gentleman. Then one of them replied *Governor, you are a liar, and guilty of that infamy*."[20] The joke here is that the black men are so innocent that they cannot even perceive that their response is an insult. This innocence constitutes an inability to perceive framings and fabrications—the tribe cannot make out the context, the series of frames, in which the "civilized" world is wrapped.

Aphra Behn's own narrative fares no better than the words of other whites. We doubt her from the opening "authentication" to the numerous lies and tall tales included in the exotica of the novel. She tells us, for example, that even the most severe wounds heal rapidly in the tropical zone—except, inexplicably, those sustained by the leg.[21] Medical wonders are compounded by zoological anomalies such as the fact that a lion may live with several bullets in his heart—a fact which even the author has the good sense to note "will find no credit among men."[22] Another wonder is the "numb-eel" which will paralyze the fisherman who holds the rod at the moment the eel touches the bait. Aphra Behn's "truthful" account of Oroonoko's life ends with his execution during which he is castrated, has his nose and ears cut off, and his arms severed while he remains in an unlikely state of calm, continuing to smoke his pipe.

In the jungle, Behn even manages to meet Colonel Martin who, as it just happens, is to be the protagonist of a new play appearing in London called *The Younger Brother or the Amorous Jilt* surprisingly written by none other than Aphra Behn herself. Such a meeting is a shrewd bit of public relations work to encourage some financial success, but also intermixes fact and fiction a bit. One wonders if Behn is consciously testing the credulity of the reader as Oroonoko's own credulity had been tested.

From the prestructure, to the presentation, through the content and even the digressions of *Oroonoko*, fiction-making and lying are central to the work. Fabrications build up into frames within frames doubling back upon themselves until every turn reveals fact warped into fiction which turns back upon itself to become fact. This novel, as others, seems to be steeped in an insecurity resulting from bad faith, criminality, lying, and fabrication.

The prefaces to the works of Mary de la Rivière Manley reveal English attitudes toward the novel and the romance, as well as toward fact and fiction. In the *Secret History of Queen Zarah* (1705), Manley writes about the differences between the English "humour" and that of the French in regard to narrative:

> The romances in France have for a long time been the diversion and amusement of the whole world; people both in the city and the court have given themselves over to this vice, and all sorts of people have read these works with a most surprising greediness; but that fury is very much abated, and they are all fallen off from this distraction.[23]

What has replaced these romances are "little histories," which Manley points out are much more agreeable to "the brisk and impetuous humour of the English, who have naturally no taste for long-winded performances. . . ." She also finds fault with the exaggerated language of romance which might refer to water as "the liquid element" or a mirror as the "council of the graces," and advocates in its place the plain style saying that conversation

> ought to be writ after an easy and free manner: fine expressions and elegant turns agree little to the style of conversation, whose principal ornament consists in the plainness, simplicity, free and sincere air

. . . for 'tis not natural for man to entertain himself, for we only
speak that we may communicate our thoughts to others. . . .[24]

This literary fundamentalism echoes the Puritans, but also places
Manley's discourse squarely in the "plain" language of news/novels.

If fiction cannot be justified by elegant language, then moral
instruction seems to have been the agent to wash away the sins of
fiction-making. Manley writes: ". . . the chief end of history is to
instruct and inspire into men the love of virtue and the abhorrence
of vice, by the examples proposed to them; therefore the conclusion
of a story ought to have some tract of morality which may engage
virtue. . . ."[25] Manley presents other literary dicta veiled in moral
terms. She discusses verisimilitude and agrees that a writer "ought
with great care to observe the probability of truth, which consists
in saying nothing but what may morally be believed." One notices
immediately a paradox here: if one is to write a probable work, one
needs to write about the world as it is, yet such a world is not
necessarily morally probable. The problem is quite similar to the
conflict between *bienseance* and *vraisemblance* that we have seen
among the French romancers. As Manley elaborates: ". . . there
are truths that are not always probable; as for example, 'tis an
allowed truth in the Roman history that Nero put his mother to
death, but 'tis a thing against all reason and probability that a son
should embrue his hand in the blood of his own mother."[26] Manley
is saying, in effect, that there are two kinds of verisimilitude—
actual and moral. It seems clear that these are contradictory types
of verisimilitude. A work that shows the world as it is will run into
the problem of allowing vice to triumph over virtue, as it does
sometimes. But a work that is morally verisimilar will always show
virtue triumphing over vice.

We are dealing with types or varieties of truth. The paradox
is that for a work to be morally verisimilar it has to be actually
*un*verisimilar. When one throws in the conception of providence,
things get even more complex. According to Christian thought,
God acts in the world to effect the punishing of vice and the
rewarding of virtue, so that all outcomes other than these, while

novelistic perhaps, would be seen as improbable—hence unveri-
similar. John Dennis comments:

> . . .'tis observable, that both in a poetical fiction and an historical
> relation, those events are the most entertaining, and the most won-
> derful, in which providence most plainly appears. And 'tis for this
> reason that the author of a just fable, must please more than the
> writer of an historical relation.[27]

Thus the fable writer must be more accurate than the historian
because human actions are more "liable to be imputed rather to
chance than Almighty conduct and sovereign justice."[28] If actual
verisimilitude is then opposed to providence, and moral verisimilitude as antinovelistic in presenting the world as it should be and
not as it is, then can we not say that the theory of the novel at this
time was a reflexive or double one since it maintained two contradictory imperatives at once? Like the newsbooks and ballads, which
maintained their reflexivity through an insistence on their verity,
these novels reclothed this fundamental reflexivity in moral terms.
Ballads maintained they were true while insuring such assertions
were actually a kind of guarantee of the opposite; novels, by cling-
ing—in theory—to moral verisimilitude, insured that their predisposition—in practice—to verisimilitude was contradicted. The
important point to remember here is that novelists were not developing a new theory of the novel so much as they were using
new terms to argue against the old inherent contradictions of the
news/novels discourse that they had inherited. It is as if the limits
and constraints of the news/novels discourse were unconscious ones
in the minds of novelists, and so these writers had to justify, as it
were, intuitively these limits in a variety of ways without ever
recognizing them overtly.

If the writer of fiction had to take more care to be morally
probable than the writer of history, who had only to write what
had happened, then it seems logical for novelists to claim that their
works were not fictional but true. This way novelists could avoid
the necessity for depicting only probable events. In other words,

the theory of the novel as it developed stood in contradiction to the actual content of novels since that content tended to be filled with improbabilities, coincidences, sensational material, exotic situations, chance events, and so on. In this sense, the theory of the novel during the late seventeenth century was a false theory or, as I shall call it, a *simulacrum* theory, that if followed in practice could never result in a novel being written. Thus, to negate the effect of the theory, authors would claim that the work was true, hence not a novel. The initial frame of fabrication ("this work is true") permits the ensuing plot-events to be improbable, fanciful, illogical—in short, novelistic. However, in this context it is important to see that there are two levels to this fact/fiction problem. First, the novel is based on a theory which is inherently reflexive in its simultaneous call for overt moral verisimilitude and covert actual verisimilitude—and on the contradiction between these two varieties of truth. At the same time, on the second level, an entirely other assertion of truth is taking place that in effect frames the first contradiction. This second contradictory assertion falsely maintains that the work is not a fiction at all.

Mary de la Rivière Manley's works themselves do not look or feel like novels, at least like the novels of Defoe, Richardson, or Fielding. The assertion has been made with works like hers that one is observing romance and not the novel. There are in Manley's works swooning lovers, aristocratic intrigues, and adventures performed by characters with classical or oriental-sounding names— Zarah, Zelinda Rivella, But since Manley insists so strongly in her introductions that she is not writing romances, we need to consider the nature of her difference.

First, of course, is the insistence that her work is true. The subtitle to *Queen Zarah* reads *Faithfully Translated From the Italian Copy Now Lodged in the Vatican at Rome, and Never Before Printed in Any Language*. This ploy echoes Mlle. Scudéry's joke about her work being taken from a manuscript in the Vatican Library, but here it seems to be proposed more seriously. Manley seems to be saying that though her work might be taken for a falsehood, the manuscript, at least, is genuine. Yet, from her introductory discussion of the theory of her novel, it is clear that this is a work with an author, and Manley suggests this when she talks about the rules that apply to the writing of fictional works. In reality though, her work is, among other things, a *roman à clef* like the works of Mme. de Lafayette. It not only tells a story of love and passion, but is also a commentary on most of the major political and aristocratic figures of the age. In this sense, it is a work that is at once true and false—as any allegory would be. The level of the allegorical can be very *outré* in Manley's work, as when Zarah attempts to ride various horses that are also representations of various politicians:

> What though Danterius [Daniel Finch, Earl of Nottingham] was made a stalking horse to the state . . . they were forward to part with him before they could catch the game Volpone [Godolphin] was hunting for; and though the Cambrian [Harley] be a tamer beast, he's but an ass at best, whose ears will scare the the partridge before they can drive them to their nets.[29]

Even the more obtuse readers could easily penetrate the metaphoric level with a key to the work that was usually printed at the end of the novel or appeared separately and could be bound into the work. In this metaphoric way, *Queen Zarah* and other works by Manley such as *The History of Rivella* and *The New Atlantis* were fictional stories and at the same time factual reports on the world. As such these works participated in both the factual and fictional components of the news/novels discourse.

Further, these works claimed to be "secret histories," that is, they were the histories of private citizens as well as public officials, laminated with a veneer of exotic names and settings, as is the case of *Queen Zarah*, set in that mysterious country of Albignion. Such works inaugurate an interest in the private life—an interest that had been more or less the exclusive province of nontypographic spiritual autobiographies and private diaries of the seventeenth century. They also sound the familiar notes of recentness and reduction of cognitive space between reader and text by allowing history to enter the nonpublic realm.

In the introduction to the second part of *Queen Zarah*, Manley counters those critics who had claimed her work was not fiction:

> . . . some have conceived [that *Queen Zarah*] . . . was a modern history, and related to several affairs at home . . . [that] the whole story is a fiction, that there is no such country in the world as Albignion, nor any such person living, or ever was, as Zarah. . . . The manuscript is so ancient that 'tis supposed to be writ by Cain in the land of Nod.[30]

Manley's assertion of antiquity may place her in a preliterate culture, but that is of little concern to her. One of the virtues of the news/novels discourse at this point is that it could go both ways in terms of its assertion of fact or fiction. Manley, in writing a political commentary on English government and society must claim that her work is fictional, if only to protect herself from the punishment of the libel laws. As it was, Lord Sunderland swore out a warrant for her arrest after the publication of her *New Atlantis*, although charges were eventually dropped. The fact remains, though, that at this juncture, for a work of literature to be part of the news/novels discourse and to claim to comment on the real world, it had to adjure that it was a fiction, while for a pure fiction to appear in print it had to claim to be true. Such was the built-in reflexivity of the rules of the news/novels discourse.

Of course, we should not overlook the fact that Manley's novels were reviled not only for daring to comment on the world, but because they were perceived as sexually scandalous. Indeed, Manley continues the tradition we have seen in the ballads which involves the reader as voyeur to sexual encounters. Ballads were in fact, along with operas and books of love, designed as devices for "heightening the passions."[31] Eliza Haywood writes that the function of such works was to be "preparatives to love and by their softening influence, melted the soul and made it fit for amorous impressions. . . ."[32] In Manley's work sexual scenes such as the following are not unusual: ". . . without further dallying he made his last efforts, and rendered those of Zarah so useless that she lay at his mercy. But it was not long e'er this transported lover had allayed his passion, when he would have withdrawn without saying a word."[33] In *New Atlantis*, Polydore and Urania, brother and sister, fall in love and consummate an incestuous passion. With such forays into erotica, it is no wonder that the *Tatler* criticized Manley, saying "where crimes are enormous, the delinquent deserves little pity, but the reporter less."[34] But Manley replied to this charge saying that without proper reportage "vice may stalk at noon secure from reproach."[34] Her defense is consonant with the simulacrum theory which seeks to deny the essential ingredients of the novel—in this case voyeurism. Given the news/novels discourse, the reader is usually in voyeuristic relation to the text since here too the reader is both subject and observer. This was so not only because these books were meant to be training devices for the passions, self-help manuals for the erotically undereducated, but because the readers would only have to lift the veil of allegorization to realize that these erotic stories were about people the reader might know personally either directly or indirectly. By virtue of the omnipresent key, these texts were brought into the lives of readers in a way new to the history of narrative.

The reading process itself was becoming eroticized through the identification of observer with subject in a way quite new to society. To be sure, pornography had existed since the Greeks and Romans if not before, and during the seventeenth century there were numerous pornographic works,[36] but there was no regularly accepted, written genre which was identified with sexual arousal.[37] It seems probable, if one looks at descriptions of the process of reading novels during the Early Modern period, there is a definite sense of the reading process becoming eroticized in a way quite new to the culture. Take, for example, a description by Manley:

> . . . the reader is filled with a curiosity and a certain impatient desire to see the end of the accidents, the reading of which causes an exquisite pleasure when they are nicely handled; the motion of the heart gives yet more, but the author ought to have an extraordinary penetration to distinguish them well, and not to lose himself in the labyrinth.[38]

The language here must strike the modern reader as suggestive. The "desire" to come to the end causes "an exquisite pleasure" when things are "nicely handled," and all this is added to by the "motion of the heart." All this stimulation presumes that the author has "an extraordinary penetration" (the word had both meanings at the time) and does not "lose himself" in this "labyrinth." What unconscious material Manley was working through will be bereft of analysis for our purposes, but the visceral and affective aspects of this description, even without a modern reading of the unconscious connections, is striking. Both consciously and unconsciously, the message of this statement is that reading a book is analogous in some way to being sexually aroused by the author. Although the reader is involved, his or her role is distinctly passive.

This language of sexual stimulation can also be found in some writings of John Dennis on reading:

> . . . authors excite our curiosities, and cause those eager longings in their readers to know the events of things, those longings, which by their pleasing agitations, at once disturb and delight the mind, and cause the prime satisfaction of all those readers who read only to be delighted.[39]

These excitations, longings, curiosities, and pleasing agitations which cause the prime satisfaction seem to be tokens of an eroticized reading process. The effects of such an eroticization are difficult to pinpoint, but Lawrence Stone suggests that the eros-laden novel as a social formation profoundly affected people's conceptions of love, family, and marriage. Stone partially attributes the growth of "affective individualism" to the reading of erotically inclined novels, and even suggests that ideas of romantic love were fostered in the culture through the widespread reading of novels.[40] As readers became more intimately associated with their narratives, voyeurism combined with action in a new way.

Manley's *The History of Rivella* (1714) is a book which combines many of the characteristics I have been discussing. Not only is the reader of this novel drawn into the eroticism of the work, but the

author herself is the book's central subject. The novel serves as a
kind of literary pimp soliciting the reader on behalf of the author.
Rivella is unambiguously meant to be Manley, and the book begins
with a conversation between an older English gentleman, Sir
Charles Lovemore, and a young, handsome French visitor, Chev-
alier D'Aumont, on the subject of the history, charms, and sexual
intrigues of Mrs. Manley *cum* Rivella. As D'Aumont is made to
say: "I have not known any of the moderns in that point come up
to your famous author of *Atlantis*. She has carried the passion
farther than could be readily conceived."[41] Lovemore's description
of Rivella takes up the rest of the book as D'Aumont listens in
rapture. Manley's modesty is certainly not one of her distinguishing
features, and descriptions of herself through the smoking-room
vision of these two men abound in the work.

> Her person is neither tall nor short; from her youth she was inclined
> to fat; whence I have often heard her flatterers liken her to the
> Greecian Venus. . . . I have heard her friends lament the disaster
> of her having had the smallpox in such an injurious manner, being
> a beautiful child before that distemper; but as that disease has now
> left her face, she has scarce any pretence to it. Few, who have only
> beheld her in public, could be brought to like her; whereas none
> that became acquainted with her, could refrain from loving her.[42]

Manley's placing of herself so directly in the novel, of placing her
physical body so centrally in the work, is unique in the history of
narrative. Each of her virtues, as well as some of her defects, are
enumerated as part of the catalogue. Her eyes: "Nothing can be
more tender, ingenious and brilliant with a mixture so languishing
and sweet when love is the subject of the discourse, that without
being severe, we may well conclude, the softer passions have their
predominancy in her soul." Her hands and arms ". . . have been
publicly celebrated . . . her neck and breasts have an established
reputation for beauty and colour."[43] Manley has done much here
for her ego, but also for narrative by greatly extending the capacity
of print to embody a life. Her every detail, every characteristic is
preserved in print.

In the same way that we saw the intersection of the real and the fictional in *Don Quixote* and *Roxana*, here too Manley transforms her narrative by intersecting the literary creation with the real and sexual politics of her time. The eroticization of the text by this means intensifies the respective roles of author, character, and reader. The process of reading this novel is the process of approaching Rivella, having her body revealed, her sexual habits displayed, and her being made immanent. Likewise, the eighteenth-century reader was given the actual possibility of approaching Manley—voyeuristically, of course—but always with the real possibility of knowing her, meeting her, or seeing her in London. Given the intimacy of literary circles in London, it is not inconceivable that most of Manley's readers had either seen her or knew someone who knew her. The novel then closes even more the perceptual distance between reader and text. In fact, the whole movement of the novel is structured to bring us closer and closer to Manley and her boudoir. At the end of the discussion between Lovemore and D'Aumont, the Englishman offers to bring the admiring Frenchman to Rivella:

> I should have brought you to her table, well furnished and well served. . . . From thence carried you (in the heat of the summer after dinner) within the Nymph's alcove to a bed nicely sheeted and strowed with roses, jasmines, or orange flowers, suited to the variety of the season; her pillows neatly trimmed with lace or muslin, struck round with jonquils, or other natural garden sweets, for she uses no perfumes and there have given you leave to fancy yourself the happy man, with whom she chose to repose herself during the heat of the day in a state of sweetness and tranquility.[44]

This description is at once a proposition on behalf of Manley to D'Aumont (and to the reader) and at the same time a fantasy of Manley's in which she offers herself to her collective readership. The incredible detail, the superabundance of flowers, the oriental suggestions all strike the reader as part of colossal autoerotic reverie the likes of which had probably never occurred so directly between author and reader in the history of narrative up to this point. While

I am not claiming that Manley would actually have welcomed all
who paid the price of the book, it is worth noting the closing of
the distance between reader and text and the eroticization of the
reading process which partially helps accomplish this change. The
reader is made to agree with D'Aumont who finally bursts out of
the confines of the book crying:

> *Allons*, let us go . . . let us not lose a moment before we are ac-
> quainted with the only person of her sex who knows how to *live*,
> and of whom we may say, in relation to love, since she has so
> peculiar a genius for, and has made such noble discoveries in that
> passion, that it would have been a fault in her, not to have been
> faulty.[45]

The book ends with a hypothetical, off-stage consummation, one
presumes, as author, reader, and D'Aumont are left the possibility
of fulfilling their fantasy. The notion offered here, even only hy-
pothetically, that the ending of the novel represents an entrance
into the real world of Rivella/Manley—a continuum between fact
and fiction—is an innovation that we would have to speculate was
made possible by the terms of the news/novels discourse which
always permits the reader to put down the newspaper and witness
the printed account as it continues in the real world.

The frame surrounding *Rivella* is worth noting for what it
reveals about fact and fiction. The work is supposed to be a translation of a French edition written presumably by D'Aumont himself
about Lovemore's account of Rivella's life. Here the reader is at
least three removes from reality. But another remove can be added
since Rivella is not presented immediately as Manley but as the
character of Delia in *New Atlantis*. Lovemore underlines this when
he says: "I must refer you to her [Rivella's] own story, under the
name of Delia, in the Atlantis, for the next four miserable years
of her life."[46] In this case, the reader would have had to consult
the *fictional* novel to get the *true* story of the *disguised* character
discussed in *The History of Rivella*. The framing at this moment is
complex enough to baffle the observer at first glance.

It was this interpenetration of fact and fiction that got Manley in trouble and provoked Lord Sunderland to bring her to court claiming that Manley's work had "the barbarous design of exposing people that had never done her injury." Manley, however, denied this intention by saying that she did not intend to reflect on any person and only wrote her book by "inspiration," not by receiving special "facts" from other sources. Indeed, Manley's book would be one of the great homages to imagination if it could have satirized so many people by mere chance. Actually, according to Manley, she was convinced after this legal trouble to avoid politics and write mainly for the theater. As Lovemore is made to say: "She now agrees with me that politics is not the business of a woman, especially one that can so well delight and entertain her readers with more gentle pleasing themes. . . ."[47] It is interesting that Lovemore concentrates on the inherently political cast to the news/novels discourse as he strikes this blow against feminism. Although we are supposed to believe that Rivella renounces her political designs in also renouncing narrative, this *History of Rivella* is clearly very much part of the news/novels discourse with its commentary on the political and social lives of the English gentry; the predisposition of novels to comment on, expose, and satirize the world is not so easily disbanded. Manley's solution is to disguise sufficiently the political content of her novel by elaborately framing it and so attempt to avoid further prosecutions. In other words, she had to make her work more overtly fictional.

In general, then, it can be said that these early novelists saw themselves as quite clearly separated from the discourse of romance, that their works tended to exhibit the type of ambivalence toward fact and fiction that has been characteristic of the news/novels discourse, as well as displaying a reduction of cognitive distance between author and reader, the development of a simulacrum theory, and the tendency to report on the events of the world. This argument is more difficult to make with writers like Elizabeth Haywood and Mary Davys whose works tend to look much more like the romance with its upper-class characters, affairs of love and passion, intrigues, and so on. Such works seem to lack ambivalence and a special attitude toward fact and fiction—even though their authors may occasionally claim to be writing true accounts, as does Haywood in *The Injured Husband or the Mistaken Resentment: A Novel*: ". . . as I have only related a story, which a particular friend of mine assures me is matter of fact, and happened at the time when he was in Paris, I would not have it made use of as an umbrage for the tongue of scandal to blast the character of anyone."[48] However, in the case of Davys and Haywood, both authors specifically refer to their works as novels. Davys, though, is using the word "novel" to refer to the French heroic romances, as is clear when she says that novels "have been a great deal out of use and fashion."[49] Given the date of this statement, 1727, it would be impossible for Davys to be referring to the novel in our sense of the word. Also her description of such works as "tedious and dry . . . four hundred pages without the least variety of events," leads me to suspect that she is talking about the long heroic romances. She is against the idea of "probable feigned stories" such as the French have written, and so opts to write a novel with only "one entire scheme or plot, and the other adventures are only incidental or collateral to it . . ." in a shorter work.[50] Davys does not claim her work to be true, and in her rejection of romance as overly complex, she seems to be setting out on her own course. She actually seems to be writing something closer to a tale or short story.

With such ambiguous works as these, one cannot finally say what kind of a genre is being described. To attempt to include all narrative in a system would constitute a kind of closure that would be, by definition, falsifying. The inability, in formal terms, of such works to create or belong to a genre points to their unique and experimental value. It is worth recalling, though, that while Haywood's and Davys' works are difficult to categorize, their prefatory material seems to take into account the complexities of the transformations of narrative that were occurring at the time. In this sense, they can be said to be part of the ongoing definition of news and novel, although each work might not conform to recognizable patterns.

CHAPTER VII

Criminality
and the Double Discourse

IN 1725 JAMES ARBUCKLE wrote an article in the *Dublin Journal* which condemned the reading of novels. He attacked those "fabulous adventures and memoires of pirates, whores, and pickpockets wherewith for sometime past the press has so prodigiously swarmed." What particularly galled Arbuckle was that members of the middle classes were being attracted now to the kind of literature which had formerly been the fodder of the lower classes. Arbuckle continued, saying that

> your Robinson Crusoes, Moll Flanders, Sally Salisburys and John Shepards have afforded notable instances how easy it is to gratify our curiosity, and how indulgent we are to the biographers of Newgate, who have been as greedily read by people of the better sort as the compilers of last speeches and dying words by the rabble.[1]

Arbuckle's words reflect a widely held view that novels were immoral, criminal, and dangerous precisely because they were part of the popular culture. What I would like to suggest in this chapter is that the precise nature of the danger of novels comes not so much from the fact that novels tend to depict "low-life" activities—robberies, sexual encounters, and so on—but that the whole project of the novel, its very theoretical and structural assumptions, were in some sense criminal in nature, and that part of the nature of this

This chapter, in a somewhat different form, was first published in *Yale French Studies* 59 (Fall 1980) under the title "Wicked Actions and Feigned Words: Criminals, Criminality, and the Early English Novel."

criminality was specifically associated with the threat of violence and social unrest from the lower classes. However, the early novel could and did fulfill the equally opposite goal of keeping that lower class in its place. The complexity of this double function remains to be explored in the following pages.

The project of reading and writing novels was criminalized from the outset. Prefaces to novels published in England during the seventeenth century are filled with apologies for their criminal associations. Richard Head begins his book *The English Rogue* (1665) by saying that in being with and writing about criminals, "I have been somewhat soiled by their vicious practices."[2] Daniel Defoe, in acting as "editor" to Moll Flander's narrative, says that he has had to translate Moll's words into more modest ones since the first-person account of a criminal is inherently illicit: "When a woman debauched from her youth, nay, even being the offspring of debauchery and vice, comes to give an account of all her vicious practices . . . an author must be hard put to it to wrap it up so clean. . . ."[3]

Another writer during the seventeenth century maintained that the literary trade was on a par with the criminal one. In fact, whores are better than authors because "a good, honest carted whore . . . Will make ye some conscience yet of turning up on the market place, whereas the other [the author] without so much as waiting for the question, prostitutes himself upon every bulk to all comers."[4] A hundred years later the same comparisons are still made equating "several low arts of beggars with the equally low arts of authors." This same critic of novels goes on to compare novelists to thieves and their works to whores:

> Here come a troop of thieves, who observing that *novelle* taste is in high vogue; have drest up a————parcel of dirty————, given them all their allurements in their out-side; tacked them in a blue gown, with a little red and white in their faces, and now they swarm all over the *Strand*, and bullies without number attend them. Many an honest country gentleman, and many a raw university boy falls a prey to them; they pick his pocket and debauch him from morning to night————The most noted of these————are Harriot Stuart, Fanny Hill, Charlotte Summers, Lady *Frail*, &c. &c.[5]

The strength of this metaphor is backed up by a topographical study made of London which revealed that during the eighteenth century "the subculture of Grub Street merged elements of criminal London (deriving partly from the actual surroundings in which the writers worked, partly from the nature of their work) with elements of the 'literary' subculture. . . ."[6] It is difficult to escape the conclusion that something about the literary trade was considered illicit, disreputable, and even criminal. And the association of the news/novels discourse with political opposition, libel, and vulgarity did little to make novels seem anything less than criminal.

Readers were no less culpable than writers. The habit of reading novels was a sure sign that a young man or woman was on the way down. A libertine in John Dunton's *The Night Walker: or Evening Rambles in Search After Lewd Women* (1696) admits that he found pleasure at an early age in reading novels; Mary Carleton, the infamous forger and thief, is depicted by Francis Kirkman as falling into the mire of criminality by reading novels at an early age and, like Don Quixote, "believing all she read to be true . . . and supposed herself to be not less than a *heroina*"; Mr. Badman of John Bunyan's allegory is linked to those who read "tales [that] must needs be adorned with lies."[7] The formula for creating a criminal in the eighteenth century was to take a youth, have him read novels, which action leads him to crime, prison, and the gallows. Defoe himself casts the responsibility for criminal use of literature on the reader saying that "if the reader makes a wrong use of the figures [in *Roxana*] the wickedness is his own."[8] Thus, those who read novels are seen as sharing in the criminality of the general enterprise of fiction.

The frequency with which the early English novel, newspapers, and ballads focused on the criminal is significant. There seems to have been something inherently novelistic about the criminal, or rather the form of the novel seems almost to demand a criminal content. Indeed, without the appearance of the whore, the rogue, the cutpurse, the cheat, the thief, or the outsider it would be impossible to imagine the genre of the novel. The image of the criminal is complex and seems to serve at least two different and opposing purposes. First, the criminal is an example of sinfulness, evil, and degeneration. His life is to be avoided and his fate to be deplored. On the other hand, criminal biographies and novels lead the criminal to repentance and salvation. Thus, the criminal serves a double function as both example to be avoided and example to be imitated.

Public execution, or the threat of execution, is a required element in the criminal novel, as is the repentance that results from the gallows encounter. Moll Flanders, for example, when faced with Newgate's "hellish noise, the roaring, swearing and clamour, the stench and nastiness" and her imminent death, experiences the feeling of being "covered with shame and tears for things past, and yet had at the same time a secret surprising joy at the prospect of being a true penitent . . ."[9] Even those unrepentant criminals like Jonathan Wild—who picks the pocket of the Ordinary of Newgate on his way to the gallows—serve to emphasize the power of the law and of religion, if only by dis-example.

It is through the moment of execution that the ordinary felon becomes transformed into a speaker of truth. According to Michel Foucault, the criminal's body became a kind of surface onto which was emblazoned the judgment of the state. But in exchange for this, as it were, the criminal acquired the temporary power to be the author of his own story "attesting to the truth of what he had been charged with." Since the criminal no longer has anything to lose, his dying speech is "won for the full light of truth."[10] The last words of the criminal, and the ritual of execution, serve then to permit paradoxically the lawbreaker to become the law-affirmer, the liar to become the speaker of final truths, and the thief to become the giver of good advice.

The ritual of execution provides the criminal a platform from which to make his words public; the gibbet authorizes a form of publication by which criminal's words are amplified. As one visitor to England observed, executions afterwards turned into occasions of honoring the criminal with "elogies."[11] While the fact of criminal execution is quite different in many ways from the fact of publishing a fictionalized criminal tale, I would like to suggest that the reading public and the crowd at the execution had much in common. The last words of the criminal were not only oral declarations but printed ones as well. Such speeches were frequently printed in advance of the execution and passed around for sale at the crucial moment. As Defoe writes:

> . . . dying men have been so often injured by the false and imperfect accounts given from those that have pretended to write from their mouths, that such people generally give (what they design to say) in writing to the Sheriff or Officer appointed to attend the execution, and desire it may be made public, leaving copies with some of their relations, in order to be sure that nothing should be added, or omitted, and so that no wrong be done them.[12]

The criminals' concern seems almost a literary one, and their fears of "imperfect accounts" certainly strike a resonance with the same concerns of earlier journalists. Accounts of executions and records of dying speeches were transformed into ballads, flying sheets, and pamphlets to be read by those who were not present. Both the execution itself and the criminal novel required, indeed presupposed, the observing presence of the reader or the crowd, who Foucault maintains was the main character in the execution.

To the reader or member of the crowd, the life of the criminal might serve two opposing functions. To the middle or upper class, the novel and the criminal were illicit because each sullied itself with low life and irreligion. However, the criminal's life as it is rendered into a discourse through its participation with either printing or the penal system has an obvious constraining social function, even if the criminal—fictional or otherwise—has rejected that function or that society. There is then an apparently conservative, punitive, authorizing power embedded in popular novelistic accounts of criminals as well as a lawless, immoral example. The discourse of the criminal in either fiction or fact is one that is constitutively a double discourse. That is to say, the criminal's life as it is contextualized by "publication rituals," if I may conflate capital punishment and printing into such a term, is both an example and a dis-example. The criminal is both the locus of fraud and the locus of truth.

This double status of the criminal was a tricky one for the middle and upper classes. It is inconvenient for such a hierarchical society to have its criminals placed in a position of reverence, even if that position is modified by the snap of a broken neck. This problem was furthered by the fact that the crowd at the exeution, drawn from the class of journeymen, domestics, apprentices, and what Christopher Hill calls "masterless men," were frequently sympathetic to the felon.[13] Especially when people were to be executed for petty larceny, the crowd might vociferously object to the work of the hangman. Accounts of the Tyburn Riots and other related disturbances in England and France demonstrate that the lower classes frequently did not support the state in its judgments, especially when the crime was only against the possessions of the "propertied oligarchy," as E. P. Thompson calls those who legislated the more than one hundred crimes punishable by death during the eighteenth century.[14] There was a strong class alliance in these reactions. Thompson notes that there was not really a clear distinction in the popular mind between political crimes and social crimes. "In many cases, we found little evidence of morally endorsed popular culture here and a deviant subculture there."[15] Indeed, Foucault sees the execution as an occasion when the true dynamics of social repression, "the disproportion of power of the sovereign over those whom he had reduced to impotence," was dramatically focused so that the execution "blew up to epic proportions the tiny struggles that passed unperceived in everyday life."[16]

The condemned felon on the gallows had a tremendous fascination for the crowd that went beyond class-consciousness. The fact that in slang usage there were about one hundred different words for the gallows—a number exceeded only by the multitude of expressions for money—indicates that the gallows experience had a transcendent quality which stood out in popular consciousness.[17] That "gallows" and "money" were such highly charged words should come as no surprise to the reader of eighteenth-century novels. These works focus almost exclusively on the permutations generated out of the themes of felony and money.

The importance of the gallows experience is most apparent in the rituals surrounding the execution of a criminal. Foucault's point that the criminal's body was a locus for truth and holiness seems to be borne out by historical accounts. A kind of mystery concerning God's intervention in man's affairs hung over the gallows. It was not an uncommon occurrence, for example (until the middle of the eighteenth century when the trap door became standard equipment on the gallows), for "executed" criminals to revive— occasionally on the dissecting table—since hanging worked by asphyxiation rather than by breaking the neck.[18] This resuscitation was popularly called "resurrection," and it does not take much imagination to link the resurrected criminal to a particularly well-known biblical forerunner. The execution and hoped-for resurrection (often facilitated by a skillful and well-bribed hangman) might have strong religious overtones, and the saving of the body—so emotional an issue at the Tyburn Riots—also had its biblical example in the hiding of Christ's body in the cave.

As with Christ's body, the corpse of the executed felon was believed to be holy and therefore to have therapeutic powers. Parts of the criminal's body—his sweat or his bones—were kept as magical charms, and people often came to executions expressly to be cured of diseases by physical contact with the dead felon. This transformation through hanging was also emphasized in popular language by the common habit of calling the hanging the "wedding day." The felon would dress up in his finest clothes and was frequently described as looking like a bridegroom. As in modern usage, "to be noosed" was either to be married or hanged.[19]

So, the criminal was in a sense one of the people—a "man of the people" as Foucault calls him—yet he was outside of normal society, acquiring special powers and subject to resurrection by God's justice. The felonious act committed by the criminal was frequently associated with the political aspirations of the poor and the lower classes. These facts lead to an understanding of the way in which novels themselves were so fascinated by the criminal. It is clear that this interest comes from more than mere prurience and lechery and seems to amount to a definite political interest and ideological stance.

This lower-class sympathy for an alliance with the criminal, the "man of the people," must have been a factor in novels' being perceived as dangerous. Of course, criminals had often been depicted as folk heroes. Popular ballads until well into the eighteenth century depicted the "spirited crime" of the Robin Hood type of folk hero. One who committed such a crime might well be considered as part of a general radical project like the one expressed by Richard Overton in 1647, which declared "it must be the poor, the simple and mean things of this earth that must confound the mighty and strong."[20] Indeed, the assumptions and desires of the criminal world, as it was and as it appeared in novels, frequently echo the demands of radical religio-political groups such as the Levellers, the Diggers, the Ranters and others who advocated a more egalitarian society through the breaking of class distinctions.[21] Of course, not all criminals were heroes in a political sense as well. But the attention paid by the populace to such criminals expresses elements of adulation and envy as well as fear and rage. The criminal action as well as the criminal tale often served as a form of social protest that expressed the class resentment of many who read novels and attended executions.

For this reason the propertied classes might have looked to these criminal biographies and novels with dismay. But it is also important to remember that such literature served the needs of the upper classes too, since the moralizing of the repentant felon amounted to a form of social control and was, as Foucault would remind us, an exercise of power and authority as tangible as that manifested during the ritual of execution. In this sense, the double nature of the criminal as both example and dis-example is carried a step further in the double nature of the novel's discourse. The criminal tale serves to locate dialectically both the act of repression and the reaction of social protest. In other words, the protest could be said to be rendered possible by virtue of the act of repression within which it was cloaked, and likewise the act of repression was rendered powerful by juxtaposition with the protest. This contradiction is inherently part of the novel's project, and this double discourse of the novel is in some ways what accounts for the novel's illicitness.

Prefaces to novels during the seventeenth and eighteenth centuries spend a fair amount of time denying this double function. Although the novel seems to be constitutively drawn to the criminal, novelists like Defoe, for example, deny or negate that necessity for including "wicked actions" by saying that these are included only to paint them in "low-prized colors."[22] Or we may recall here Mary Manley's defense of the portrayal of vice on the grounds that such a depiction will reveal injustice. In other words, for these authors the criminal content is not inherently part of the novel's discourse but is only included to exemplify deviant behavior.

However, English novels of the seventeenth and early eighteenth centuries were perceived by many of the middle and upper classes as immoral and illicit not only for their criminal content but for their very enterprise of fictionalizing, inventing, forging reality, and lying. Novelists not only made up their stories, they also denied that their invented stories were fictions, as did Defoe when he wrote of *Moll Flanders* that "the world is so taken up of late with novels and romances that it will be hard for a private history to be taken for genuine. . . ."[23] Like *Moll Flanders*, most of the "true" accounts of the dying words and confessions of criminals, as well as the autobiographies and biographies of criminals were—as we might suspect—fabricated despite their authors' claims to the contrary. Even in the case of the actual thief Mary Carleton, for example, Francis Kirkman, who wrote *The Counterfeit Lady Unveiled* (1673), pledged that his account was "the truest account I can get of her life" which is presented to the reader exactly as "she hath related it."[24] Yet Kirkman merely plagiarized an earlier account of Carleton's life that was in turn also not written by her. In this case, and more generally, writers were culpable of telling lies, but their more significant problem was that they were forced into denying the very structural assumptions of the novel—that the discourse was fictional.

Novelists in the seventeenth and eighteenth centuries were placed in an extremely odd position. They had to construct an elaborate false theory of the novel to mask the inherently illicit discourse of writing about criminals in a fictional form. This simulacrum of a novel, this false novel, is depicted as being univalent, as opposed to the genuine news/novels discourse which is double and reflexive. Novelists, being forced to lie about the fictionality of their work, for example, are going against the constitutive structure of the novel. This position is all the more ironic since one of the stated aims of the novel is to bring the reader to accept a set of ideological truths about the value of salvation, virtue, honesty, and so on. Yet, the novelist must lie to bring the reader to truth. In this sense, the novelist is very close to the criminals about whom he or she writes, whose lies and deceptions were the precondition for their repentance. Thus, the novelist's participation in the doubleness of the fictive discourse is very similar to the criminal's doubleness as example and dis-example.

Much of the early theorizing about the novel was an attempt to rationalize and deny the essentially immoral and illicit givens of the novel's discourse. Bishop Huet wrote in his treatise on romance, reprinted in England as a defense of novels, that fiction was not necessarily morally irredeemable. If put to a moral use, fictions might "carry a signification, and suggest an hidden meaning (and are not lies, but the figures of truth) which . . . even our Saviour himself . . . used upon honorable and pious occasions."[25] This moral-use doctrine was frequently invoked by English writers to deny the doubleness of their discourse. The moral corrective, such as the one we have already seen suggested by Manley, acts as a kind of dispensation or retraction that, like the special quality of truth assigned to the dying criminal's speech, reverses or annuls the illicitness of what came before. This tactic is a crude one, but it recognizes and tries to make explicit the doubleness of the novel's discourse.

Moral realism or moral verisimilitude—as opposed to actual verisimilitude—is another element of the false or simulacrum theory of the novel, since the actual novel is filled with the improbable (morally or otherwise), the impossible, the coincidental, the morally reprehensible, and the like. For novelists actually to write the morally verisimilar novel, they would have had to abandon realism and the novel's form itself. The rules and limits of the simulacrum theory of the novel seem to be in direct conflict with the discourse of the novel itself. Thus, paradoxically, in order to write novels that were morally verisimilar, novelists had to abandon the factually realistic. However, as we have seen, such a choice would in fact have meant the end of the novel's form since it was so bound up with the realistic. Therefore, novelists had to claim that their works were true—true accounts after all do not have to be morally probable, they just have to have happened. In this case, though, novelists become liars, perpetrators of the crime of fiction. And worse, novelists are not merely liars by virtue of the fact that they make up stories; they are liars twice over since they deny that they have done so.

Part of the motive for the elaborate denials illustrated in the last chapter was a denial of the apparent criminality of the novel form. As I have been trying to show, the simulacrum theory of the novel amounted to a massive denial of the inherent doubleness of the fictional discourse. For example, when John Bunyan accounts for his use of "feigned words" in *Pilgrim's Progress*, he says that his special use of the normally disreputable fictional form will "make truth spangle and its rays to shine." But of course the work is saved by the fact that it is really "delivered under the similitude of a dream."[26]

The injunction against fiction was all the more powerful because of its religious component. While actual criminals might recount the steps by which God led them through crime to repentance, the novelist must impersonate God in sending his character through a series of "divinely" inspired—but really "writerly" inspired—revelations. Authors, then, put themselves in the blasphemous position of equating plot with providence. Since the theory of "second" or "natural" causes emphasized that God's intentions could be understood through examining not miracles but the ordinary events of everyday life, writers like Defoe relied on their readers to understand that the key incidents in, for example, *Robinson Crusoe* were actually messages from God. In Crusoe's reading of his life, and in the reader's simultaneous reading of that life, these incidents stand out; of course it is not God but Defoe who provided the intentionality behind these plot elements (see Chapter 9).

Defoe's presuming to transform plot into providence, taking on the mantle of divine intentionality, was blasphemous to such contemporaries as Charles Gildon who attacked Defoe, saying that "the Christian religion and the doctrines of providence are too sacred to be delivered in fictions and lies." For Gildon, it was utterly evil to allow "lies to mingle with the holy truths of religion."[27] What is significant about Gildon's attack was that it assailed not the content of *Robinson Crusoe*, which Gildon admitted was fundamentally religious and exemplary, but the form of the work. The very enterprise of fiction was blasphemous because one cannot make up stories in which God's actions figure as central plot devices.

The connection between journalism, fiction, criminality, and novels is a powerful one. News had long been associated with stories of criminals from the earliest days of sensational ballads through the eighteenth century and beyond. In the eighteenth century, the more popular newspapers relied on criminal and sensational matter as the main, if not exclusive, material they published. The move from newspaper to history to novel was easily accomplished with the recording of the lives of various criminals. Jonathan Wild, for example, was first written about in the newspapers, then later by Defoe and Fielding. Accounts of recently executed criminals were published periodically. Paul Lorrain, the chaplain at Newgate, issued at irregular intervals *The Ordinary of Newgate* which was printed on single sheets and gave details of the executions to which Lorrain had access. Other publishers took up this practice and printed similar types of collections at regular intervals. Such works were clearly part of the news/novels discourse if only because they combined the traits of recentness, seriality, and criminality. These accounts of criminals were, in turn, collated into larger editions. The first notable compilation of this sort was Captain Alexander Smith's *Complete History of the Lives and Robberies of the Most Notorious Highwaymen*, published in 1714.

The content of these criminal catalogues suggests a further link between journalism, the novel, and execution rituals. Moralizing combined with voyeurism is a central characteristic of such works, as can be seen in the following example from Smith's collection. One George Caddel, who murdered his fiancée, is condemned to death:

> We have no particular account of the behavior of this malefactor while under sentence of death, or at the place of execution: yet his fate will afford an instructive lesson to youth. Let no young man, who has connections of any kind with one woman, think of paying his addresses to another.[28]

The stories in Smith's *History* read like the plots of Defoe's novels. Mary Adams, one criminal, moves from free sexuality to prostitution to pickpocketing, and in doing so seems to rehearse the pattern Moll Flanders will follow. Or the account of Thomas Gray uses elements that it shares in common with the novel—the story is told in the first person but is presented by an "editor," and it is filled with interpolated letters, tales, and poems that seem reminiscent of the novel form. All of these criminal narratives passed through many incarnations as news items, fictionalized biographies, segments in anthologies of criminal stories, and perhaps serializations in newspapers. So, for example, Captain Smith's history eventually came to be reprinted in journals. Thus the same material might circulate through several forms from the pages of the news to separate, numbered parts, to a yearly volume of collated numbers, to a more systematic collection, and back finally into the

columns of the newspaper. Because of the nature of the news/novels
discourse, narrative might pass through all these contexts of fact
and fiction.

Thus the news/novels discourse—in its various forms of news,
fiction, tale, *recit*, novel and so on—maintains a basic predisposition
toward criminals, and this predisposition is not to be seen as characteristic merely because narratives depict scenes of low life or
irreligion. Rather, the news/novels discourse is constitutively illicit,
and its illicitness is directly linked to the novel's double discourse—
a discourse which embodies opposing political and moral functions.
That is to say, the novel is not simply dangerous because it is a
reaction against social repression, but because it also authorizes that
very power of repression at the same time. Likewise, criminality
is depicted in novels both as a state of error, as a straying from the
light, and at the same time as a nostalgic reaction against power
and property. This doubleness is carried through the parallel fact
that the criminal's crooked path of sin is a necessary precondition
for repentance, but repentance also carries with it the negative
signification of endorsing the repressive power of religion and the
state. Further, what I have been calling the moral-use doctrine
stands in opposition to the continual use of criminal scenes and
actions. Continuing the elements of the double discourse, verisimilitude, the necessary structural precondition for the novel's existence, flies in the face of the simulacrum theory's demand for
moral probability. Finally, religious edification is undermined by
the novel's formal requirements for fictiveness and immorality.

All of these contradictions are bound up with the total structure of the early English novel. However, the authors of these
works were necessarily forced into a stance of denial which served
to decriminalize or neutralize the illicit and even subversive aspects
of the genre. So the effect of this massive act of denial was to create
a false or simulacrum theory of the novel which proposed for each
illicit aspect of the novel an antithetical, negating element. Thus,
the inherently double discourse of the novel would be simplified,
and thus defused, by this conflicting simulacrum theory. Of course,

such a tactic contains the seeds of its own destruction, since to deny the inherently double discourse is to create that discourse. It is in the play between criminality and protest, realism and moral probability, fictions and truth, plot and providence that the novel's energetic principle is revealed. It is the doubleness of the discourse that distinguishes it from others, and it is the dialectic between wicked actions and feigned words that powers the novel's form.

CHAPTER VIII

The Language of Print: Embodiment, Legitimation, Signification

IN THE MIDST of these tranformations in the nature of narrative I have been describing, certain profound changes were occurring in the general attitude toward language—at least insofar as we are discussing the language of prose narrative in print. As will be seen in this chapter, printed language was being assigned new tasks and being attributed new capacities. Print was becoming not only legitimate but the guarantor of immortality, fame, and public existence, taking on the capacity to embody within its representation the entire scope and shape of a human life in the form of biography and pseudobiography. At the same time, because of the enforcement of libel laws, printers and writers had to become more and more circumspect in their references and representations. As a result, a kind of confusion of signification developed. To a certain extent narrative became so interpretable that it became difficult to know for sure if a reference to one thing might not be a disguised reference to something else. All of these developments had significant effects on the differentiation of the news/novels discourse.

It was during the second half of the seventeenth century that print became legitimized. The early history of print, as we have seen, reveals that typography was regarded dubiously by the state. At certain historical moments print equalled subversion. Then, during the seventeenth century as we have seen, with the growth of political parties and the civil war came the development of the notion that print was an ideological and political tool to be used by either side. By the end of the seventeenth century, the Bank of England began to print paper monetary notes, and it is clear that printing by this time could act as a guarantee of the value of the money and the authority of the institution.

At the beginning of the seventeenth century, print carried no such guarantee of authenticity or legitimacy. Upper-class poets, for example, rarely voluntarily committed their works directly to print; the preference was to circulate manuscripts among friends and allow the work to slip into print by devious routes and means.[1] It was considered vulgar to print one's works, and even popular plays came to print quite slowly if at all before 1600.

Shakespeare is a case in point. His sonnets were published secretly, and the First Folio edition of his plays was published posthumously. The grounds for publishing the First Folio edition were not to confer immortality on the opus of Shakespeare's work but more likely to secure money for the actors of his company who were trying to block others from printing forgeries. It seems that this was the reason the folio was entered in the records of the Stationers' Company, a measure which tenuously preserved copyright in an age before the Copyright law was enacted. The preface to the First Folio claims its authenticity as the only true version of the plays, all others being ". . . diverse stolne, and surreptitious copies, maimed, and deformed by the frauds and stealthes of injurious impostors, that expos'd them: even those are now offer'd to your view cur'd, and perfect of their limbes";[2] It was far from the minds of the publishers to immortalize Shakespeare through print. Rather, they wished to claim possession of the text, secure the financial rights, and in some sense keep the text somewhat uniform. As they wrote to their prospective readers, ". . . whatever you do, Buy."[3]

It would be difficult to imagine writers like Shakespeare and Sidney conceiving of the immortality of the work as being tied up with typography rather than being confirmed by the preservative value of pure art. For Shakespeare, the poetry itself would preserve the memory of the young man in the sonnets.

> But thy eternal summer shall not fade,
> Nor lose possession of that fair thou ow'st,
> Nor shall Death brag thou wander'st in his shade,
> When in eternal lines to time thou grow'st;
>
> (18: 9–12)

Even when Shakespeare refers to "my books" (23: 9–10), it seems likely that he is referring to manuscript books, not printed books. One would be hard pressed to say that Shakespeare conceived of print as assuring him any kind of special immortality.

Yet by 1664, when Joseph Glanville translated his book *Scepsis Scientifica* into the English version *The Vanity of Dogmatizing*, print seems to have attained another status in the culture—it had become a guarantor or preserver of cultural immortality. Glanville writes in his introduction "I found so faint an inclination toward publishing a second edition that I could have been well content to suffer it to have slipped into the state of eternal silence and oblivion."[4] The idea that unless thoughts be fixed or anchored in print they face "eternal silence and oblivion" seems to have been a relatively new one. Glanville's statement, in contrast to Shakespeare's, emphasizes that it was not so much the act of creation, nor even the setting of the idea to paper that confers immortality on an idea, but solely the act of print.

What Glanville is describing in effect is the creation of a vast record or repository of society's thoughts and discoveries that was made possible through the printing process. Print guaranteed that discourse would be preserved and even assembled into what Foucault has called the "archive." I am using "archive" in the very particular sense ascribed to the word by him in *The Archaeology of Knowledge*. The archive is the sum of all knowledge in a society. Further, the archive embodies the rules by which that knowledge is governed. It is so vast and complex as to be unknowable to the person who inhabits the cultural moment of a particular phase of the archive because, as Foucault says, that person thinks and speaks from within these rules, and therefore cannot perceive them.[5] However, though the rules of the archive are unknowable, a society can be aware of the existence of the concept of an archive. Glanville's statement suggests that a conception of the archive was coming into being which included all knowledge and not merely ancient knowledge. This idea appears to be related to the battle of the "ancients" and the "moderns." What seems clear is that print was increasingly becoming one of the prerequisites for entrance to the archive. Although written discourses *may* be included in the material a culture preserves, writing does not always act as a passport to the archive; however, print seems to have become a sufficient guarantee that the material in question will be preserved by a culture.

As the idea of the archive began to be established, the rise of the public library—the public analogue in English history to the archive—becomes significant. During the seventeenth century, libraries came to be considered more than mere collections of one's own books; they become cultural repositories. (According to Burkhardt in *The Civilization of the Renaissance in Italy*, such repositories were formed earlier on the Continent.)[6] This is not to say that antiquarian interest at least in England did not exist before this time in history, but English libraries of the past were more concerned with the preservation of the writings of the ancients rather than the whole spectrum of human knowledge at the present moment.[7] This preservative tendency is evident in a proposal made during Elizabeth's reign by the Society of Antiquaries who requested the establishment of an academy of antiquary and historical studies "to preserve old books concerning the matter of the history of this realm, original charters and monuments . . . to be well furnished with ancient bookes and rare monuments of antiquity, which otherwise may perish."[8] One notices here that the process being described is a kind of embalming. Rather than discussing the possibility of establishing a library to house living knowledge, or of perceiving the existence of an "archive," the medieval and Elizabethan British librarians were proposing a preservation of the past

to the point of excluding the present. Even the architecture of
medieval libraries suggested more of a "noble reading room,"[9] than
a storehouse or catalogue.

But, a new conception of the library arises during the middle
of the seventeenth century when John Drurie, a keeper of the Royal
Library, published *The Reformed Library Keeper* (1650). In it he posits
a library which sounds very much like the prototype of the archive.
The library's function, according to him, is "to keep the public
stock of learning, to increase it, to propose it to others in the way
which may be helpful to most."[10] The idea of a "public stock" of
learning is indeed a remarkably new notion. Knowledge no longer
belongs to the decaying arm of the past but to the present just as
journalism came to imply a vivification of history. And knowledge
belongs not only to the present, but to the public—as if that access
to knowledge were a kind of right, and not the eccentric privilege
of the priest's sanctum sanctorum or the scholar's desk. In addition,
the collection of books is proposed to be "arranged in a way which
may be helpful to most." The aim of this proposal is to introduce
the concept of generic order to cataloguing and to provide system
and continuity to seemingly random and occasional books and
writings.

The use of the phrase "public stock" is significant. The *Oxford
English Dictionary* defines "public stock" as "the property held for
public purposes by a nation, municipality, or community." In this
financial sense, libraries, in addition to books, have become com-
modities. The libraries are now part of the cutural economy, books
have an exchange value, and as the conception of an "archive" which
is *precious* arises, so does the perception by society that it cannot
do without its *stock* of knowledge. From the years 1650 to 1700,
domestic libraries like those of Samuel Pepys, which were the
collections of books based on individual whim, receded in importance in the face of the rise of public libraries.[11] The public stock
of knowledge became an accepted concept in England by the eighteenth century—and by extension, the archive came more readily
into being. The London Library Society, established in the latter

half of the eighteenth century, a forerunner of the London Library, issued a catalogue which shows how firmly entrenched these conceptions had become: "It is intended that the London Library shall contain all those great works in science and literature which it is difficult for individuals to procure. . . ."[12]

This emphasis on modern learning certainly is part of the larger debate of the ancients and moderns—and the outcome reflects this. The development of the archive—both in its material form of the library and in its abstract form of the sum of all written and printed discourses—emphasizes the growing importance of the preservation of contemporary ideas and lives, and particularly by the modality of print. The technology of typography now permitted the assembling of the basic unit of discourse—the book—into a collection greater than itself, and arranged these books as if they were building blocks to form a structure that is the collective consciousness of mankind.

The rise of the printed history and the biography as a form during the latter half of the seventeenth century reinforces this growing interest in the preservation of an individual life by typography. (This interest also develops outside the modality of print in the unprinted autobiography.)[13] Just as the archive was the collection of the units of discourse, so too the collected lives of individuals in some way or other amounted to history. A curious shift in values began as histories and biographies gained importance as recreations of the past. To have one's life recorded in print was in a sense to have it validated and enshrined. Recall Glanville's characterization of not being in print as "eternal silence and oblivion." A later writer gives a further testimony to this notion by saying of her history of Anne of Austria: "I have interspersed in her histories some of her speeches, thoughts and actions which deserve to be known to the whole world, and which would never have seen the light if I had not immediately committed them to writing."[14] There is a sense of urgency and tenuousness in the words "if I had not immediately committed them to writing." It is as if only by recording the details of life through transcription that one can grasp the evanescent slipperiness of experience. The author says that by writing the thoughts of Anne of Austria she will make them "known to the whole world." Clearly, she is referring not to the writing down of such thoughts but to the printing of them—which has by now the predominant way to make writing known to the world. The idea expressed here that to be in print is to be in the "light" is in sharp contrast to not being in print, according to Glanville, which is to be in "oblivion." Clearly, the paradigm here seems to be one of salvation and oblivion, at least as far as the archive is concerned.

The correct use of language advocated by those who favored the plain style embodied the religious obligation to present things in words as they were in the world. Thus the accurate recording of a life would reduplicate God's work, recreating either the journey of a soul toward salvation or toward damnation—either of which would be an instructive or hortatory example. To allow life to slip by unrecorded would be to lose it forever beyond the salvation of writing and/or print. While the official culture, its ideas, and its public persons are preserved for the future ages in the archive, the culture of the lower classes is invisible except as it has been committed to print through the news/novels discourse, and in its incidental appearance in parish records, tax books, and the records of criminal trials, especially as printed in the *Proceedings* of famous trials, pamphlets, ballads, news accounts, and criminal tales.[15] In this sense, the preservation of a life through typography was a uniquely overdetermined event. Not only did the news/novels discourse lean in this direction through its orientation toward reportage, but religious teachings as well as the growing power of print all contributed to this act of "embodiment," the preserving of a life in print.

There are many possible reasons why such a reliance on print to recreate, embody, and even displace life should have occurred. One possibility is that this development reflects a growing trend toward specialization and with this specialization the familiar correlative—alienation. I do not wish to misuse this term, but there seems to have developed slowly a sense that to truly "be," one had to be set in print—to have a preserved existence one had to be where one was not, that is in the embalmment and embodiment of print. If news was becoming not what *happened* out in the world but what was *recorded* about what happened, then the very notion of reality and existence had to be perceived somewhat differently. Indeed, as Raymond Williams has suggested, since literature is social language or activity, the development of this social capability must also have had much to do with the growth of specialization.[16]

How then can we view language of this sort as reflecting at the same time alienation and social activity? In a sense specialization, by breaking down community, hierarchy, and so on, might be said to have shifted the social gathering place from the daily world to the printed page. That is to say, as groups of masterless people—part of the great shifting population of the unemployed that began developing during the seventeenth-century in England—ceased to be associated with particular locations, print in effect became the new locus of stability, of ideological allegiance which might replace clan, village, or familial allegiance.[17] The news/novels discourse became the voice of the ideological community, the memory of the past, the collective manifestation of the individual. Thus, one could argue that though print represents an alienation of people's lives that necessitates the creation of a displaced world embodied in print, at the same time print can be seen on the positive side as the newly available form of social activity made necessary by that same alienation.

If print may be said to have taken on a quality of being the locus of embodiment, it has a further function in this context. Since so much of the news/novels discourse is based on the contradictions inherent in the double assertion of truth and falsity, the value of print as a reliable medium is also put into question, at least until some consensual agreement about how to distinguish between factual and fictional narratives is made. So, although print has been given the capability of preserving a life, that capability can be seen as a negative or dubious one. What then results is frequently a struggle on the part of authors to prove that their work is truly the most accurate, the most true account—although, finally, such writers lack the tools, the proofs, the guarantees that would make such accounts possible.

In looking at a work like *The Counterfeit Lady Unveiled* (1673) by Francis Kirkman, for example, we can see a process in futility much like someone trying to prove 'a theorem about the nature of the relativity theory with only a knowledge of Euclidian geometry. Kirkman wrote his book about the criminal Mary Carleton, who had recently attained notoriety under the alias of "The German Princess." Between 1663 and 1673 there were as many as twenty-four publications about her life and crimes. Kirkman's book is a collation of these accounts, frequently lifting pages of text directly from these earlier works. *The Counterfeit Lady Unveiled* is less of a publication of what is *new* than an attempt to establish what is *true*. The author takes great care to assure the reader of the certainty of the facts of Mary Carleton's life as he now sorts them out. For example, Kirkman evaluates his information in the following:

> Having now given you the best and truest account of her birth and extraction, the place where and the persons who, I should proceed to tell you the time when, but that I can give you less certainty than the other. For I altogether believe her own report to be false, but as she related I must give it you, not knowing how to disprove her. . . .[18]

Kirkman seems to spend a good deal of time in his book evaluating the relative degree of certainty or uncertainty in other accounts of Carleton's life. It is difficult to tell, as is perhaps fitting, to what extent Kirkman saw his own work as fictionalized; he does continually assure the reader that the work is "the truest account I can get of her life." Kirkman must of course rely on earlier publications although he clearly is unable to say whether such works are accurate. His very technique is based on dubious practices, as when he turns the narrative over to Mary Carleton herself, quoting from her first-person account in an attempt to "give it to you as she hath related it."[19] However, Kirkman's supposedly genuine first-person account is taken extensively from an earlier work entitled *The Case of Madam Mary Carleton* (1663) that in all likelihood cannot have been written by Carleton. In this latter work, Carleton is supposed to be correcting yet an earlier pamphlet written about her, allegedly by her husband, entitled *The Replication or Certain Vindicatory Depositions* (1663).

In each attempt to correct the accuracy of the previous account, each author is frustrated by the impossibility of proving in any way the veracity of his or her version. Each account of Carleton's life appears to be less of a narrative than it is a disquisition and a guide to previously printed versions of the criminal's life. Kirkman admits this inauthenticity of printed accounts when he writes that *The Memoires of Mary Carleton* (1671), yet another book on the subject, contains a letter in which "she [Mary Carleton] or the author that writ it" gives an account of a voyage.[20] With the words "or the author that writ it," Kirkman seems to allow that "hard" sources might indeed be fictionalized if not altogether fictional. He presents the material and allows the reader to evaluate the reliability of the evidence.

Further, continuing in the upstaging of earlier texts, Kirkman claims to actually have been in Newgate himself during the final days of the German Princess' life (a fact that is certainly open to doubt). It is Kirkman himself who reminds Carleton that she can repent in the short time left, and she replies "The Lord grant me true repentance."[21] Kirkman thus uses his eyewitness testimony to refute the claims of earlier writers that Carleton was merry and unrepentant in her last hours, and by virtue of his own account he established, within the limits of his work, the ultimate claim of verity. In doing so, he ends futilely by falling back on the inherent contradiction of the news/novels discourse—that affirmation is denial. There is no way to claim certainty under these conditions, since verifiable certainty is beyond the scope of the discourse at this time.

Not surprisingly, Carleton's life itself, as the story is told by Kirkman, is a series of forgeries, imitations, deceits, and disguises. Carleton, posing as a princess, forged letters, maintaining that "to deceive the deceiver is no deceit."[22] It is fitting that Kirkman's efforts to attain the true account of Carleton are as quixotic an attempt as any, and that the account itself should be a history of deception and deceit. In fact, no confession, history, or memoir could guarantee veracity. Indeed, Isaac Bickerstaff noted wryly in the *Tatler* that

> there are others of that gay people who (as I am informed) will live half a year together in a garret, and write a history of their intrigues in the Court of France. . . . I do hereby give notice to all booksellers and translators whatsoever that the word "memoire" is French for novel; and to require them that they sell and translate it accordingly.[23]

Interestingly, "novel" is used here to indicate that the writing is not as accurate as a memoir, although it is clear that the general usage of the word "memoire" gave no assurance of verity either. This state of affairs seems to reflect an ongoing fuzziness in the definition of fact and fiction. Donald Stauffer, who has made a study of biography in eighteenth-century England, points out that biographies particularly blur the distinction between true and false. It might not have been considered out of the ordinary to have written a biography of a real or contemporary person and included fictional characters and encounters, or to have written a novel and included historical figures, as we have seen. In fact, at some points in his book, Stauffer has so much difficulty in trying to squeeze these works into the modern categories that he admits, "One wonders with some trepidation how many works of fact and works of fiction are incorrectly listed in this present volume."[24]

The uncertainty concerning fact and fiction, linked to the concept of embodiment, proves to be a strange wedding in the development of the narrative. Bodies appear, lives are represented, and their existence, due to the growing legitimation of print and of the archive, becomes sanctioned with an existence more "real" than real life. But the discourse still cannot convey the ultimate veracity of the image. In this sense, the representation is more real than the object, but in another sense it is constitutively an eternally unprovable invention, a shadow of legitimized form that cannot be grasped. In considering this dilemma, it is necesary to say that something profoundly wrong has happened within the news/novels discourse by the first quarter of the eighteenth century—a breakdown, as it were, in signification has occurred. Of course, this breakdown is hardly new in the sense that the news/novels discourse is predicated on its doubleness and reflexivity. But the growing legitimacy of print and the growth of its capacity for embodiment has tilted the scales to a certain extent. When ballads had circulated or when criminal tales were printed, the inability to distinguish fact from fiction was less of a liability. But ironically, with the authority of print comes a need to distinguish and define fact. This need, along with the sharpening of the laws defining news, created a state of profound difficulty in the news/novels discourse.

Not only in fiction but also in what we would call reportage there were problems. In order to talk about the real world, writers had to create a kind of indirect or allegorical language to avoid the edge of the newly honed law. For example, when Dr. Johnson acted as a reporter of parliamentary debates for the *Gentleman's Magazine*, he had to transcribe his accounts under the name of the Senate of Liliput using "feigned denominations of the several speakers, sometimes with denominations formed of the letters of their real names, in the manner of what is called anagram, so that they might be deciphered," according to Boswell, who added that "Parliament then kept the press in a kind of awe, which made it necessary to have recourse to such devices."[25]

In the case of Richard Steele, as we have seen, even writing in an allegorical style which might allow variant readings was considered illegal (see chapter 5). What all this meant to writers in the news/novels discourse was that almost any writing could be ascribed a treasonous meaning through a process of interpretation. Swift in *Gulliver's Travels* mocks this paranoia of interpretation. Gulliver notes that in the kingdom of Tribnia [Britain] people are accused of plots, their papers seized, and

> delivered to a set of artists very dextrous in finding out the mysterious meaning of words, syllables and letters. For instance, they can decipher a close-stool to signify a privy council; a flock of geese, a senate; a lame dog, an invader; the plague, a standing army. . . .

By using anagrams and acrostics, these same interpreters can turn
all writing into political import.

> Thus, N., shall signify a plot; B, a regiment of horse; L, a fleet at
> sea. Or secondly, by transposing the letters of the alphabet, in any
> suspected paper they can lay open the deepest designs of a discon-
> tented party. So for example, if I should say in a letter to a friend,
> Our brother Tom hath just got the piles; a man of skill in this art
> would discover how the same letters which composed that sentence,
> may be analysed into the following words; Resist,—a plot is brought
> home—The Tour.[26]

This state of affairs resembles the old medieval controversy
over polysemousness, except that now instead of trying to determine whether the figurative or eschatological level was to be accepted, the question at hand was whether the literal narrative or
the hidden political account was the preferred sense of the text.
The fact that journalism had to conceal its language under the cloak
of oblique references and fictional situations is all the more bizarre
in light of the fact that the plain style was concurrently the dominant mode of discourse in other areas. This new type of allegory
differed from the older form in the sense that the surface—which
in the case of medieval allegory and biblical interpretation had a
pretense to a meaning—is now a mere tactic or ploy for the concealed message. The surface now is the alibi for the genuine material
it conceals. People's opinions and careers now hung on the interpretation given to their writing, as was the case with Steele.

What writers of the time seem to have been faced with was
a threat to the mechanism of signification caused by a reading which
demanded that the reader look beyond and discard the literal text.
Reading of this type can be seen as becoming something of a paranoid venture in which seemingly insignificant details would yield
the true, but concealed, meaning of a written work, and endless
levels of meaning could be plumbed without certainty as to which
was the "real" text.

No one knew this better than Swift, who may have been
mocking the interpretive paranoia of the government in his famous

allegorization performed by the Grand Committee in the preface to *A Tale of a Tub*. Swift was certainly concerned that he and his fellows were caught in a moment particularly dangerous to language, as his proposal for the founding of an academy to fix the constantly shifting English language indicates. In the preface to *A Tale of a Tub*, Swift seems to satirize the government's interpretations of allegorized literary works by going them one better. The Grand Committee, it may be remembered, says that the mariners' custom of throwing a tub out of their ship to divert whales from attacking the frigate is suitable for allegorical interpretation. The frigate is to be considered "Government and Religion"; the whale is Hobbes' *Leviathan* "which tosses and plays with all schemes of Religion and Government."[27] But when it comes to assigning a meaning to the tub, the Committee is unable to come up with an interpretation and decides that the tub is to be taken literally. Without pausing to examine the boggling number of levels created by turning the allegory upon itself in this kind of linguistic Möbius strip, we may note that Swift is perhaps ridiculing the current dissolution of meaning. By taking the literal level as *true* for the tub, while allowing the Committee to *allegorize* the whale into Leviathan, Swift pulls down the supporting pillars of signification— Hobbes' book could not sanely be said to joust with a tub. And if it could, what would that mean? Swift further manages to mock the paranoid reading of texts by having the Committee allegorize not a literary work but an actual practice of mariners. This *reductio ad absurdum* points the finger at interpretation, saying why not interpret life as well as words? Moreover, the entirety of *A Tale of a Tub* is nothing if not an ingenious series of contradictory fragments of information that at once seductively demands and prevents a polysemous reading. Swift's footnotes are the cream on this pie thrown in the face of hypersignification.

   The stress on interpretation was perhaps more apparent to those politically outside the government who suffered from the abuses of the law's reading into their writings and pronouncements. A Tory member of Parliament, Archibald Hutcheson, expressed his rage against this device:

> I have at this time by me a long dissertation upon innuendoes
> wherein I have proved, that all the sense clapped upon all heathen
> authors by their scholiasts, and all the tenets charged upon the
> inspired writings by Dutch commentators, were not so wild, absurd,
> and arbitrary, as what the single force of an innuendo can fix upon
> any passage when played *secundum artem*, in the hands of a nice state-
> empiric.[28]

The reference to religious and scholastic hermeneutics shows an
awareness that there was a prehistory to the present linguistic state
of affairs. Clearly, no side was innocent. Writers did in fact write
books in this veiled manner, and no doubt many of the interpretations made by government prosecutors were valid. Yet, beyond
this, a kind of obsession does seem to exist which persistently seeks
"keys" and interpretations to any text. Even by mid-century Tobias
Smollett, in his introduction to *Roderick Random*, still found it necessary to warn the reader not to assume every character in his book
was based on an original in life:

> Christian Reader, I beseech thee, in the bowels of the Lord, re-
> member this example while thou art employed in the perusal of the
> following sheets; and seek not to appropriate to thyself that which
> equally belongs to five hundred different people. If thou should
> meet with a character that reflects thee in some ungracious partic-
> ular, keep thy own counsel; consider that one feature makes not a
> face, and that, though thou are, perhaps distinguished by a bottle
> nose, twenty of thy neighbors may be in the same predicament.[29]

One of the effects of this instability was a confusion and distrust
concerning the meaning of a text. Novelists exploited this confusion
in writing their narratives and, as I will argue in the following
chapters, *based* the novel precisely at this starting point.

I should note here again that I am describing a problem within
the news/novels discourse—which is now rapidly breaking down
into its two more clearly defined subdiscourses. However, I must
stress that I am not saying readers of news or novels were doltishly
unable to say what was true and what was false, simply wandering

around in a dazed, anomic state devoid of language or signifiers. (Although it should be noted that people like Laurence Sterne were having their problems as well as their rewards with linguistic matters.) But it does seem that a major problem for the Early Modern reader and writer was how to create a narrative that would be clearly and unambiguously either factual or fictional. While not all language was disintegrating, clearly the language of the news/novels discourse had to undergo so many transformations, interpretations, translations, reverse interpretations, allegorizations, and so on that it might be difficult to assign it a clear and unambiguous capability for signification. The paradox, of course, is that this crisis comes at the same moment that typography is gaining an ability to embody a life, to be—in theory—a veracious discourse. In a sense, this is the moment of truth for the news/novels discourse—the need for a veracious narrative discourse is there, but so too is the inability of language to fulfill the need. And it is perhaps out of this conflict that the novels of Defoe, Richardson, and Fielding emerge.

CHAPTER IX

Daniel Defoe:
Lies as Truth

DEFOE IS THE single writer who is usually pointed to as the originator of the novel in England. Countless anthologies and critical works begin here at the famous landmark of the literary pilgrimage, and one always hears first the strange story of the industrious man on the island who spends his days listing his provisions and walling himself deeper into his isolation against a danger that fails to materialize for twenty years. *Robinson Crusoe*, in many ways, seems like the wrong locus—the exquisitely wrong place— to begin a consideration of the origins of the novel. Crusoe is such an atypical work, so devoid of society, of human interaction, so full of lists and micro-observations. Crusoe's isolation is even atypical of the circumstances of Defoe's other protagonists—Moll Flanders or Roxana—who roam through the midst of society and live off it. Of course, one could argue that Moll and Roxana are isolated egos just as is Robinson, but even in isolation they are dependent on society. Crusoe lives alone, independent, and is so domineering that he makes the first human he encounters in twenty years his slave. And unlike Moll and Roxana, Crusoe does not end up married and settled, but goes off on further adventures.

Given all this atypicality, why have *Robinson Crusoe* and Defoe been chosen as touchstones for the great tradition of the novel, and why are they the point of origin? In some ways this fact simply resonates from the popularity of the book. Certainly no story written, except perhaps *Pilgrim's Progress*, was so widely read in the eighteenth century, so often reprinted, and serialized in so many newspapers and journals. But there is another reason for Defoe to stand out beside this imprinting in the cultural memory, and that is that his works remain odd to us because they seem not fully novels. *Pamela* and *Tom Jones* (even *Tristram Shandy*) strike the modern reader as recognizable novels whose tradition has been endorsed by many subsequent imitators. But Defoe's works seem still plainly to bear the marks of their intimate connection with the news/novels discourse. There is not enough "art" about them, no dazzling plots, not much in the way of form—just a kind of dogged attention to the cumulative details, to getting the story down on record. I believe we can still sense the confusion of attitude toward fact and fiction. When *Robinson Crusoe* was written in 1719, there was no clear distinction between news and fiction, and Defoe's work rests uneasily in that world of a discourse which is more and more inclining to separate into two subdiscourses but which still has not broken apart. Defoe strikes us as necessary to, yet subversive of, the history of the novel, and perhaps this quiddity has installed his work in the position of *primum mobile* of the novelistic tradition.

Defoe seems to be a perfect writer for the purposes of this study. And in some ways this study itself is ultimately about Defoe, about his centrality to the English novel—this strange centrality which places him outside the mainstream of what is to come. His early training as a journalist combines with his later career as a novelist in a poignant way; he has both feet in the news/novels discourse, but each foot in a different position. The oddity of his own life, so filled with disguise, lies, indirection, forgery, deceit, and duplicity seems to place him constitutionally at the center of questions about the truthfulness of narratives, about the problem of framing and ambivalence, about the breakdown of signification and reliability.

Defoe's writings run the gamut from outright fabrications to the pseudoreportorial works like *Duncan Campbell*, *Journal of the Plague Year*, and *Jonathan Wild*. Even *Robinson Crusoe* seems to have been an imaginative working-up of the life of Alexander Selkirk who had been shipwrecked on Juan Fernandez Island. Defoe's fictional works are quite frequently not fictional at all but based on some story or tale making the rounds. These are extended stories of the type that appeared in newspapers or ballads or pamphlets. But over the course of Defoe's writing career his attitude toward the nature of fiction seems to have undergone a significant change, and it is this change I would like to explore briefly. Why should Defoe's attitude toward the kinds of writing he had been doing for quite a while have changed? I would argue that as the news/novels discourse began to subdivide, and as the culture began making clearer demands for factual or fictional narrative, the old claim that a work was true became harder to substantiate. As that happened, the possibility arose that a work could be purely fictional. There is a movement in Defoe's writing that we can describe as a shift toward the fictional. Defoe uses a series of dodges, feints, and poses to rationalize the use of fiction, and even in his last phase, he is very careful not to say outright that his work is not factual.

In the preface to *Robinson Crusoe*, Defore simply claims, as had Aphra Behn and others, that his work is true. Defoe calls himself "editor" and says that he "believes the thing to be a just history of fact; neither is there any appearance of fiction in it. . . ."[1] This is a claim with which we are by now familiar, and it is not especially worthy of note. However, what is significant about Defoe's assertion is that it was openly challenged. Charles Gildon in *An Epistle to Daniel Defoe* claims that *Robinson Crusoe* is really no more than a "fable."[2] One wonders why this attack should have come at this time; why should Gildon have been so outraged about a conventional act of authorial disavowal? If everyone knew authorial disavowal to be a mere convention, as some have argued, why should Gildon's main attack on Defoe be about something that everyone knew all along? In reality, Gildon's book is one of the few I have been able to find which specifically attacks a work on the grounds that it is fictional—that is not a lie, a libel, or a distortion, but simply a fiction. The *Epistle* seems interesting to me precisely because it spends so much time attempting to out-fox Defoe and prove that because his work is inconsistent it must have been fictional, that is untrue or a lie, hence damnable.

In the *Farther Adventures of Robinson Crusoe*, Defoe attempts to elude Gildon's arguments by saying that "the just application of every incident, the religious and useful inferences drawn from every part, are so many testimonies to the good design of making it, and must legitimate all the part that may be called invention or parable in the story."³ Defoe is here allowing that parts of his story are indeed fictional, but that those parts are actually parables like those of Bunyan. In fact, in the *Serious Reflections . . . of Robinson Crusoe*, Defoe does not hesitate to include himself in the biblical tradition by saying that the only kind of falsehood that is excusable in narrative is the parable or allegory: "Such are the historical parables in the Holy Scripture, such *The Pilgrim's Progress* and such, in a word, the adventures of your fugitive friend Robinson Crusoe."⁴ Gildon, however, is unconvinced and writes that *Robinson Crusoe* can hardly be seen as an allegory since

> the design of the publication of this book was not sufficient to justify and make truth of what you allow to be fiction and fable; what you mean by *legitimating, invention,* and *parable,* I know not; unless you would have us think, that the manner of your telling a lie will make it truth.⁵

Gildon means his comment to be a snide one, but there is an element of truth beyond what Gildon intends. The fact is that Defoe does precisely mean that his manner of telling a lie will make it truth. That is, Defoe is keeping well within the bounds of the news/novels discourse intreating the reader to an inherent doubleness or reflexivity. Crusoe is at once true and false; he is a fiction with a true existence and a true story with a fictional structure. As was the case with so many of the works considered in this study, the distinction between fact and fiction is deliberately unclear. The significant point, however, in this interchange between Gildon and Defoe is that for the first time the whole issue of a discourse based on fact or fiction as a discriminant is brought up front. For Gildon, the genre of *Robinson Crusoe* depends on the external criteria of its truth or falsity.

Defoe was caught in Gildon's exacting demands and his response was to retreat to the defense of allegory. As we have seen, the recourse to the claim of allegory was quite popular and natural in the eighteenth century as a means of avoiding the censure of the courts. Defoe is clearly trying to back out of the issue by changing the terms of the argument. No longer claiming to be writing truth, Defoe claims that his message will be true only after it is interpreted. Defoe, rather than reply as editor to the charges that his book is feigned, has Robinson Crusoe himself in the preface deny the charges that "names are borrowed, and that it is all a romance; that there never was any such man or place, or circumstances in any man's life; that it is all formed and embellished by invention to impose upon the world."[6] Having Crusoe swear in the first person that his story is true is reminiscent of the authentication by eyewitness so common in the news/novels discourse and particularly in works about criminals. The brilliance of Defoe's defense rests in its mastery of confusion and its high tone of outrage. Witness:

> I, Robinson Crusoe, being at this time in perfect and sound mind and memory, thanks be to God, therefore, do hereby declare their objection is an invention scandalous in design, and false in fact; and do affirm that the story, though allegorical is also historical; and that it is the beautiful representation of a life of unexampled misfortunes. . . .[7]

The legal tone of the passage is impressive, especially considering that the character who is affirming his truthfulness is himself a fiction. Defoe is going the libel laws one better here by creating his own court of law and taking with a serious face the deposition of the legal and existential nonentity Robinson Crusoe. If this manipulation of fictional and real were the only thing Defoe does to confuse Gildon and like-minded followers, we should have to marvel; but Defoe takes us into new realms of framing by having Crusoe say in the above deposition that his story is allegorical and at the same time historical.

What can it mean to say that a work is both allegorically and historically true? On the one hand such an assertion has a familiar scriptural ring to it since the Bible is at once an historical account of the patriarchs, and at the same time subject to allegorical interpretation on various typological and eschatological levels. But, on the other hand, Defoe can hardly be claiming that Crusoe's life is able in any way to share this special attribute of biblical narrative. To make any sense of Crusoe's life in this way, one would have to believe that every incident occurring to Crusoe was designated by God to have an allegorical significance. How else could the virtual historical record of a human life be allegorical as well?[8]

And if Robinson Crusoe's life is an allegory, whose life does it allegorize? Of this Crusoe hints that "there is a man alive, and well known too, the actions of whose life are the just subject of these volumes." This well-known man, Crusoe hints further, was one who was forced to be confined in jail, and that the island is the symbol of that jail since "it is reasonable to represent anything that exists by that which exists not." And of whom could Defoe have been thinking—both famous and imprisoned—but himself? The tone of smug self-pity apparent in Crusoe's statement points directly to Defoe, especially when Crusoe says that the book is an allegory of "the life of a man you knew, and whose misfortunes and infirmities perhaps you had sometimes unjustly triumphed over."[9]

Now comes the problem to which I alluded earlier—how can this book be both an allegory of Defoe's life and a true history of Robinson Crusoe's? How can a real person's life be the allegory of fictional character's life? Defoe attempts to explain how this paradox can be possible, but in so doing, he muddies the waters beyond obscurity. First he has Crusoe claim:

> When in my observations and reflections of any kind in this volume
> I mention my solitudes and retirements, and allude to the circum-

stances of the former story, all those parts of the story are real facts in my history, whatever borrowed lights they may be represented by.[10]

Crusoe is saying that every event in *Robinson Crusoe* is to be considered true, to have actually happened, even if that event can also be interpreted allegorically. Then he continues to say that "there is not a circumstance in the imaginary story but has its just allusion to a real story, and chimes part for part and step for step with the inimitable life of Robinson Crusoe."[11] Here the "imaginary story" is juxtaposed to a "real story." However, is Defoe's life the imaginary story or is Crusoe's? We must remember that Crusoe is telling us all this, swearing on his own word, so he cannot be calling his own life "imaginary." If Defoe's life is imaginary, then things are strange indeed; of course, Defoe could be maintaining only that his life is the hidden allegory behind that of Crusoe. But things get stickier yet when Crusoe is made to say that

> when in these reflections I speak of the times and circumstances of particular actions done, or incidents which happened, in my solitude and island life, an impartial reader will be so just as to take it as it is, viz, that it is spoken or intended of that part of the real story which the island-life is a just allusion to. . . .[12]

This train of thought now seems to stand the previous one on its head. Instead of Defoe's story being the imaginative or allegorical one, now it is the island-life of Crusoe which is the allegory to the "real story" of Defoe's life. But, lest one rest comfortably with that interpretation, another paragraph flips things back again, saying that "all these reflections are just history of a state of confinement, which in my real history is represented by a confined retreat in an island. . . ."[13] So here again the island story is the "real history," and the allegorical one is Defoe's story.

What is going on here? Defoe seems to be spinning himself and his readers beyond confusion and ambivalence. He states an impossible case, that one man's life should be the allegory of another's; he compounds the impossibility with imprecisions; and his use of the words "real" and "imaginary" seem to be interchangeable.

If we try to map out the frames implicit in this work, we come up with something more troubling than the already confusing frames of the news/novels discourse. Not only do we have an editor claiming a work is true, but we have the assertion that the work is allegorical, which makes the story neither true nor false but adds the additional kink that the author must have divine or superhuman powers to make one man's life the allegory of another. Defoe's flight to the allegorical cannot be taken seriously (although Arthur Gold has attempted to do this) since it is such a confused defense. Rather his whole deranged set of tactics should be seen as a reaction to and a statement about the shifting nature of the news/novels discourse. Defoe apparently could not find a category to define the nature of his work, which for our purposes we might call the partially or provisionally true narrative. The only preexisting category that defined a type of narrative both true and false was allegory. Admittedly, Defoe did not do particularly well in choosing such a term, but he was, after all, groping in the dark.

One thing we may observe about the first quarter of the eighteenth century is that now narrative could no longer fall back on the old reflexive theory with its claims to verity since critics like Gildon were seriously pursuing the veracity of novels on a point-by-point basis. Defoe, Richardson, and Fielding each claimed to be beginning a new type of narration, a new species of writing, but since no clear conventions had been determined, and no real terminology had been used to define their attempts, they each had to create crudely the categories into which their works might fall. For Defoe, this category took advantage of the news/novels discourse's attitude toward fact and fiction but never quite made a transition to a clearly defined commitment to fiction, as perhaps Gildon would have liked. So Defoe continued to hedge, to fall back on the old category of allegory because he had no new term to define what it was he was doing.

Defoe began to change his allegation that his novels were true—allegorically or otherwise. The shift is a gradual one, but in *Colonel Jack* (1722) Defoe hedges as to whether or not the work is veracious; he writes that it should be of no "concern to the reader, whether it be an exact historical relation of real facts, or whether the hero of it intended to present us, at least in part, with a moral romance."[4] The shift in emphasis is noticeable. Defoe characteristically places himself out of the frame of the work implying that he is merely editing the autobiography of the hero. But the presentation differs from that of previous works because the hero himself may not have been telling the truth. A frame of doubt intercedes between the editor and the text. The editor still claims that he is not fabricating anything, but neither he nor the reader can ever know if Colonel Jack himself is putting something over on them. It is this element of doubt that Defoe will use for his remaining novels. As it turns out, the device is as good as allegory for outfoxing critics. The editor can always account for "problems" in the work by heaping blame on the protagonist. This tactic also lets Defoe sneak in the idea that the work may indeed be a complete or partial fiction. And so, the ambivalence characteristic of the novel-reading experience is now incorporated permanently into the novel's structure. The ambivalence fills the first two frames—neither the reader *nor* the editor knows whether the work is true or false. The moral imperative of the simulacrum theory that the *story* must be true is avoided entirely; now the only fact to which the editor swears is that the *text* exists. But the editor cannot account for the verity of the incidents in the text. In a very definite way, the novel moves covertly closer to proclaiming itself a fiction, and the novel's audience seems to be prepared to accept this sliding over.

Moll Flanders, which appeared in the same year as *Colonel Jack*, seems at first glance a return to Defoe's defense that his work is not a fiction but a factual account:

> The world is so taken up of late with novels and romances, that it will be hard for a private history to be taken for genuine, where the names and other circumstances of the person are concealed; and on this account we must be content to leave the reader to pass his own opinion upon the ensuring sheets, and take it just as he pleases.[15]

Defoe seems to be saying that his work is a factual history of a private life and not a novel or romance. But a closer reading reveals that Defoe actually does not claim anywhere in the preface that the work *is* true, he only quite skillfully implies this. Ingeniously, he lets himself off the hook by leaving the final judgment about the factuality of the work up to the reader, who may "take it just as he pleases." Defoe seems to be searching for a way to say that the work is at once true and not true, or, as Gildon had put it, Defoe is trying to tell a lie in a way that is true.

Continuing to use the frame of doubt, Defoe writes:

> The author is here supposed to be writing her own history, and in the very beginning of her account she gives the reasons why she thinks fit to conceal her true name, after which there is no occasion to say more about that.[16]

In the phrase "the author is here supposed to be writing" the word "supposed" is clearly operating in two ways: either Moll is *intending* to write or else she is *deceiving* the reader by doing other than she is supposed to be. The ambiguity, which I would say is deliberate, permits Defoe to cast doubt on the reliability of the narrator. As in *Colonel Jack* a frame is interposed between the editor and the text implying that even Defoe does not really know the intentions of the "author." This tactic brings about a state of affairs in which even if Defoe were the most trustworthy of people, which he is not, the reader still would be placed in a situation of never knowing whether or not the work is a fiction. Ambivalence, in this sense, becomes a given in one's experience of the novel if the frame of doubt is accepted.

Things get further complicated, as they have a way of doing with the novel, when Defoe reveals that the text, which in *Colonel Jack* was the only thing that could be sworn to be true, is not the actual text of Moll's written story but rather a tampered-with transcription of her words, which were too coarse to be presented to the more refined reader.

It is true that the original of this story is put into new words, and the style of the famous lady we here speak of, is a little altered, particularly she is made to tell her own tale in modester words than she told it at first; the copy which came first to hand, having been written in language more like one still in Newgate, than one grown penitent and humble, as she afterwards pretends to be.[17]

Defoe goes somewhat farther here than in *Colonel Jack* in suggesting that Moll Flanders is not trustworthy as an informant or a narrator. How can Moll, who now speaks like "one still in Newgate," be "penitent and humble?" Defoe casts more aspersions when he adds, at the end of the sentence "as she afterwards pretends to be." He uses the word "pretends" in a double sense. Both the *Oxford English Dictionary* and Dr. Johnson's *Dictionary* allow the modern use of "pretend"—"to simulate"—to have been in use during the eighteenth century alongside the earlier meaning "to propose." Is Moll Flanders simulating penitence or is she actually penitent? Defoe seems to have neatly straddled the line but entertains the possibility that Moll might be gulling the editor along with the reader.

Here Defoe also assigns a more active and deceptive role to the editor. Rather than being simply a "relator," Defoe claims to have changed the text by creating gaps in the continuity of the "original" text. The crudeness of Moll's language indicates the limits of verisimilitude, which must not portray the world as it is but as it should be. Defoe is specific on this point: "In a word, as the whole relation is carefully garbled [cleansed] of all the levity and looseness that was in it; so it is applied, and with the utmost care to virtuous and religious uses." But Defoe has done more than simply bowdlerize the language and omit risqué incidents; he tells us that he has left out two entire parts which are "too long to be brought into the same volume."[18] Of course, Defoe may simply be leaving open the possibility of a sequel to *Moll Flanders*. But, the effect of these excisions is that Defoe has taken on the role not only of disowner but, in this sense, of mutilator.

Defoe continues to avoid the issue of whether his work is fact or fiction in his next novel, *Roxana* (1724), which makes the claim that the "foundation of this [work] is laid in truth of fact; and so the work is not a story, but a history."[19] Although openly claiming to be factual, saying that his work differs from other "performances of this kind" by being based on a "foundation" that is true, he does not actually state that the story itself is true. In this case, what can "foundation" mean? Can we say that the editor has loosely construed the story or that the character of Roxana is based on the life of another?

One thing worth noticing in this statement is that Defoe distinguishes between his work and most other narratives; his work, he says, is based on fact. This assertion may well be simply one in a series of assertions of veracity that we have seen in other novelists. However, I would argue that Defoe is trying to demonstrate that his works are different from the works of Manley, Haywood, and others precisely because he does stay much closer to journalism—that his characters are almost always based on some kind of actuality and that his lies are varieties of truth.

In *Roxana*, as in *Moll Flanders*, Defoe poses as the "relator" of Roxana's story whose "words he speaks."[20] One notices here that Defoe is no longer editor, he is much closer to story-teller. He can now allow that his work is a meta-text, a retelling, based only on fact, but itself not fact, not the original text as Defoe had first claimed in *Robinson Crusoe* and *Colonel Jack*. Yet, Defoe still has not severed the cord between reporting and fictionalizing, so he claims that while he is only "relator," nevertheless he knew Roxana's first husband, thereby asserting the power of eyewitness. However, we have to wonder if Defoe is not playing a joke on himself or the reader since Roxana's husband is consistently described throughout the novel as a fool. Is Defoe deliberately damaging his own testimony by keeping bad company? Further, Roxana's husband disappears from the novel after the first several pages, and so to know such a man would only give the relator the most limited knowledge of the events of Roxana's life. Yet Defoe writes that he hopes his intimacy with the husband may "be a pledge for the credit of the rest [of the work], though the latter part of her history lay abroad, and could not so well be vouched as the first."[21] One might think twice before redeeming such a pledge, especially considering the vacuity of the husband and the unreliability of the wife.

What kind of a voyage has Defoe taken through the straits of fiction-writing? He started out asserting flatly that his work was true, that his text was original, and that the reader should accept all this. Then he allowed that though the text was true, it might be interpreted allegorically where it was inconsistent with reality or even where it was not. From this stance, he began to introduce the idea that though the text before us was either a true account or a moral romance, it was still definitely written by the protagonist and Defoe, as editor, was only transmitting the text to the reader. From this stance, we move to the idea that the text of the protagonist is unprintable as it is, for a variety of reasons, and that Defoe's version is a rewriting of some original but absent text. Finally, we see that Defoe now says only that his text is a retelling, based on fact, but perhaps dubious fact at that. In the course of this journey, we have passed from text as document to text as meta-text. One senses that Defoe has, unwillingly and always under fire, moved from a pure assertion of veracity to a highly contextualized and qualified one. In this movement, he has responded to a cultural demand for a more explicit definition of a work's factuality or fictionality. Yet Defoe has kept to the salient features of the news/novels discourse throughout: the report, the reduction in cognitive distance, a relatively median past tense, embodiment, and so on.

Defoe's complex attitude toward fact and fiction was not something restricted to the writing of novels, and many of Defoe's political writings—even his political actions—are perfect examples of framing, fictionalizing, and fabricating. I am not implying a simple causality between Defoe's life and his works.[22] But I think that a consideration of Defoe's milieu and actions will give a better sense of the extent to which Defoe was the eminently correct person, in a sense, to fall into writing works like *Robinson Crusoe* and *Moll Flanders*. Defoe's first major production of a framed document was *The Shortest Way With Dissenters*, written in 1702. The pamphlet was a reaction to a bill pending in Parliament that attempted to abolish the possibility of "occasional conformity," a practice which had permitted Dissenters to hold political office without completely giving up their religion. Defoe, himself a Dissenter, opposed the bill, but rather than attacking the bill outrightly, he decided on a typically Defoean fabrication. He would state the case for his opponents, the High Tories and High Church supporters, with such virulence that moderates would be disgusted by those who supported the bill and vote to continue occasional conformity. Much in the way Swift later used *A Modest Proposal*, Defoe advocated that Dissenters ought to be banished and their preachers hanged. The book had its effect. When it was published, it was hailed by the more extreme Tories, while Dissenters were frightened.[23] Yet, when it was discovered that the work was a hoax, neither side was pleased. The Tories realized that they had been parodied, and the Dissenters felt that the harangue had too much of the provocative about it to be treated lightly.

The Shortest Way With Dissenters is a characteristically news/ novels production. The pamphlet is inherently double and relexive; it denies its own authenticity; it creates frames around itself; and it creates ambivalent perceptions. Its position as a reflexive work is what remained, even after the fact was revealed that the book did not really reflect Defoe's own feelings. There is a sense about the work that denial is affirmation, and that the subversiveness of such a work goes beyond all attempts to remove ambiguity from it. In fact, Defoe was arrested, pilloried, and jailed for this pamphlet—an intersection of the legal and the literary which should serve to remind us of the seriousness and the care with which writers had to behave in the arena of print.*

Defoe was released from jail by striking a politic bargain with Robert Harley to write *A Weekly Review of the Affairs of France*,

---

* Defoe was not content to learn from this lesson and in 1713 wrote two new pamphlets, *Reasons Against the Succession of the House of Hanover* and *What if the Pretender Should Come*, which advocated in an exaggerated form the political viewpoint opposite to his own. He was again jailed for his writings.

Purged From the Errors and Partiality of the Affairs of Newswriters and Petty Statesmen of All Sides. The *Review* was Defoe's first serial publication of importance, and it is here that we can mark him as a journalist proper. What is significant is that Defoe was now in the employ of the Tories, whereas before he had written exclusively for the Whigs. In the secret employ of Harley, Defoe now wrote what Harley wished. In fact, Defoe's career was one in which his political ideology seemed to change with the winds of power and opportunity, and his writings always had the nature of a disguise, a fiction contrived for whoever would pay. There is even reason to believe that while Defoe was writing his Tory *Review*, he also wrote some issues of the opposition paper—the Whig *Observator*, the arch rival of his own paper—when he was asked to do so by the editor John Tutchin who had fallen ill.[24] To say the least, Defoe's politics were labile.

If Defoe could shift with such ease and write for a rival paper, or for a rival political cause, then writing must have been quite a different act for him than it was for others. Writing must have carried a quality of deception and inauthenticity; political allegiance must have been seen as essentially of linguistic, artificial manufacture; and the whole enterprise must certainly have been infused with disguise, trickery, framing, and fabrication. Defoe's knee-jerk reaction to politics was always a resort to the tactic of fictionalizing. For example, when Defoe wrote Harley a letter in 1704 suggesting ways of routing the High Church party, Defoe had instinctive recourse to duplicity. His idea was to propose, rather than oppose, the bill against occasional conformity. It may be recalled that Defoe's opposition to the same bill's passage two years earlier led to his writing *The Shortest Way With Dissenters*. Now Defoe felt that the time was ripe to propose the generally unpopular bill by having it put forth by "trusty hands" in the Whig party, an action which would "blacken and expose" the Whigs, "blast" the bill once and for all, and cause fewer Whigs to be reelected in the next session.[25] Here Defoe is even willing to risk the passage of the bill in exchange for attacking the Whigs, and his method is again one of indirection, disguise, and plotting.

Defoe's own body was a locus of fabrication. He used disguises in his role as secret agent for Harley and Godolphin. He also assumed linguistic disguises, as it were, calling himself on different occasions Alexander Goldsmith or Claude Guilot as he would use false names for his novelistic characters.[26] From 1704 to 1717, Defoe's job was to provide information on the friends and foes of the government by traveling incognito throughout England and Scotland. To his discredit, Defoe himself proposed a scheme for the establishment of a permanent information gathering system— a sort of FBI—to check on the morals and politics of the clergy, justices of the peace, and leading landowners. This tendency to the covert and the deceptive is the underside of Defoe's operations— literary and otherwise. His continued desire and pleasure in this reflexive mode is clear in a letter written to Harley in 1709.

> . . . I act the part of Cardinal Richelieu. I have my spies and pen-sioners in every place, and I confess 'tis the easiest thing in the world to hire people here to betray their friends.
>
> I have spies in the commission, in the parliament, and in the assembly, and under pretence of writing my history, I have every-thing told me.[27]

Defoe possessed the ability for massive denial of accusations and culpability, and it is difficult to tell to what extent he was convinced by his own rhetoric. When Defoe was accused of writing for the Tories and being in their pay, he wrote with characteristic indignation in the *Review*:

> . . . all the world will bear me witness it [the *Review*] is not a Tory paper. The rage with which I am daily treated by that part will testify for me. Nay the Tories will honestly own that they disown it. Yet, because I cannot run the length some of the others would have me, new scandals fill their mouths, and now they report I am gone over to the ministry.[28]

Defoe is performing here with the kind of irate virtuosity that he uses in his prefaces to *Robinson Crusoe*. In both cases, genuine ac-cusations are denied in tones of outrage. One almost has the sense that Defoe believes himself. But, of course, the previous disclaimer is written for the eyes of the public. However, even in private correspondence, Defoe seems to be just as deceiving if not self-deceiving. He appears to be trapped by his own fabrications. To Harley, who more than any other man certainly knew the kinds of intrigue with which Defoe had been involved, Defoe writes the most barefaced of denials:

> God and your Lordship are witnesses for me against this generation in that your goodness to me was founded on no principles of bribery and corruption but a generous compassion to a man oppressed by power without a crime and abandoned even then by those he sacrificed himself to serve. . . .
>
> Your Lordship has always acted with me on such foundations of meer abstracted bounty and goodness, that it has not so much as suggested the least expectation on your part that I should act this way or that, leaving me at full liberty to pursue my own reason and principle; and above all enabling me to declare my innocence in the black charge of bribery. . . .
>
> . . . This, my Lord, gives me room to declare, as I do in print everyday, that I am neither employed, dictated to, or rewarded, in what I write by any person under heaven. . . .[29]

Everything Defoe says in this letter, based on what is known of his life, is completely false. He had accepted money from Harley and had written at Harley's behest. So, in private correspondence to a man who certainly knew the extent of Defoe's complicity, why did Defoe reassure Harley about what both men knew to be patently false? One possible answer is that Defoe might have been engaging in an eighteenth-century equivalent of Richard Nixon's taped conversation with John Dean in which he recorded his "innocence" for posterity. Though we may credit Defoe with somewhat less foresight, it seems more likely that he had been able to rationalize his actions so thoroughly that he actually convinced himself that his motives in this affair were innocent. His job of fabrication may have succeeded in convincing his most dubious reader—himself. If this was so, then Defoe can be said to have performed the supreme act of novelistic fabrication by enclosing himself in a framed situation without consciously knowing it. Only Borges or Calvino could sufficiently do justice to the ramifications of such an act.

Perhaps more directly related to the news/novels discourse is Defoe's connection with the press. As we have seen, his authorship of the *Review* is certainly steeped in duplicity. When he writes, his works seem to express so inherent a quality of ambivalence—especially because Defoe's own motives seem to be so unclear—that there is a problem not only in trying to decipher his politics but also in accounting for the moral stance of his novels. So when Defoe finally comes to write novels at the end of his life, he has had a considerable prehistory of controlling language and narrative in a way that deliberately confuses fact and fiction, relying on inauthenticity and duplicity.[30]

For example, Defoe was so entangled in secret control of the press that it is difficult to know the true extent of his involvement in various newspapers. He was accused of writing the *Mercator*, a paper which supported Queen Anne's policy of free trade for France, after the demise of the *Review*. Defoe publicly denied that he had control of the paper:

> What part I had in the *Mercator* is well known: and would men answer with argument and not with personal abuses, I would, at any time defend every part of the *Mercator* which was of my doing. But to say that the *Mercator* was mine is false! I neither was the author of it, had the property of it, the printing of it, or the profit by it. I have never had any payment or reward for writing any part of it; nor had I the power to put what I would into it.[31]

Yet a letter to Harley reveals that Defoe did have charge of the *Mercator* for at least two months,[32] and the record of the Secret Service funds for the first seven months of 1714 indicates that Defoe was paid £500 for what appears to be his services in publishing the *Mercator*.[33]

Defoe's fiction-making became more profound as his involvement with the press continued. Although he was working for Harley, a moderate Tory, Defoe insinuated himself into the position of writer for a Whig paper called the *Flying Post*. His aim was to defuse the political content of the paper by taking off "the virulence and rage of the *Flying Post*."[34] In this sense, he was writing in the voice of a Whig for a Whig newspaper while he was a paid Tory publicist. His opinions in the newspaper were supposed to be Whig ones, but muted or shaded in the direction of Tory positions. As duplicituous as this position was, Defoe was to go himself one better and turn counterspy. When he was sent to jail for a libel which appeared in the *Flying Post*, he was approached by the Whig Lord Townshend who offered him a secret pardon if he would continue in his position as a Tory spy who was writing for a Whig newspaper. Only now would Defoe really write from the Whig point of view. It almost seems that word had gotten out in government circles that if you wanted Defoe to write for you, all that had to be done was to throw him in jail for a week and then strike a bargain. In any case, Defoe agreed to "appear as if I were as before under the displeasure of the government and separated from the Whigs; and that I might be more serviceable in a kind of disguise than if I appeared openly."[35] The frames that are involved here are almost mind-boggling. Defoe, originally a Whig writer, was persuaded to write from the Tory point of view for Harley by insinuating himself into the control of a Whig paper. However, Defoe then secretly agreed to push the original Whig position while pretending to write as a Tory infiltrator. One has only to consider the possibilities for deception inherent in such an arrangement, as well as the complexity of the various contextualizations of any statement written by Defoe, to appreciate the depths of Defoe's commitment to the framed document, not to mention the framed existence.

As if this were not enough, Defoe also agreed to infiltrate *Dormer's Newsletter*, which was a Tory opposition paper, and to cause "the sting of that mischievous paper to be entirely taken out, though it was granted that the style should continue Tory, as it was, that the party might be amused and not set up another, which would have destroyed the design. . . ."[36] One has only to imagine the subtlety of style required to produce the Whig *Flying Post* that would allow the Tories to think they had infiltrated it while at the same time expressing the Whig hard-line point of view. And Defoe did all this while writing *Dormer's Newsletter* in such a way that the Tories would believe he was writing from their viewpoint while in reality he was infusing Whig ideology.

I have paused here to analyze the masterful architecture of Defoe's ideological hall of mirrors, but I have only given the barest glimmerings of the true extent of Defoe's use of this type of framing. Defoe had under his influence *Mist's Weekly Journal, Dormer's Newsletter,* and *Mercurius Politicus*—all of which were billed as Tory newspapers, and all of which were controlled by the Whigs through Defoe's manipulation—I am not including in this list the *Flying Post*.[37] When one considers the total number of newspapers appearing in London at this time, Defoe seems to have controlled the total flow of political information to no small extent. This fact is all the more interesting in analyzing the relevance of this deception to the fact/fiction problem. As a journalist, Defoe was perhaps closer to the fictional than he was as a novelist. It would seem that for Defoe, fact was just another form of fiction, and fiction was just a particular category of fact. Disguises were part of Defoe's commitment to news, and news was merely a tactic to arrive at whatever was most practically expedient. In this sense, Defoe adheres to the basis of the news/novels discourse. Indeed, he must be one of the heroes of that discourse since his entire life seems to be predicted on the notion that what appears in print is neither true nor false—only ideological.

In *Serious Reflections of Robinson Crusoe,* Defoe speaks out in no uncertain terms against lying in an essay entitled "On Talking Falsely." He says that "there is a spreading evil in telling a false story as true, namely that you put it into the mouths of others, and it continues a brooding forgery to the end of time. . . ."[38] Given this strong statement, how ironic to have Defoe continue making his own brooding forgeries. This contradiction in Defoe is at root the contradiction of the novel. The doubleness of the discourse remains intact not only in a literary sense, but in a personal one for Defoe. Defoe has woven such a web of uncertainty into his works that readers and critics can only respond with multilayered ambivalence. Given Defoe's life, it comes as no surprise that he should have become a novelist since his devotion to fictionalizing fact seems to have indicated that he had been a novelist all along anyway.

CHAPTER X

Samuel Richardson:
Disavowal and Spontaneity

THE NOVELS OF Samuel Richardson seem to be so wholly different from those of Defoe as to place them squarely outside the news/novels discourse. They are hardly pseudobiographical or journalistic; their focus on romance themes, the world of virtuous ladies, the ruminations of individual characters—all seem to place the works beyond the world of criminals, pickpockets, pirates, and castaways that informs Defoe's creations. As we have seen, Defoe has seemed more or less obviously related to the news/novels discourse. In fact, he seems like a set-up for the argument of this study. Richardson's obsessive dwelling on the details—psychological and otherwise—of the moment, the endless digesting of relatively few plot events seems qualitively quite different from the episodic plots of Defoe. However, I would argue here that Richardson, in his own neurasthenic way, was very much part of the news/novels discourse, and that much of his writing too emerged from the rupture between factual and fictional narratives. Indeed, Richardson's life was so implicated in the technology of typography—in the taint of ink, press, and production—that it is not surprising that his work should carry the imprint of his trade. In this sense, his novels lean anaclitically on the collection and repro-

This chapter, in a different form, was presented at the English Institute, Harvard University, in September 1978 and published in Edward W. Said, ed., *Literature and Society* (Baltimore: Johns Hopkins University Press, 1980), under the title "A Social History of Fact and Fiction: The Beginnings of the English Novel."

duction of a series of handwritten letters. His job as printer is merely recast as that of novelist bringing into print "found" documents.

In this respect, as we will see, Richardson lines up with those other authors who not only wrote novels but were also associated with journalism; Eliza Haywood was a journalist; Defoe and Fielding wrote and edited newspapers; Aphra Behn was also the writer of political pieces, as was Mary Manley; Bunyan was a pamphleteer; Swift not only wrote journalistic pieces and political pamphlets but also was deeply involved in politics. Like these writers, Richardson had his links with the news/novels discourse, but his access was on the production side. He printed newspapers, pamphlets, and other pieces, although he was not predominantly a printer of newspapers.

Richardson was connected with the news/novels discourse, however, in a more formal and structural way. He shows this connection, in the first place, by denying his authorship of *Pamela*. He claims to be the editor of an essentially factual and true work. However, Richardson wrote privately to a friend that he wanted his books "to be thought genuine; only so far kept up, I mean, as that they should not prefatically [*sic*] be owned not to be genuine." Richardson added that he did this because he wanted to "avoid hurting that kind of historical faith which fiction is generally read with, though we know it to be fiction."[1] The wording of the letter is somewhat paradoxical in saying that Richardson wanted the novel to be *thought* genuine but really not to be considered genuine. That is, he wanted the novel to be seen as partially or provisionally true only to the extent that it could not be charged with being outrightly false. Here, he describes a credence in this type of fiction that is permitted to be *provisionally* factual. Richardson's intent is similar to Defoe's in desiring to create a work that was a new category of provisionally true narrative (although it is true that Defoe was hounded to that stance by his critics and did not begin with this intent). Richardson, according to his now well-known letter to Stinstra, suggested that the foundation for *Pamela* was true in some very limited sense of that word; he claimed to have overheard in a tavern the story of a poor girl made rich and noble through marriage and then years later to have written *Pamela* with this story in mind. Richardson's claims to authorial disavowal and veracity are also similar to Defoe's in his introduction to *Roxana*. But here again we must ask the question: if the foundation for the story is true, in what sense can one say that the story itself is true? Richardson's claim would be rather like Flaubert's saying that *Madame Bovary* was based on a story he once heard about a woman who committed adultery.

Authorial disavowal and the linked assertion that the work in question is true are two distinct signifiers of the news/novels discourse. However, one striking fact is that almost one hundred years have passed between Aphra Behn's affirmation of veracity and that of Richardson. Why have novelists continued to deny what must have been a more and more obvious connection between authors and their works? If, as has been traditionally asserted, authorial disavowal was merely a convention to steer around the Puritan sanction against nondidactic, imaginative tales and stories—why should it have remained operative for one hundred years of novel writing? Puritans must have been pretty slow to catch on to this trick if this simple convention lasted so long. Or, if one can dismiss the technique as conventional humility on the part of an author who did not want openly to besmirch his reputation by writing novels, could such a by now hackneyed device have had any effect at all? Another way of putting the question is, could a convention survive one hundred years and still be useful?

As is perhaps obvious, such attempts to account for authorial disavowal seem insufficient or incomplete. If authors were trying to avoid the Puritan sanction against writing fictions, it is difficult to see what the benefits of lying about the factuality of a work would have been. Essentially religious men, like Defoe and Richardson, would by lying only compound their sins—hardly fooling anyone, least of all God. Defoe himself specifically condemns lying of all sorts in *Serious Reflections . . . of Robinson Crusoe*, pointedly chastising authors who make up stories but "vouch their story with more assurance than others, and vouch also that they knew the persons who were concerned in it."[2] If, on the other hand, authors were being conventionally humble, it is hard to believe that so many could have been so humble. Defoe, for example, not known for his humility in other respects, seems unlikely to have gone in for this kind of self-effacement. Or Richardson, so full of pride and pomposity, cannot be imagined to have shielded himself under the aegis of editorship merely to prevent the applause which he seemed to have courted so strenuously anyway.

Another possible way of accounting for authorial disavowal has been to see the device as a means of making novels appear more realistic. According to this view, writers more or less deliberately increase the "distance," to use Wayne Booth's term, between themselves and their novels by implying that the narrative has a legitimate autonomy of its own, the author being merely the editor of a manuscript *trouvé*.[3] This technique is then seen as simply another device in the early novelist's repertoire to achieve what Ian Watt has called "formal realism."[4] So writers who want to achieve this formal realism need only maintain their work to be true, talk in great detail about the variety of objects that are part of daily life, and introduce low-life characters into their work. Although this last attempt to explain authorial disavowal is perhaps the most persuasive by virtue of its justification on the grounds of formal realism, it is also an explanation which is incomplete insofar as it attempts to explain only the stylistic effect of disavowal—not the origin, significance, or even necessity of such a device. The more pressing concern is why a writer should have cared to make his narrative more realistic in the first place? Even the use of the word "realistic" or "realism" begs the question by implying that there was available to particular writers during the seventeenth century the concept of realism which they might freely choose to adopt. In fact, according to the *Oxford English Dictionary*, the word "realism" itself was not used in English until the mid-nineteenth century, and there was no parallel word to describe the concept before that time, it would appear. Fielding's use of the term "comic epic-poem in prose" hardly seems a handy substitute.[5] It is possible that a concept of factual verisimilitudinous narrative could have existed without the specific nomenclature. However, as we have seen, there seems to have been much confusion abut the nature of that narrative discourse we have come to call realistic. The important issue for English culture at that time seems not to have been how to be more realistic, or even how to achieve formal realism, but whether it was possible to write fictions at all without maintaining that they were factual.

One further point: since the use of authorial disavowal was so widespread in the beginning of the eighteenth century, it should be clear that its effect on the reading public surely would have become hackneyed and overused. If the aim of distancing an author from his work is to create heightened realism, the technique could only have worked if most readers had a dulled if not retarded sense of observation after seeing the same device for so many years. More likely, it seems that readers would have attained a kind of perceptual fatigue over some four or five generations and could no longer be expected to believe that narratives beginning with authorial disa-vowal were automatically more realistic. Indeed, as Harry Levin has noted, realistic "fiction approximates truth, not by concealing art but by exposing artifice."[6] That is, realism is based not on the extended and continued use of a particular convention, but in the continual rejection of earlier accepted conventions.

Therefore, as I have been suggesting, in order to understand the phenomenon of authorial disavowal, we need to go beyond the idea that its use is only conventional. In effect, we need to look at the convention of authorial disavowal as something more than a neutral tic or habit of novelists, and to consider this phenomenon as a significant and historically particular sign of a transformation in the discourse of narrative. Further, if authorial disavowal were an empty convention, why did its use by Defoe and now by Ri-chardson provoke such a strong attack as Gildon's against an issue that had been taken for granted for at least seventy years? The liveliness of the debate about the nature of true and false narratives, of the correct definition of various types of narrative, arouses the thought that a rather new type of consideration was being focused on the nature of narrative and, as I would suggest, this consideration was a consequence of, an perhaps a cause of, the breakdown of the news/novels matrix.

An attack on Samuel Richardson by an anonymous author of a pamphlet entitled *Pamela Censured* reveals much about the extent to which the debate over fact and fiction was still ongoing, detailed, and serious. The attack begins by saying that although Richardson offers us letters as "originals" and says that these constitute a "narrative which has its foundation in truth," in reality anyone can reduce Richardson's formulation to its "modestest construction" in common sense and say that "*Pamela* is a romance formed in the manner of a literary correspondence founded on a tale which the author had heard, and modeled into its present shape . . . and however true the foundation may have been, yet a few removes and transitions make it deviate into a downright falsehood."[7] What the critic of *Pamela* here engages in amounts to no less than a thoroughgoing analysis of the types, degrees, and categories of veracity that are embodied in the work. He considers that *Pamela* is founded on a tale, modeled into a shape, and thereby removed from the truth. Still, the critic refuses to say outrightly that *Pamela* is entirely a fiction. His analysis seems to reflect an awareness that narratives can be both true and false in the special senses of those words, but his attitude also reflects a profound ambivalence about these categories.

The readers of *Pamela* and *Robinson Crusoe* must have been in a state of considerable ambivalence too, when they picked up their novels, as to whether or not the works they were reading were true. Many did consider *Pamela* to be a true story, and one went so far as to write to the putative editor demanding, "Let us have *Pamela* as Pamela wrote it."[8] Gullibility aside, even the French translator of *Pamela* considered that the story was "a true one" and that Richardson, as editor, "often sacrificed the story to moral instruction."[9] There were, on the other hand, those who refused to believe that Richardson was only editor; the anonymous author of *Pamela Censured* called Richardson a "half-editor, half-author."[10] But significantly even this attack allowed Richardson the title of "half-editor," as if it were too much a violation of the news/novels discourse to say that a work of such popularity could be entirely fictional. So, for an eighteenth-century reader of Defoe or Richardson, it would be literally impossible to know with any certainty that books like *Pamela* were true or not. And as we have seen, this ambivalence and uncertainty was itself one of the hallmarks of reader response to early English novels.

This state of ambivalence was no doubt furthered by the incidents that followed the publication of *Pamela* in 1740. In the following year there appeared a *Memoir of the Life of Lady H., The Celebrated Pamela*. This book averred that Lady Hesilrige, who did actually marry into the aristocracy, was the real Pamela, and other such publications as this no doubt caused many readers to wonder about the truth or falsity of Richardson's work. In early 1741, things grew murkier yet, when two booksellers, Chandler and Kelley, published a work called *Pamela's Conduct in High Life*, a sequel to Richardson's first two volumes. Richardson responded to this literary ambush by advertising that Chandler and Kelly were writing "without any other knowledge of the story than what they are able to collect from the two volumes already printed. . . . [And that Richardson was] . . . continuing the work himself, from materials that, perhaps, but for such a notorious invasion of his plan, he should not have published."[11]

Although Richardson calls himself an "author" here for the first time, he still perpetuates the necessary state of ambivalence by implying that he was editing "materials"—presumably some actual record or further letters—to which his rivals did not have access. However, Chandler and Kelly claimed in an advertisement in the *London Daily Post* that it was their book, not Richardson's sequel, that was published directly from Pamela's "original papers," and was "regularly digested by a gentleman more conversant in high life than the vain author of *Pamela*."[12] The actual work itself is a pretty fair imitation of Richardson's novel. It claims to be based on its own "original" papers found among Mrs. Jervis' possessions by her niece Mary Brenville who succeeded her at her post. A brilliant touch on the part of Chandler and Kelly is made clear in the introductory exchange between one B. W. and Mary Brenville in which the claim is made that the profits from the publication of these letters will be used to "be a relief to the modest poor," so that Mrs. Brenville may succeed her aunt in "the post of almoner."[13] Thus Chandler and Kelly argued not only that their edition was more accurate and superior to that of Richardson, but that the profits from the sale of their edition would help the poor.

Richardson had argued himself into a corner, and his dilemma illustrates the tangible disadvantages of authorial disavowal. By denying that his work was fictional, Richardson had to maintain that *Pamela* was based on actual records and documents. But taking this tack, he had no way of preventing other authors from claiming to possess those very records. His problems were compounded by the fact that Richardson himself was not really conversant with upper-class life and therefore could not even have claimed to be the best or most suitable editor of Pamela's letters. In this sense, Chandler and Kelly could openly boast that their usurpation of Richardson's book was not theft but an actual improvement and of benefit to the poor as well. Clearly, at this time when the Copyright law of 1709 was still easily circumvented, authorial disavowal became distinctly unsuited for maintaining financial control over one's writings. To claim that a novel was purely fictional would be an advantage to writers like Richardson since they could then maintain that the uniqueness and originality of a novel came from its connection to a particular author's imagination and not from its source in actual records.

However, for Richardson, it was morally and artistically important to maintain that his works were in some major sense genuine. His objection to novels in general were that they paid so little attention to fact, to the real. To him the Behns, the Manleys, and the Haywoods were no better than a "set of wretches."[14] It was the untruthful aspect of continental romances that disgusted Richardson when he wrote, "I hate so much the French marvelous and all unnatural machinery." *Tom Jones*, too, was "a rambling collection of waking dreams in which probability was not observed," and *Shamela* received vituperation—predictably—as a misrepresentation of facts.[15] Richardson's concern here is with establishing in narrative what he considered an innovative attention to factuality. He wrote that narratives must be "very circumstantial" so as to best "maintain an air of probability" and "represent real life."[16]

Richardson, like Defoe and Fielding, claimed that he was founding a "new species of writing."[17] I think he meant his kind of narrative to be different precisely because it had a new relationship to the problem of fact and fiction. Each of these early novelists had to invent a new definition and type of writing to place him or herself in this new order of discourse. What then was Richardson's innovation? Clearly not his epistolary style itself since, as Katherine Hornbeak has shown, this form of writing was quite popular before Richardson.[18] Richardson's real innovation, it would seem, was what he called "spontaneous writing," that is, "letters [written] by parties themselves at the very time in which the events happened." His method of organizing letters so that they appear serially and maintain a continuous account of events is clearly his own invention. Not shy of stating his own merits, Richardson cites "a candid foreigner" who says that *Pamela* and *Clarissa* are written in this special way "and this method has given the author great advantage which he could not have drawn from any other species of narration."[19] This observer notes the technical advance, as it were, invented by Richardson as a mark that distinguishes spontaneous writing from "any other species of narration." The description "new" and "new species" occurs over and over again in describing what Richardson has done. He claims in another context that he had introduced "a new species of writing that might possibly turn young people to a course of reading different from the pomp and parade of romance writing, and dismissing the improbable and marvelous, with which novels generally abound. . . ."[20] Reverend Skelton calls *Clarissa* "a rather new species of novel."[21] Even the characters within Richardson's work are aware of spontaneous writing. As Lovelace tells his correspondent, "though this was written afterwards yet (as in other places) I write this as it was spoken and happened, as *if* I had retired to put down every sentence as spoken. I know thou likest this *lively present tense* manner, as it is one of my peculiars."[22] Or, as Harriet writes in *Sir Charles Grandison*:

> What a great deal of writing does the reciting of half an hour or an hour's conversation make when there are three or four speakers in company, and one attempts to write what each says in the *first* person! I am amazed at the quantity, on looking back. But it *will* be so in narrative letter-writing.[23]

Richardson's self-consciousness, and the self-consciousness of his own characters within the text, points to the genuine sense of a break with earlier kinds of writing.

What was significant and unique in this new method of spontaneous writing was the ability to recapture recent time past and to forcibly decrease the interval between event and transcription. Lovelace called this technique a "lively present tense manner." One of its effects, of course, seems to have been the decreasing of the cognitive space between language and reality, as well as between reader and text. Spontaneous writing permits Richardson to fashion language and narrative so as to cleave closer to the real in terms of both time and space—time, in the sense that when Pamela writes, she writes close to the moment of doing; and space, in the sense that the reader is presented with the letters themselves. Lovelace, perhaps more than any other character, comes closest to this ideal since he writes not only spontaneously but in shorthand as well, so that he can attempt to approach asymptotically the immediacy of the originating moment. Because Richardson assembles these units of immediacy into a series of letters rather than a retrospective narrative, he is better able to give a continuous and coterminous account of reality by virtue of the serial format letters afford.

In effect, what Richardson seems to have done in a surprising way is to isolate in his "lively present tense manner" the essence of the news/novels discourse—the median past tense, which was made possible in the first place by the regular, serial printing of news. In both Richardson's novels and journalistic discourse, se- riality, recentness, immediacy, decreasing of cognitive space, and even dissemination of information are paramount. Just as journal- ism had permitted language to become in some sense an embodi- ment of and a memorial to those public events it recorded, so too spontaneous writing allowed Pamela, for example, to leave behind the only valid record of the events that transpired between herself and Mr. B.

While I am not saying that Pamela is a journalist—though she does keep a journal—it is significant that she is in some sense much sought after precisely because she does regularly and obsessively transcribe reality, although this is clearly not her only charm. Mr. B becomes quite early on the regular and even obsessive reader of her letters. He frequently expresses his readerly devotion with such comments as "I long to see the particulars of your plot . . . and . . . [am] desirous of reading all you write." He also respects the attention to factuality in her narratives reflected in her "great regard to truth," and even says that she writes a "very moving tale."[24] Moreover, Lady Davers, who has heard about Pamela's journal- izing, wants to read her writings—precisely because she looks to Pamela's work as the only authentic record of what actually hap- pened: ". . . I understand child, says she, that you keep a journal of all matters that pass . . . I should delight to read all of his [Mr. B's] strategems, attempts, contrivances, menaces, and offers to you. . . ."[25] So Lady Davers becomes part of Pamela's reading public, joining Mr. B and, of course, Pamela's parents, who value their daughter for her writings too, which they read as if these communications were actually the monthly parts of a serialized novel. To Goodman Andrews and his wife, Pamela's accounts of her travails were "the delight of our spare hours" and, like many novel readers, they could not wait to finish the story and "so turned to the end; where we find . . . her virtue within view of its reward. . . ."[26]

So effective, in fact, is Richardson's attempt to have language cleave to reality that frequently Pamela is all but subsumed or replaced by her language. Thus, ultimately Pamela's complex taming of Mr. B and his would-be seduction of her are worked out initially through his penetrating her epistolary integument by reading her private correspondence. He is "overcome" by her "charming manner of writing."[27] The scene in which Mr. B attempts to rape Pamela is virtually paralleled by his attempt to undress her forcibly in order to secure the letters that are hidden under her petticoats. Mr. B warns: "Now . . . it is my opinion that they [the letters] are about you, and I never undressed a girl in my life; but I will now begin to strip my pretty Pamela; and I hope I shall not go far before I find them." As he stoops to see if they are "about your knees with your garters," Pamela yields up her secret manuscript in despair.[28] The metonymy of this scene of private letters in proximity to private parts is not to be overlooked, and the attempted forcible removal of Pamela's deepest secrets from under her petticoats sets up an equation between her physical and spiritual being and the handwritten account of that being, which for the moment, is as important for Mr. B to possess as it is for him to have her maidenhead. In this symbolic sense, Pamela-the-heroine becomes replaced by Pamela-the-linguistic simulacrum. This situation is repeated in *Clarissa*. Lovelace combines the theft of a letter, taken forcibly again from under Clarissa's skirts, with the "most fervent kiss that I ever had dared to give her before."[29] Richardson seems to have unconsciously linked the state of his female character's sexual integrity to the state of the privacy of their discourse.

This state of affairs is emphasized throughout *Pamela* by the particularly textual nature of the heroine's existence. To the reader, Pamela is manifestly constituted through the omnipresent machinery of spontaneous writing—letters, journals, texts. This machinery stands perpetually between the reader and the writing heroine and has the effect of rendering Pamela's incarnation profoundly typographical—certainly more typographical than any written narrative before the work of Richardson. Even Mrs. Jewkes bears witness against Pamela's constant textualization of experience when she says to Pamela in understandable despair that certain matters "would better bear *talking* of, than *writing* about."[30]

Richardson's textualization of experience requires that language replace, in a sense, reality. It is not simply that language becomes verisimilar, as we have seen was true of earlier novels, but that the narrative itself becomes an object in reality. The letters, the journals, the documents are the baseline of the novel. The feel and shape of the text becomes itself the object of scrutiny. This characteristic becomes most obvious in the notion that a character's writing style, his or her orthography (unavailable to novel readers), the turn of phrase, and so on become the marks or signs that reveal personality, inclination, and intent. The letter is not merely the graphical trace of the protagonist's personality; it is the only tangible and directly available information that the reader may scrutinize. It is perhaps fitting that Pamela's only love poem is written not to a person but to a letter.[31] For Richardson, then, it is the letter, language, that has taken on a primacy, and through the technique of spontaneous writing, language has become both action and document, both signified and signifier, both present moment and past event.

Clarissa shares this quality of typographical existence. She literally becomes the sum and total of the written account that she herself actively pushed into publication. Clarissa's last act, the writing of her will, "published in compliance with the lady's order on her deathbed," as a proposed original subtitle to the novel stated, suggests the final replacement of her being by her language and her will incarnate in language.[32] Clarissa says that she is "solicitous to have all those letters and materials preserved which will set my whole story in a true light." She continues, "The warning that may be given from those papers to all such young creatures as may have known or heard of me, may be of more efficacy to the end wished for, as I humbly presume to think, than my appearance could have been in a court of justice. . . ."[33] Clarissa's existence is more efficacious, as she says, in language than in personal appearance. Her purpose is journalistic, according to Richardson, to issue a "warning to unguarded, vain, or credulous innocence."[34] With this aim in mind, Clarissa selects Belford to be the "protector of her memory" and asks Reverend Lewen to preserve and publish "all letters and materials" as well as her Last Will and Testament.[35] It is Clarissa's written/printed story which is paramount, displacing Clarissa and her temporal existence. As she writes of herself, "One day, sir, you will perhaps know all my story."[36] Even Anna Howe, seeing Clarissa's mortal remains, responds not as if she were viewing a corpse, but as if she had seen the concluding punctuation mark at the end of a novel when she says, "And is this all! is it all of my Clarissa's story!"[37] Clarissa's conscious attempt to put her writing in the hands of the public, to replace herself by her language, goes Pamela one better in the attempt to journalize experience.

One of the keys to Richardson's work in this respect is the idea of making the private public. What could be more personal than the intimate letters of a woman written in the privacy of her most protected room—that locus of privacy in eighteenth-century architecture—the closet? And then what could be more visible than these letters and materials brought through print before the eyes of the public? Clarissa starts out reluctant to be published and writes that she is "concerned to find I am become so much public talk," but she winds up deliberately consigning her complete correspondence to the printers.[38] That movement outward is certainly a movement toward the journalistic discourse, toward the notion of the publication of experience.[39]

That movement also leads toward a kind of eroticization of the text. Richardson's work demands that the reader continually be the voyeur, placed in much the same position as Lovelace or Mr. B in intercepting the letters of the heroines and penetrating their private discourse. The experience of reading *Pamela* or *Clarissa* is the experience of staring through the keyhole along with the libertine kidnappers. Bared bosoms, stolen kisses, and supine, helpless figures are the essence of Richardson's eroticism, and the reader of the work is placed within the text as voyeur much as were readers of the news/novels discourse. Thus, the reduction of cognitive space between reader and text, between subject and observer, carries on the pattern of the discourse as we have seen it in seventeenth-century ballads. Certainly, eighteenth-century readers were aware of this voyeuristic component in the technique of spontaneous writing since Richardson was much criticized for titillating readers, as the author of *Pamela Censured* did not fail to point out. The issue was a hot one, and the authors of *Pamela's Conduct in High Life* were faced with the task of defending themselves against the critic who wrote *Pamela Censured* by saying that

> he is unfair in his quotations and gives us such an idea of his own vicious inclination, that it would not (I fear) wrong him to think the shrieks of a woman in labour would excite his passions, and the agonies of a dying woman enflame his blood and stimulate him to commit rape.[40]

This ad hominem attack aside, the issue was more than an individual matter, and much debate centered on the scene, for example, in which Pamela faints and Mr. B observes her lying on the floor. The heated question was whether in fact she had been seen by Mr. B in an indecent posture. Chandler and Kelly argue casuistically that "as her gown was caught in, and torn by the door, she must fall too near it, in whatever posture, to show any *latent* beauties."[41] The author of *Pamela Censured* clearly thinks otherwise. Whether or not Richardson's intent was to inflame his readers with this supine revelation, the point behind this debate is that both the defenders as well as the detractors of Richardson's morality are equally positioned, along with Mr. B, squarely behind the keyhole peeping in on the scene. They may be trying to decide whether Pamela was accidentally exposed or safely covered from their own gazes, but their gazes are the constant in the equation. Voyeurism is one of the preconditions of the novel, and it is also the essence of the private world-made-public, which is to say, voyeurism is inherent in the news/novels discourse.

The private-made-public also extends in Richardson's world, beyond the pages of his novels. The method he chose for writing his works was to pass various drafts around to his correspondents and ask for criticism, revisions, and so on. While Richardson rarely listened to anything anyone had to say about his work, unless praise or flattery was involved, his method of prepublication publication is noteworthy. With Richardson, even novel-writing had gone public. As he wrote to Aaron Hill:

> Mr. Cibber has had the patience to read it [the manuscript] through, and is for taking away whole branches, some of which, however, he dislikes not: But these very branches Dr. Young would not have parted with, and Dr. Heylin says that Mr. Cibber . . . thinks I have built a house, whereas it is rather a town and a new peopled colony; and his lady, who is a woman of fine sense, begs me not to rob her of any of her acquaintance.[42]

Writing by committee is not exactly how Richardson composed his work, but his method does seem unusual and new in being so public a composition. Certainy few if any writers before Richardson had engaged in such a practice. As Richardson wrote to Sophia Westcomb, after sending her some sheets from *Sir Charles Grandison*, these "having been seen by very few, might be said to be written only to those few? When they are laid before the world, then they are written to that world. . . ."[43] This curious way of conceiving of writing and publication gives us the sense that the public/voyeuristic quality of Richardson's work mirrors the private-made-public aspect of its composition. Richardson even advocated, perhaps in jest, that because he was unwilling to write a concluding volume to *Sir Charles Grandison* "every one of my correspondents, at his or her own choice, [could] assume one of the surviving characters in the story, and write in it."[44] Richardson would then "pick and choose, alter, connect, and accommodate" until he had made up this last volume. Even the idea of such a project should point out the very public way Richardson thought of his works, so much so that readers here would become not only the characters but the authors as well. Some readers actually tried to extend the scope of spontaneous writing by immediately recording their own responses to the novel as they read the work.[45] With all these possibilities—readers becoming authors, readers becoming characters, readers beginning meta-texts of their own spontaneous reactions to the spontaneous writing of characters—cognitive distance would have decreased so profoundly as to collapse against itself. The novel had the possibility of becoming a kind of circulating news/novel-letter, a work perpetually in progress, perpetually added to, and as such would become a parodic, fictionalized, serialized form of news. As is perhaps obvious, this interactive process did not become an integral aspect of the dominant technology of the novel.

I have been suggesting that the innovativeness of spontaneous writing lies in its ability to reduce the cognitive distance between thought, reality, and language. In so doing, language itself comes to the forefront and takes the place, as it were, of the events or people that it describes. In journalism, the printed account becomes through the passage of time the archival record; in *Pamela* the character is memorialized and preserved in time by virtue of her own written account. As I have been arguing throughout, this new capacity of language should be seen as a major shift in culture—one that is indebted to the establishment of the news/novels discourse and its subsequent breakdown. Michel Foucault has detailed this transformation of linguistic capacity in *The Order of Things*. Foucault notes that language, at least formal narrative language, in the Middle Ages served mainly as a mark or sign for another level of meaning that had to be reached through some hermeneutical or allegorical process. However, the late seventeenth and eighteenth centuries, this interpretative demand of language had been dropped and replaced by the "discursivity of representation."[46] Language is no longer a sign for some other level of meaning and reality, language becomes itself capable of verisimilitude, the representing of meaning and reality. So Foucault might not find it odd that in Richardson's novel the heroine is not so much Pamela as Pamela's

language. There is no demand for interpretation in the novel—
only a meticulous care for the material aspect of language—the
fetishization of style, penmanship, the concern with the minutiae
of sending and receiving, intercepting, forging, and the logophilia
which demands that every event be obsessively incarnated into the
word.

In suggesting this "text-ualization" of experience, I am not
saying that eighteenth-century novelists were really twentieth-cen-
tury French semiologists in powdered wigs and waistcoats. And
I certainly do not mean to reduce all experience to language and
so aestheticize literary phenomena into an infinite regression of
signifiers and signifieds. Far from having such an effect, the primacy or centrality of printed language in eighteenth-century novels
shows us how fictional narrative is actually part of a powerful
discourse associated with journalism. This discourse, it is true, did
transcribe reality into language—but did so with the aim of increasing the numbers of those privy to information, of creating
political ideologies, and of embodying social consciousness in the
printed word. The nexus between news and novels is a powerful
one because it allows us to see that fictional narratives, by partic-
ipating in a journalistic discourse, are also part of an information
disseminating system that is by definition social. Raymond Williams has aptly referred to literature as social language and social
practice—and I think by seeing that novels were part of the journalistic discourse, we can add dimensions to the concept of "social
language."[47]

If we can consider eighteenth-century novelists as actually part
of a public and popular news/novels discourse, then I think it is
possible to understand better the problem of authorial disavowal
with which I began this chapter. Further, if even a writer like
Richardson who has been seen traditionally as a novelist in "recoil"
from his environment seeking in his writing "the emotional satisfaction which ordinary life denied," can be seen as actually part
of a social language and practice, then the usual notion of the novel
as being an escape from experience is open to challenge.[48] Authors

who denied their authorship and insisted on the factuality of their works were, I would argue, attempting to make a statement about the real difficulties of finding their place in the midst of a discourse that was in the active process of rupture. As the news/novels discourse grew into the specialized subdiscourses of journalism, fiction, and history, novelists still saw themselves as part of a news-synthesizing and disseminating system, but the works they were writing, while embodying the qualities of recentness, immediacy, voyeurism, memorialization, preservation, transcription, and dissemination, no longer could be seen as news.

Richardson spoke about his role as novelist as if he were actually a journalist or editorial writer when he wrote, "And it is a glorious privilege, that a middling man enjoys who has preserved his independency, and can occasionally (though not stoically) tell the world what he thinks of that world. . . ."[49] Richardson here places novels by the side of newspapers, saying in effect that novelists, instead of writing news of public events of a nation, were writing news of the ideology, as it were, of that nation. If he and other novelists refused to concede that they were writing fictions, perhaps it was because fiction was too limiting a concept for them; they were in their own sense of themselves still writing news—only, in this case, news stripped of its reference to immediate public events.

Richardson's contribution to the novel, as we have seen in this chapter, was to adopt the structural elements of the journalistic discourse while creating his own romantic and psychological content. His novels could be filled with plot elements seemingly quite divergent from the news/novels discourse while at the same time remaining formally linked to that discourse. The strength of Richardson's narratives seems to derive from that fusion—the static, sentimental threads are enlivened and socialized by the vital connection to the world of publication, reportage, dissemination, and ideology. Yet the sentimental and psychological elements interiorize and deepen the world of factual discourse. This fusion, in a sense, was able to create a kind of factual fiction quite different from anything that had come before.

CHAPTER XI

Henry Fielding:
Politics and Fact

FIELDING WAS, among other things, a journalist who also wrote political pamphlets and worked closely with the government, so it seems to follow that he was a novelist as well. Like Defoe and Richardson, he saw himself as introducing a new species of writing, breaking new ground with previous narrative forms. However, unlike any of the major novelists I have examined, he presented his works in an unframed, unambivalent form. Fielding did not claim that his stories were real or factual, and he did not pretend to edit some other writer's work. Rather, he presented himself as author, included willingly the voice of the author in his work as commentator and observer, and allowed his work to be openly fictional rather than provisionally factual. In this sense, it is with Fielding that fictional narrative of the outright variety was born. But why should Fielding have been the one to remove the sacred frame from the novel form? What developments had by this time permitted the subdivision of news/novels to pure novels? And how much news remained in a novel?

To understand some of the problems, it might be helpful to begin by seeing the intersection between news and fiction in Fielding's own career. As was the case with so many early novelists, Fielding's career was deeply implicated in the public, political world. His career as a playwright was thwarted when the political content of his plays *Pasquin* and *The Historical Register* aroused so much ire that Walpole succeeded in closing down the unlicensed

theaters en masse and censoring other plays to counter Fielding's
attacks against the government. Fielding was credited in his own
time with inventing a "new method" of playwrighting that "laid
the foundation for introducing politics on stage." The same writer
accused Fielding of having turned the stage from a "general mirror"
to a "private looking glass [that] displays objects without any regard
to truth, decency, good manner, or true judgment."[1] In effect,
Fielding stands accused of rendering theatrical discourse ideological. Further, one notes that the word "truth" here does not mean
factual but rather ideological veracity. In some sense, Fielding has
journalized theater, extending the scope of plays to include political
comment. And it is significant for our purposes that the play with
which Fielding had decided to attack Walpole was *The Historical
Register* (1736). It takes its name, appropriately enough, from an
annual journalistic publication which printed domestic and foreign
news of the past year along with notices of births, marriages, and
deaths. Fielding's use of this compilation of news of the year as a
parodic device is revealing. Fielding might have been attempting
to graft elements of the news/novels discourse onto the theatrical
form. In this attempt, one notes Fielding's interest in linking the
imaginary creation to a broader social commentary. Fielding's aim
was apparently not merely to comment on human nature and foibles
in general but, as his choice of a news annual as format indicates,
on particular events and the people who shaped those events. Walpole's response to this play, his shutting down of the theater and
licensing plays, should show us the strength of the legal grid that
restricted ideological commentary in literature. Although one is
mainly concerned with prose narrative here, it is important to note
that contemporaries saw that this action against Fielding and the
theater had similar implications for news and novels as well. As
the Earl of Chesterfield said in speaking against the Licensing Act,
"Though it seems designed only as a restraint on the licentiousness
of *the stage*, I fear, it looks farther, and tends to a restraint on the
liberty of the press. . . ."[2]

Fielding's impulse, then, like those of other writers in the

news/novels discourse, was to extend his writings toward the journalistic—making private public, reporting, taking advantage of serialized news, pushing his writing toward the ideological. Fielding's
commitment to the news/novels discourse was serious and not accidental. The fact that he went from playwriting, now no longer
possible for him, to writing a newspaper called *The Champion* and
three novels over the next six years seems more than coincidental.
His work on these newspapers and novels is all the more overdetermined when we consider that at the same time he was studying
law, tending to a dying wife, and caring for a dying child. To
illustrate this point, in 1741 Fielding was editing and writing the
Champion, he had written a political pamphlet *The Opposition*, his
novel *Shamela* was published, and *Joseph Andrews* composed, Fielding attended assizes, was crippled by a severe attack of gout, all
the while his daughter Charlotte, six years old, was dying in one
bed and his wife in another.[3] I mention these conditions not to
marvel at Fielding's productivity or fortitude, which are admirable,
but to point to the seriousness and equality with which Fielding
treated his novels and his political work. It would be quite difficult
to imagine someone writing novels only for amusement under such
circumstances. The point is that Fielding seems to have seen his
novels, his plays, his periodicals, and his politics as part of a continuum, part of a general political project, and not as the idle fluff
of his leisure hours. Whereas Defoe's novels, if one can isolate
them, seem for the most part to be devoid of overt politics, although
they retain their connection with newspapers; and while Richardson's works refrain from directly commenting on the political
world, although they too retain formal elements of the news; Fielding enters into current political issues and events in his work while
by and large abandoning the formal aspects of journalism. Fielding
has dissociated his own work from news in a formal and structural
sense, while keeping his allegiance in an ideological sense.

   Shamela and *Joseph Andrews* can hardly be called openly political
works, it is true, but they are more or less direct reactions to
contemporary events—at least to the extent that Fielding was at-

tacking Colly Cibber (who he thought was the author of *Pamela*) and Richardson in *Joseph Andrews*. In the latter work there is criticism of some aspects of contemporary morality and legal practices, although it is in *Tom Jones* that Fielding unleashes all of his anti-Jacobite sentiments. What Fielding does in *Tom Jones* that is unique in the previous history of the novel is to make the political commentary in his work an integral part of the structure of his own novel. The broad politicizing of *Tom Jones* has echoes of other such intra-literary injections of politics, as in the work of Mary Manley or Jonathan Swift but, as I will demonstrate, the scope of Fielding's conceptualization and use of public events is unique in a work which is openly pronounced to be fictional.

With Fielding we approach an interesting paradox. Here is an author who is different because he both admits his work is fictional and yet seems to be speaking about public events more openly than most earlier novelists. How can Fielding justify being at both ends of the news/novels continuum at the same time? In the preface to his *Miscellanies*, Fielding explains that his purpose in writing *Jonathan Wild* was not to present "a very faithful portrait of Jonathan Wild" as Defoe had done: ". . . my narrative is rather of such actions which he [Wild] might have performed, or would, or should have performed, than what he really did." For Fielding, Defoe was "that excellent historian, who from authentic papers and records, etc., hath already given so satisfactory an account of the life and actions of this great man."[4] Although Fielding seems to be reading Defoe rather unambivalently, the criteria for a documented history seem fairly firmly established, and Fielding himself openly declares that his aim is quite simply to make up portions of the life of Wild. There will be no frame, no false documentation, no denials, no assertions of veracity—all we have before us is pure fiction based loosely, if at all, on the life of Wild. Of course, one should recall that Fielding's aim is superscribed by the hidden aim of assigning an allegorical interpretation to a work in which Jonathan Wild stands for Sir Robert Walpole. For Fielding, the metaphor is appropriate—the head of state is seen as a great thief at the head of a bureaucracy of corruption.

This hidden agenda notwithstanding, we must mark the pre-fatory statement by Fielding as a sign that the old double discourse of news/novels has apparently come undone. Apparently, works may now be legitimately fictional. However, one notes an inherent paradox that while Fielding's works are more fictional than those of previous authors, they are also more factual. In this sense, they are less like newspapers, but also more like them; these works make no claim to being actual documents but do claim to report on public events from an ideological and political viewpoint. If we begin with this paradox, I think we can begin to get a sense of Fielding's project in writing novels. For example, Fielding takes pains to say that his type of narrative is distinctly different from what has come before:

> As it is possible the mere English reader may have a different idea of romance with the author of these volumes; and may consequently expect a kind of entertainment, not to be found, nor which was even intended, in the following pages; it may not be improper to premise a few words concerning this kind of writing, which I do not re-member to have seen hitherto attempted in our language.[5]

In *Tom Jones* Fielding calls his narrativity a "new province of writ-ing,"[6] and in *Joseph Andrews* it is "a species of writing . . . hitherto unattempted in our language."[7] I think that Fielding can be taken at his word, and one could say that he was in the midst of impro-vising the form that we now comfortably call the "novel," although as we have seen the word "novel" during the eighteenth century had no single, precise meaning. It is important to recall that Fielding uses the words "life" or "history" rather than "novel" to describe his works. He might be said to be trying to distinguish his writings from the earlier works mentioned here, by calling himself an his-torian or biographer.

Reading the author's definition of his work, one becomes con-vinced that Fielding is improvising or formulating a language—as did Richardson and Defoe—to describe what he must have intuited was a new trend in narrative, but which he was unable to define except by retooling an antiquated critical language. It is the break-down of the news/novels matrix which might be said to be causing these problems in terminology, creating a cognitive locus for a type of narrative that was strikingly new but without articulated characteristics or definitions. Thus we might say when Fielding calls himself an historian in a work that is openly fictional, he is trying to recast the concept of history and attempting to distinguish it from news and novels.

In this context Fielding's puzzling and awkward definition of his novel as a "comic epic-poem in prose" begins to make sense.[8] Why, in the first place, should he have called his work an "epic?" In classical terms, there were really only three forms of linguistic art—epic, drama, and lyric. Only the first two could even remotely apply to a work like *Tom Jones*, and epic is the only actual term even vaguely appropriate to a long, invented narrative.* Fielding's taxonomy further subdivides epic into two types—tragic and comic. For Fielding's purposes, only comic represents the actions of the lower and middle classes, who are, however, presented as good people and not merely buffoons.[9] Given Fielding's use of classical terminology to describe a form which really is outside the limits of that terminology, as the Einsteinian universe cannot be described in Newtonian terms, Fielding has used roughly the right terminology to describe a longish piece of prose fiction that depicts the life of the common or middling man or woman. His tactic becomes clearer when he writes that Fénelon's *Telemachus* appears "of the epic kind," and adds that it is "much fairer and more reasonable to give it a name common with that species from which it differs only in a single instance [meter], than to confound it with those which it resembles in no other. (Such are the voluminous works commonly called romances . . .)."[10] Here we see Fielding marking off his turf, sharply dividing himself from French romancers, dividing the novel from the entire romance tradition, but being at a loss to define his new discourse. As he says, he is in wide open space since "no critic hath thought proper to range it under any other head, nor to assign it a particular name to itself."[11] Taxonomy fails, hence the atavistic and awkward "comic epic-poem in prose."

* Length rules out such classical terms as *erōtika pathēmata* or *mythoi*.

All of this is well and good, but Fielding still has to reckon with the fact that his work is a fiction. He seems unwilling to severe himself totally from the ethic of the news/novels discourse by justifying his work for fiction's sake alone. Therefore, he must explain in some larger sense how a fiction can be true—that is to say, how a made-up story can have a bearing on our judgment and consciousness beyond mere frivolity. Fielding's solution is to say that even though the particulars of his work are invented, he has captured the essence of the truth of human nature. As he says in *Tom Jones*, true historians are not those writers of national history— these he would call "topographers or cartographers"—but rather are biographers since "truth is only to be found in the works of those who celebrate the lives of great men" (III, i). Truth is arrived at through fiction. Fielding turns the tables on historians, saying that though they are bound to adhere to the facts of the event, they often disagree on the interpretation of those events; therefore their works really are fictions, "romances" created by authors who "indulged a happy and fertile invention." The novelist, on the other hand, may get the factual details wrong, but on the whole he depicts people as they truly are; the novelist's truth depicts the type and variety of human nature "though we often mistake the age and country . . ." (III, i). This argument recalls Sidney's defense of poetry, but is given new credentials by the fact that historians such as Lord Clarendon, Echard, Rapin, and Whitlock had begun to write polemical histories supporting either Whig or Tory points of view. Thus, in Fielding's eyes, history indeed had its hermeneutical quality and its fictional bent.

Fielding spends a good deal of time telling us what he is not. He is *not* an historian, nor is he a romancer.* His work is *not* a newspaper or a chronicle destined to record everything that happens and to "fill up as much paper with the detail of months and years in which nothing remarkable happened . . ." (II, i). Novels "of plain matter of fact must overpower every reader . . . [and amount to a] newspaper of many volumes" (IV, i). Likewise, char-

* "Truth distinguishes our writings, from those idle romances" (IV, i).

acters in novels should never be "trite, common, or vulgar; such as . . . may be met with in the home articles of a newspaper" (VIII, i). In telling us what his work is not, Fielding continues to sever his work from romance as we have seen earlier novelists do. What is worth considering, though, is the explicit way Fielding takes pains to separate himself from history and journalism. In this sense, Fielding is cutting at both ends the umbilical cord that connected him to the news/novels discourse. However, as we will see, Fielding is tied to journalism in ways too profound to be severed by prefatory assertions. Yet, in other ways, Fielding has made his break with the news/novels discourse by claiming to be writing not a document, but a fiction, and in so doing disbanding the simulacrum theory of the novel. This action would permit his work to be subsumed under the new and unheard of subdivision of purely fictional prose narrative.

Yet Fielding's concern is to make sure that the subdivision, which he would call "comic epic-poem in prose," will not be considered fictional in the perjorative sense of mere falsehoods either. As Fielding points out, since the novelist is not bound by public records, as the historian must be, the novelist must conform to probability more than must an historian: "As we have no public notoriety, no concurrent testimony, no records to support and corroborate what we deliver, it becomes us to keep within the limits not only of possibility, but of probability too . . ." (VIII, i). Fielding wants to avoid "the universal contempt" heaped on those "who do not draw their materials from records." Fielding's solution is to rely on a record of sort—the "Doomsday Book of Nature" (IX, i). By saying that nature rather than document and testimony will provide his factual base, Fielding shifts the argument from one of sources to one of morality. Human nature will be revealed and analyzed through the vehicle of fiction. Yet nature is not a book that can be judged by its cover, and so Fielding's use of that record is by no means an unambiguous one. He strikes an interesting political stance when he says that since nature is his source, he is bound by the limits set by nature; in this sense, says Fielding, he cannot be a *"jure divino* tyrant" over the content of his work. He is picking up on a Jacobite buzzword, and almost seems to imply that his democratic-parliamentarian principles are woven into his concept of the novel's theoretical principles. Rather than inventing at will, Fielding accepts the moderation of nature—as opposed, perhaps, to earlier romance writers whose totalitarian control over subject matter resulted in the marvelous, the supernatural, and the implausible.

While it may be pushing the issue to suggest that Fielding conceived of his novel's form as an ideological rebuke to Jacobitism, it is striking to consider that Fielding in *Tom Jones* did attempt what no novelist before had ever attempted. He wove into his work an actual, ongoing political and historical event—the Jacobite Rebellion of 1745. One could argue that French romancers had included historical battles and political feuds as a backdrop to their tales. However, Fielding is unique in using an event contemporary to the writing of the work, an event that informs the work, and that seems to have been included for explicitly ideological purposes. Further, Fielding does not merely tack on the rebellion as a vague event occurring in the background, but he keys his own novel to the events with a then unheard of degree of accuracy. It has even been suggested that one can coordinate Tom Jones's actions with the day-by-day activities of the invading Bonnie Prince Charles. In fact, F. Homes Dudden, in his biography of Fielding, has been able to date all of the key plot events in *Tom Jones* from November 24, 1745 when Tom leaves Allworthy's estate until December 31, 1745 when Tom and Sophia are married. Although Dudden's dates can be disputed, it is remarkable that Fielding decided to set his plot in any way parallel to the historical events of the rebellion. Fielding even went so far as to place the full moon on the appropriate date.*
Although this full moon is also the subject of critical controversy, it is remarkable that Fielding would have attempted to make his

---

* Fredson Bowers points out that the full moon which Fielding had described as occurring on the morning of February 30, 1745 had actually set five hours earlier and could not have illuminated Mrs. Water's escape. See below for a tentative solution to this problem.

narrative conform to minute details of reality. Indeed, Fielding's readers took note of this innovation in narrative.[13]

Why should Fielding have taken such pains to coordinate fiction to reality? Why have the full moon fall on the correct night? Why have Tom Jones run into the King's soldiers marching against the rebels precisely after the Duke of Cumberland was appointed Commander of Forces on November 23, so that the reader could date the event as late November or more precisely, if we believe that Fielding placed the full moon on the correct night, November 23 (VII, xi)? And why later have the news that the rebels had given Cumberland the slip and had gotten a day's march toward London—a detail that allows readers to date the event around December 6? Fielding himself reported this rumor in the *True Patriot* on December 10. One could argue that he was simply trying to make his work more "realistic," but such an argument is fraught with all kinds of self-fulfilling and retrospective problems, as I have argued (Chapter 1). Rather, I would say, Fielding seems to have kept his alliance with the news/novels discourse in the sense of making his work a journalistic and ideological commentary on the public world. Although Fielding dissociates himself from the more overt side of journalism, his reportorial functions are still fulfilled through fiction. Fielding was clearly interested in keeping a record of the significant ideological events of his time. The *Champion*, the *True Patriot*, and the *Jacobite Journal* all served this function—but so did *Tom Jones*.

The very fact that so many characters in *Tom Jones* take strong stands on the issue of Jacobitism is itself an unusual if not unique innovation in novels at this time. Squire Western, Partridge, and the landlord of the inn at Upton all support the rebellion, while Tom, Mrs. Western, Squire Allworthy, Sophia, and the Man of the Hill are Hanoverians like Fielding who oppose the rebellion. Never before had the reader's point of view in a novel been so directly linked to particular characters' politics. While Swift may have ridiculed political stances in *Gulliver's Travels*, to have done so without the express and exclusive aim of satire is unique to

Fielding. Readers of *Tom Jones* were subject to a new kind of political manipulation by virtue of the fact that so many admirable characters were Hanoverians and so many foolish ones were Jacobites, although to be fair to Fielding, Mrs. Western can be said to do little for the King's cause.

The integrity of the rebellion as a formal part of *Tom Jones* is also unique. The idea of a rebellion fits in structurally with the general themes of the work—themes that I can only suggest here. Tom's defiance of Allworthy, along with Sophia's resistance to her father, are a kind of rebellion against the authority of the kingdom and parallel the rebellion of Bonnie Prince Charles—although in the case of Tom and Sophia the rebellion is ultimately proven to be just because it conforms to human nature and eventually satisfies tradition and authority. Allworthy's mistaken judgment against Tom and the insinuations made by Blifil to gain Allworthy's favor signal that something is wrong in the orderly succession of land, property, and law from one generation to the next. The Tory reverence for rules of tradition, order, and community based on the just rule of the all-worthy Allworthy are overturned. The mayhem that results is the novelistic analogue to Fielding's view of the Jacobites' threat of disorder. In his essay *History of the Present Rebellion*—the journalistic counterpart of *Tom Jones*, also written during the rebellion—Fielding calls on every man to "leave at present the calling which he pursues" and "enure" himself to arms because *"His All is at stake . . .* your religion, my countrymen, your laws, your liberties, your lives, the safety of your wives and children; *the whole* is in danger. . . ."[14] Fielding's view of the Jacobite rebellion as a total destruction of the moral and political order must have led him to include this world-historical event in his novel. The extent of his vision of destruction can be seen in the *True Patriot*, also written during this time, when Fielding fantasizes about the world that might result if the rebels managed to capture London—Protestants are being roasted on the streets, young women are being raped, habeas corpus is repealed, the law courts are travestied, abbey lands are restored, liberty of the press abolished, and Fielding himself is brought to trial and executed.[15] For Fielding, the rebels embodied the total destruction of society, tradition, and order, and as such the rebellion enters the world of *Tom Jones* as a premonition, a report, and an analysis of the greater disruption that the lesser events of the plot threaten for the microcosm. The happy resolution of the novel, the pastoral solution to the political upheaval, restores and reestablishes the sacred and logical rule of Allworthy, now subsumed and incorporated into the reign of Tom, who is not only the morally correct heir to Allworthy's estate but the genetic one as well. The novel thus justifies ideology, and ideology informs the literary solution of the plot in a way that was certainly unique at this point in the history of the novel.

There is another sense in which the inclusion of the rebellion is a mark of the news/novels discourse. It has been suggested that Fielding did not originally intend to include the rebellion in his work but that he inserted the event at the last moment because it was happening just when he was writing book six.[16] This argument is supported by the fact that the first mention of the uprising occurs in book seven when a group of soldiers enters the inn a Hambrook at the same time Tom was there. Fielding writes that

> the reader may perceive (a circumstance which we have not thought necessary to communicate before) that this was the very time when the late rebellion was at the highest; and indeed the Banditti were now marched in England, intending, as it was thought to fight the King's forces, and to attempt pushing forward to the metropolis. (VII, xi)

This sounds like an attempt to patch up the fact that Fielding had just been struck by the idea of including the current uprising into the ongoing work. Such an innovation, as we have seen, had been prepared for in an overdetermined way. What Fielding might have been doing, in effect, was to improvise on the capacities of the median past tense. By writing about the rebellion as it occurred, he was accomplishing in a different way very much what Richardson had attempted when he created a form that would allow language to embody actions and events as they happened in "reality." Fielding's use of reportage is merely a variation on Richardson's use of spontaneous writing. The fact that Fielding makes no reference in *Tom Jones* to the rebellion or the events preceding it until book seven, as Battestin points out (except for one oblique mention of the trial of the Jacobite lords—II, vi), indicates the way in which Fielding permitted reportage to take over from fiction-making. Battestin concludes that Fielding, in revising the novel, failed to correct inconsistencies in the time scheme created by his abrupt decision to include the rebellion in his work.[17] Therefore, when Fielding leaps from a sultry June day in book five to the winter of the rebellion in book seven after only three weeks of plot-time, we are probably observing his hasty jump to include the rebellion rather than his making a simple error in plotting the story.

If this hypothesis is correct, it is distinctly possible that Fielding was actually writing *Tom Jones* synchronically with the daily or weekly news of the rebellion. Such a technique would be remarkable since writers had never before so carefully interlarded ongoing, current events with the plot of a fictional work. Fielding merely had to read his newspaper or talk with his neighbors to stock up on plot events for that day's writing.* The intersection of news and novels here seems intimate and quite different from the kinds of ambivalence noted in reactions to earlier works. That

---

* This thesis of the ongoing rebellion would help explain how Fielding placed the moon on the correct night but at the incorrect time. Bowers sees this inaccuracy as proof that Fielding did not attempt to sequence the plot events to coincide with calendar time since if he had consulted an almanac he would not have said that the full moon was shining when it had obviously set five hours earlier. Such a conclusion seems to be splitting hairs a bit. Fielding may well have consulted an almanac and not thought that canny critics 200 years hence would have minded a slight difference in time. But according to my thesis Fielding may have well been writing that chapter just as the full moon had risen. By looking out his window he might confirm that there was a full moon that night (or, for the sake of expanding the argument, he might have remembered that there was a full moon a week or a month earlier), and he might have included that fact in his work. Fielding, like most writers, might not have taken the care to wake up at 1:00 A.M. to see whether or not the moon had set. In fact, he may not have cared terribly much, certainly not as much as Professor Bowers does, about this matter. No doubt, he was not expecting such a future rigorous follow-up to what may have been for him an engaging and significant whim.

is, paradoxically, by virtue of the admission of fictionality, Fielding can now incorporate news without really causing ambivalence in the reader. In effect, a broader notion of factual fictions had arrived.

One could say that Fielding was writing a kind of news in his novel. He was after all possibly witnessing the events of the day and fashioning them into plot elements, simultaneously recording these same events in the *True Patriot*, *A Serious Address to the People of Great Britain*, *A Calm Address to All Parties*, and later in *A History of the Late Rebellion*. The journalistic element is made all the stronger by virtue of Fielding's continued use of the immediacy of the rebellion. For example, in the Man-of-the-Hill section of *Tom Jones*, Tom says to the hermit that the rebellion is "now actually raging in the very heart of the kingdom" (VIII, xiv). Of course, given the narrative frame, this statement is obviously true. But given our understanding that Fielding was indeed writing "to the moment," as Richardson would have said, Tom's words take on a new significance. The fact that Fielding changed this paragraph in the third edition to read: "'I promise you, Sir,' says Jones, 'all these facts, and more, I have read in history; but I will tell you a fact which is not yet recorded, and of which I suppose you are ignorant. There is actually now a rebellion on foot in this kingdom. . . .'"[18] Fielding's emphasis on a "fact not yet recorded" is worthy of note. While both versions just quoted emphasize the kind of immediacy characteristic of the news/novels discourse and the median past tense, the revision conveys Fielding's pleasure, we may imagine, in happening upon the idea of having a novel convey a report that might scoop the daily paper. Indeed, given our hypothesis, Fielding might have been recording events at the time of his original composition of *Tom Jones* that were unrecorded elsewhere.

Actually, one of Fielding's motivations for being so journalistic in this section of the novel could have been his desire to correct the mistaken accounts of other newspapers. As he later wrote in his *History of the Late Rebellion*:

> Whosoever recollects the accounts which the newspapers gave us of the first landing of the Pretender, must remember with what in-

certainty they spoke of a few men being landed in the west of
Scotland . . . every subsequent account actually contradicting the
former, so that few, except the most credulous, gave any belief to
it, imagining it was rather a story devised by some persons for
particular purposes which need not be mentioned.[19]

Fielding claims to have taken the "utmost pains to procure the best
intelligence" in his own version of events.[20] His interest in correcting earlier texts, in insisting on veracity, and so on, strikes a
familiar note.

   Fielding's motives in including news in the novel form seem
to have been journalistic in origin. There are also other vestiges of
the news/novels discourse in Fielding's work that were apparent
to his readers. One was the previously unheard of custom of using
chapters and chapter headings in a narrative of this sort. The innovation of this now routine practice seems to have been an atavistic
device borrowed from newspaper format. The heading of a chapter
in *Tom Jones* that reads "A Warning Not to Rely Too Much Upon
Prosperity" does not sound very different from a ballad headline
such as "A Warning For All Desperate Women."[21] That the head-
lining of chapters must have come from the practice of journalism
was noticed by at least one contemporary reader of Fielding who
wrote:

> . . . Mr. Fielding had another intention besides making the world
> laugh in the lines prefixed to each portion of his history. Permit me
> therefore . . . to banish from all histories above the rank of those
> printed in Blackfriars [i.e., newspapers, ballads, and pamphlets] and
> sold at the small price of one penny, to tell us—as how Thomas
> Hickathrift carried a stack of corn. Or—Thomas Thumb was swal-
> lowed by a cow, in a title longer than the chapter itself.[22]

The reference to ballads in this quotation is obvious, and the implication is that Fielding borrowed the use of titles from the news/
novels discourse. In fact, the idea of having a narrator who comments on each book in the work—another Fielding innovation—
seems to derive from the practices of the editor of the weekly
newspaper or essay whose job it was to report the news and com-

ment on it, but who also became a character within the work. Fielding's narrator in *Tom Jones* is unique for the time in a novel but not in the newspapers. He is a virtual character introjected into the body of the work much as Isaac Bickerstaff was introjected into the *Spectator* or as Fielding himself was in his own newspapers.

While I am not arguing that works like *Tom Jones* are merely permutations on newspapers, I think it is essential to see how much of the news/novels discourse has been retained, despite Fielding's assertion that his work is entirely different from a newspaper—as it indeed is. From this view, we can see how Fielding's open admission of his work's fictionality leads him to an entirely other form of factuality. Fiction seems to open a door to direct commentary on the world in a way that was unavailable to previous narrators and novelists.

Ironically, Fielding's new species of narration was perceived by readers as being in some sense too journalistic to be considered a novel, despite the extraordinary fact that the work was acknowledged to be a fiction by the author. This general view of Fielding was grounds for praise as well as blame. Allan Ramsay, on the praising side, wrote that "the more the reader is acquainted with nature, the more he is deceived into a belief of its being true; and is with difficulty recalled from that belief by the author's confession from time to time of its being all a fiction."[23] The unusual idea to Ramsay is that Fielding continually reminds the reader that the work is not fact, a practice which strikes Ramsay as odd since the representation is too much like nature to be fabricated. Dr. John Hill observed that Fielding was unique in creating a "new road of entertainment" by relating "occurrences, like those of real life."[24] Thus, in some sense, Fielding's new species of writing is new in its reportorial, journalistic quality.

However, it was precisely this quality that made Samuel Richardson and others like him irate. Richardson claimed that Fielding's works were too verisimilitudinous and therefore not artistic enough. Fielding was charged with copying too directly from life without the intervening grace of invention. Richardson wrote of

Joseph Andrews that the characters were merely taken from experience, and that "Parson Young sat for Fielding's Parson Adams, a man he knew, and only made a little more absurd than he is known to be." Richardson continues:

> In his *Tom Jones*, his hero is made a natural child, because his own first wife was such. Tom Jones is Fielding, himself, hardened in some places, softened in others. His Lady Bellaston is an infamous woman of his former acquaintance. His Sophia is again his first wife. Booth, in his last piece, again himself; Amelia, even to her noselessness, is again his first wife. His brawls, his jarrs, his gaols, his spunging-houses, are all drawn from what he has seen and known.[25]

What particularly galls Richardson here is that Fielding had the bad taste to take the substance of his novels from life. Despite the inaccuracies and caviling on the part of Richardson, the sanction against drawing material from what Richardson sneeringly refers to as "what he has seen and known" is quite fascinating. Richardson would decisively separate news from novels, confining one to the realm of experience and the other to the world of artistic imagination. While this point is by no means new or shocking, its context in the fact/fiction, news/novels problem is illuminating.

Richardson was not alone in his criticism of Fielding. Lady Henrietta Luxborough wrote in 1748 that the adventures in *Tom Jones* are filled with "personages but too like those one meets with in the world."[26] And to confirm this oddity, Captain Lewis Thomas wrote that in *Tom Jones* Fielding "has drawn a portrait of my friend Mrs. Whitfield at the Bell in Gloucester such as painters commonly draw."[27] Even Dr. Johnson noted in the *Rambler* that writers like Fielding are "engaged in portraits of which every one knows the original, and can therefore detect any deviation from exactness of resemblence [and are therefore] . . . in danger from every common reader."[28] The commonplace notion for us that a good writer draws from his own life and makes a portrait of that observation is here seen as not only an anomaly but a defect. One notices again and again criticism of writers for being portrait painters, as if verisimilitude itself in narrative bore too much of an association, by now, with the craftsman rather than the artist. And, as Johnson points out, the writer who draws from life stands in danger of being found to be inaccurate or inept by readers who may compare the original with the artifact. Thus the factual fiction, the novel separated from the journalistic matrix, is seen not only as an innovation, but as a deviation. The picture of life is too reportorial without actually being reportorial. Fielding is not only a journalist *manqué*, he is a writer *manqué*; he fits neither category given the eighteenth-century-narrative worldview.

One could of course say that much of Richardson's criticism and that of his circle derived from the prudish objection to scenes of overt sexuality and general "low" living. I would argue, however, that the real objection to Fielding's novels is to the overt depiction of ordinary life in a reportorial way. The fact that Aaron Hill's daughters, who frequently corresponded with Richardson, found *Tom Jones* to be not really shocking at all (they wrote that the work "*seems* wantoner than it was meant to be"), points to lack of universal condemnation for the work's sexuality.[29] However, as we have seen, the brunt of contemporary reaction to *Tom Jones* seems to have been against the idea that novels could or should be factual, commenting on and representing the real world, yet being overtly fictional at the same time. England seems to have been only half-ready for such an innovation, and Fielding himself was never widely considered to be a great writer for this reason. His novels, *Tom Jones* aside, were not exceptionally well-received, and even *Tom Jones* received harsh criticism. *Amelia* was almost universally panned and parodied, her noselessness being the butt of many jokes for years to come. The *Voyage to Lisbon* was treated gingerly with the respect that the posthumous work of a well-known man might deserve. But on the whole, one might say that factual fictions were regarded much more suspiciously than works which openly claimed to be true or works that were pure fantasy.

There is in Fielding's work a profound ease with the category of pure fiction. Fielding intrudes his authorial being into the nar-

rative, displays his craft, and comments on his own artistic creations. In so doing, he is demonstrating the finality of the separation
between fact and fiction, between news and novels. But, at the
same time, he—like Defoe and Richardson—holds on to various
essentials of the news/novels discourse. While abandoning the overt
simulacrum theory, Fielding retains an essential doubleness by
having the fiction he writes become in some respects analogous to
journalism. The inclusion of the rebellion permits fiction to ap-
proximate the daily reportorial account of "lived" experience. So,
by virtue of abandoning such devices as authorial disavowal and
the "found" document, Fielding can shift his median past tense
much closer to contemporary reality. In this sense, he was indeed
founder, or cofounder, of a new species of writing—a form that
was far more capable of producing and promulgating ideology because it at once had the theoretical freedom to report as well as
invent. Fielding was a novelist, then, not because he made up
stories (or even longish stories), not because of his attention to
realism, not because his audience was middle class—Fielding was
a novelist because he had hit upon a way of writing about the world
in a manner that exploited the novelistic limits of fact and fiction,
news and novels, reportage and invention. In the disjunction and
dialectic between these apparent contraries rests the foundation for
the power of the novel in society and in the bourgeois imagination.

CHAPTER XII

Conclusion: Ideology and the Novel

IN SUMMARY, IT can be said that novels are framed works (even if they seem apparently unframed) whose attitude toward fact and fiction is constitutively ambivalent. The frame, context, and prestructure serve to place the narrative in a complex attitude toward "lived" experience—whether or not novels openly claim they are true, disavow particular authorship, or act as pseudo-allegories. Verisimilitudinous writing or techniques of creating a pseudoreal textuality increase this complexity. In this sense, the novel is about reality and at the same time is not about reality; the novel is a factual fiction which is both factual and factitious. It is a report on the world and an invention that parodies that report. This double stance toward experience can be traced in part to the predisposition of the news/novels discourse to comment on and report on the world by virtue of its connection with journalism. It is through the reportorial function that the novel arrived in its privileged position of observation and commentary. The distinguishing characteristics of embodiment, recentness, the median past tense, seriality, continuity, reduction of cognitive space, voyeurism, collapsing of subject and object—all were made possible by the intervention of typography and by the legacy of the news/novels discourse, and the novel retains this microtechnology of the matricial discourse in its structure. This legacy of the news/novels discourse is a complex blessing, carrying with it a constitutive ambivalence toward fact and fiction, an inability, as it were, to strongly mark a sense of difference. Ambivalence is the foundation for the double or reflexive nature of the novelistic discourse. This ambivalence is a precondition for the simulacrum theory which both denies the novel's true nature and its mode of production by substituting a false explanation for the novel's existence.

The novel's fictionality is a ploy to mask the genuine ideological, reportorial, commentative function of the novel. Defoe, Richardson, and Fielding were all more or less aware of this problem—that the novel talks about the world in way that is both inventive as well as cognitive and referential—and had to apologize for, defend, and complain about this state of affairs. Each of these writers was writing from within the limits of the same discourse, yet each had to invent a terminology and a rationalization to explain and define these unique narratives. The particular problem these authors faced was how to justify a new relationship between language, text, and "lived" experience. As we have seen, the fact/fiction problem seems to have been struck in particularly bold relief during the Early Modern period in a way that would have been unheard of in earlier cultural epochs. It is hard to imagine Plato, Aristotle, Augustine, or Rabelais spending much time puzzling over the fact that a tale was both true and false (although to Plato's credit this is an issue in an entirely different way for the rulers of the *Republic*). But during the Early Modern Period, narrative suddenly becomes problematic in ways I have shown. Novels—whether they claim to be found documents, edited texts, or invented stories—now have a more profound and complex relation to "lived" experience that changed the character of prose fiction.

This deeper relation is problematic and overdetermined, as I have tried to show, and is characterized by a confusing double function. To borrow some terms from Marxian criticism, we might say that novels seem to fulfill the contradictory functions of writing from both an ideological and a scientific position at the same time. I am using "scientific" here in the broad sense of *wissenschaft*—systematic knowledge or organized learning linked to theory—as opposed to "ideology" which is theory separated from knowledge,

the opposite of science. The following definition by Louis Althusser
might be of some help:

> Ideology is the "lived" relation between men and their world, or a
> reflected form of this unconscious relation, for instance, a "philos-
> ophy," etc. It is distinguished from a science not by its falsity, for
> it can be coherent and logical (for instance, theology), but by the
> fact that the practico-social predominates in it over the theoretical,
> over knowledge. Historically, it precedes the science that is pro-
> duced by making an epistemological break with it, but it survives
> alongside science as an essential element of every social formation,
> including a socialist and even a communist society.[1]

In saying that the novel is written from a scientific and ideological
position at the same time, what I mean is that the reportorial or
cognitive function of the news/novels discourse is overlaid or pre-
dominated by the ideological function. This is not to say that
ideology is opposed to cognition, but rather as Terry Eagleton has
written, the nature of ideology is such that "the cognitive structure
of an ideological discourse is subordinated to its emotive structure."[2] The novel originates from just such a subordination in which
the factual discourse, the reporting, the comment on "lived" experience is disguised, channeled, and directed into an imaginative,
emotive, practico-social structure. Now this fact in and of itself is
hardly profound, but given the previous assumption, it is possible
to say that novels operate on a formal level much in the same way
as does ideology.

    One might pause here for a moment to flesh out the concept
of ideology, as I am using it, before further applying it to literary
forms. The word "ideology," it should come as no great surprise,
is also a term of ambiguous complexity.[3] The word first appeared
in English in 1796 as a translation of the French *idéologie* coined by
the rationalist philosopher Destutt de Tracy to describe a systematic
study of the mind or a science of ideas such as those of Locke or
Condillac and to distinguish it from the older metaphysical or ide-
alist sense. Destutt's taxonomy placed ideology under the larger
category of zoology. Napoleon used the word in its more modern

sense of "impractical theory" or "abstract illusion." He was attacking proponents of democracy when he wrote:

> It is to the doctrine of the ideologues—to this diffuse metaphysics,
> which in a contrived manner seeks to find the primary causes and
> on this foundation would erect the legislation of people's ideas,
> instead of adapting the laws to a knowledge of the human heart and
> of the lessons of history—to which one must attribute all the mis-
> fortunes which have befallen our beautiful France.[4]

This derogatory sense of ideology was turned against not democracy but German idealism by Marx and Engels in *The German
Ideology* (1845–1847). The ruling ideas of the age, they wrote, "are
nothing more than the ideal expression of dominant material relationships, the dominant relationships grasped as ideas."[5] In his
book on Feuerbach, Engels called ideology an "occupation with
thoughts as . . . independent entities, developing independently
and subject only to their own laws."[6] If only people would realize
that material conditions determine ideas then ideology would come
to an end. In a letter to Mehring in 1893, Engels wrote that

> ideology is a process accomplished by the so-called thinker con-
> sciously indeed but with a false consciousness. The real motives
> impelling him remain unknown to him, otherwise it would not be
> an ideological process of thought [that] derives both its form and its
> content from pure thought, either his own or his predecessors.[7]

In this sense, ideology is false thought or consciousness, but as
Raymond Williams points out, ideology is used in at least three
different and occasionally overlapping ways:

1. It is a system of beliefs characteristic of a particular group or
   class.
2. It is a system of illusory beliefs—false ideas or false consciousness—which can be contrasted with true or scientific knowledge.
3. It is the general process of the production of meanings and ideas.

This historical ambiguity of the term came to be further confused
by the adoption within left critical circles of semiological terms to
describe ideology (a by no means certain term itself). Louis Alt-

husser initiated this approach by calling ideology "a system of representations" that constitutes and symbolizes the " 'lived' relation between men and their world."[8] In doing this Althusser is brokering a shotgun marriage between the previously feuding discourses of Marxism and structuralism by imputing a semiological foundation to help explain social formations. Such marriages tend to be uneasy ones and much remains to discuss about the success or failure of the arrangement. However, to return to Althusser's theory, ideology is seen as a mask concealing the real relation between people by investing it in the "imaginary relation, a relation that *expresses a will* (conservative, conformist, reformist, or revolutionary), a hope or a nostalgia rather than describing a reality."[9] Terry Eagleton and Pierre Macherey, among others, have followed Althusser's lead in ascribing a largely linguistic or semiological function to ideology. Eagleton, certainly the more penetrating and less obscure of the two critics, has called ideology a kind of "discursive closure" which embodies "the class-struggle at the level of signifying practice."[10] For Macherey, ideology is also a discursive closure; it is

> enclosed, finite, but it mistakenly proclaims itself to be unlimited (having an answer for everything) within its limits. . . . These abiding limits, which are both permanent and permanently latent, are the source of that dissonance which structures all ideology: the dissonance between its explicit openness and its implicit closure.[11]

These semiological approaches to Marxist theory have been helpful in laying bare some of the processes inherent in cognitive practices, but finally suffer from a lack of grounding in history. Not one of the critics I have quoted has tried to explain and describe historically, materially, with documentation the development of the process of ideology which they have described so minutely from an abstract viewpoint. I mention this state of affairs not merely to signal my own predispositions, but to point to a partial explanation not only of the historical basis of ideology but also to the ideological nature of the novel.

Here we can return to the idea that novels seem to embody

within their structure the same processes inherent in ideology. This is not to say that novels *are* ideology or are reducible to manifestations of ideology, as Eagleton asserts when he writes that "the closest analogue we have to ideology is nothing less than literary fiction," or that narrative is "the very form of the ideological."[12] Nor do we have to see novels as mechanistically described as a "production of ideology"[13] since there are certainly other less abstract forces that produce novels, including novelists, reading public, literary conventions, and printers. Indeed, to say that novels are the production of ideology is to fall into a kind of osmotic fallacy—since we have no particular description accompanying such a statement that would tell us of the microtechniques that lead from the discursive closure of ideology to the particular story of an English castaway or of a servant girl with a sexually active master. I am not disagreeing with the idea that novels and ideology seem to work in similar ways by masking "science" (or factuality) with the emotive or practico-social ideological function (and here we might read "fictionality"), but I am saying that there must be material explanations for this congruence that go beyond theory.

It should come as no great shock if I suggest at this point that both ideology and fiction share this structural congruence because they share a similar origin—that is, both can be said to originate with the journalistic news/novels discourse. In support of this notion, I would like to return to the idea, discussed in chapter 4, that ideology itself began with the beginnings of a regularly occurring press. My point is that it was only with the development of a means for assembling a mass consciousness and a mass-signifying system that ideology could arise in the way we know it today. As Alvin Gouldner explains, ideologies are "defined as symbol systems generated by, and intelligible to, persons whose relationship to everyday life is mediated by their reading—of newspapers, journals, or books—and by the developing concept of 'news'."[14] People could be assembled into a modern, ideologically-bound group only when they became perceivers and readers of a mass-signifying system so that their consciousness of events became contextualized. Thus events and happenings could transcend the particular and become the highly ideologized and value-laden entity called "news."

Of course, one could argue that ideologies have existed as lo..g as societies themselves have existed—that ideology is no more a form of consciousness that requires typography than does the folk tale. Why make literacy a precondition for ideology? Christianity, for example, is an ideological formation that antedates the Early Modern period. To all of these arguments I would say that the ideology I am discussing is qualitatively a different thing from enforced religion or ritualized social practices. Christianity seems to be a quite different type of social formation than laissez-faire politics, bourgeois idealism, or romanticism. Because people in the fifteenth century shared certain beliefs does not mean that these amounted to an ideology of the same type and power as that shared by the middle classes in nineteenth-century England. It is, however, fair to say that one of the salient characteristics of modern ideology is that it appears to be invisible, as it were, without a hierarchical set of enforcers, without an origin, appearing merely as common sense, or more appropriately merely as "thought." Such a state of affairs was not the case with the hierarchical, juridical, legislative role of the Catholic church, whose edicts and beliefs were handed down from above, from a clear source of power and authority. I should add, too, that ideology requires literacy not so much because it is necessary for all members of a culture to read the news and learn what is "really" happening in the world, but merely because without literacy there cannot be an information-distributing system that can galvanize large groups of people— people independent, that is, of totalitarian or feudal control—over a long period of time. The oral/aural information system is of use only in limited political cataclysms, but for the formation of large political parties and mass-signifying systems, literacy—at least among a sector of the population—seems a necessary precondition.

In following the assumption, then, that the social formation of ideology arose alongside the social formation of the news/novels discourse, one can move to the consideration that novels share with ideology similar cognitive processes as well as similar origins. The historical reasons for this interpenetration should now be obvious— indeed it has been the burden of this book to demonstrate this similarity. That is, fiction shares in the processes of ideology be- cause it arose historically from the same discourse as ideology. Once this has been established, certain of the more abstract dis- cussions of ideology can be given a material ground in the history of the novel.

For example, the notion that ideology is both true and false, both imaginary and real, is a central area of concern to the critics referred to in this study. As Althusser puts it: "Ideology, then, is the expression of the relation between men and their 'world,' that is, the (overdetermined) unity of the real relation and the imaginary relation between them and their real conditions of existence."[15] For Althusser, ideology is the fusion of the real and the imaginary that creates "lived" experience. Ideology contextualizes and naturalizes experience by mediating it through a mass-signifying system that exists, in part, to make those who are exploited appear bereft of an explanation for their real conditions. Eagleton, however, disa- grees with Althusser's notion that ideology constitutes a false or imaginary view of reality, and says that ideology is "not to be reduced to miscognition, but is to be seen as signifying a set of practical relations with the real. . . ."[16] Ideology is not a set of ideas, according to this view, but a form of practice—an active set of social relations and significations—and as such cannot be imag- inary or false since only theories can be incorrect, not "lived" re- lations. Raymond Williams tends to agree with Eagleton, saying: "There has been a convenient, dogmatic retention at some levels, of ideology as 'false consciousness'." This has often prevented the more specific analysis of operative distinctions of "true" and "false" consciousness at the practical level, which is always that of social relationships, and the part played in these relationships by "con- ceptions, thoughts, ideas."[17]

While such a disagreement may seem to constitute no less than the splitting of one of Marx's many hairs, the nature of the discussion is significant if only because it repeats in slightly different terms the eighteenth century's controversy over the novel—that these works were both true and false, factual and fictional. This problem arises because both ideology and the novel employ double or reflexive processes. While Eagleton and Althusser are hardly latter-day Defoes and Gildons arguing over the capacity of fictional language to be able to secure within its verisimilitudinous net the actual nature of truth, the same epistemological difficulties face all the parties concerned. As Eagleton and Althusser are more or less aware, ideology is so effective precisely because it eliminates the possibility of talking about fact and fiction as such. Ideology is "a complex encodement of certain 'lived' relations to the real which may be neither verified nor falsified. . . ."[8] Within an ideological structure there is no possibility of contradiction since ideologies operate by eliminating the terms for discussing contradiction. Without laboring the point, one sees that ideologies cannot be said to be imaginary or real, any more than one can say that novels are imaginary or real. The nature of both these phenomena is to exploit and obscure these dichotomies. Thus, the argument over the novel and the argument over ideology are more or less identical because these are similar, historically related enterprises.[19]

Another aspect of ideology much discussed in abstract terms can be illuminated by the history of the novel. Althusser and Eagleton both assert that ideology works by "naturalizing its signs"[20] to appear apparently free, universal, and self-generating. Althusser notes that when, for example, during the eighteenth century, bourgeois idealism began its hegemony as an ideological formation, the effectiveness of its power was that it universalized the particular qualities of equality, freedom, and reason. The middle class "gave its own demands the form of universality since it hoped thereby to enroll at its side, by their education to this end, the very men it would liberate only for their exploitation."[21] One might like to divorce the rather mechanistic and utilitarian approach here from its more important message that ideology works to appear as a natural, unprejudiced truth—a common-sense notion (to use

Thomas Paine's term here appropriately)—while it actually constitutes a motivated, class-oriented rationalization. In this sense, ideologies work by repressing "the mechanism of their generation."[22]

We can understand this function in material terms by recalling that novels operate theoretically under the same assumptions. Early novelists, as we recall, were trying in effect to naturalize the nature of their production by claiming that it was life they were producing and not some simulacrum of it. That is, authorial disavowal, insistence on verity, false editorship, and so on were the material grounds for the later nineteenth-century assumption that literature is a more penetrating depiction of life than life. Novels work, then, by denying their own mode of production as mere fictions and also by creating the illusion through the use of the median past tense and mimetic techniques that the text is somehow close to—if not completely—reality. The frame of the novel insists the work is true while the technique of the novel aims at creating the illusion of reality. In effect realism, as a technique, is a function of the ideological mode since it allows the work to refer to some "reality" that is cut off from the actual historical continuum. In this sense, the text is "cut loose from any particular real conditions to which those representations refer."[23] Thus, like ideology, the novel's point of reference is not history, from which the novel stands autonomously aloof, but the social process of signification, the world of "lived" as opposed to "actual" experience. In this view, realism can be seen as a function of ideology and ideology can be seen as embodying the same processes as are used in the realistic novel. This congruence, again, is not the result of theoretical symmetry but derives from the historical conjuncture of news/novels and ideology. The news/novels discourse, as we have seen, had always naturalized its signs, always appeared to be self-generating, and always denied its mode of production. Ballads, criminal tales, news reports, and novels all insisted on a connection to reality which was finally illusory since the reality they reported was largely one they were in the process of creating. That is to say, the reality of the news/novels discourse was an ideological one in that it was created as a system of signification rather than as a virtual reproduction of material reality.

Once it has been said that the novel and ideology share these characteristics, one must add that the novel and ideology have quite different functions in actual society. As I have shown, novels came about partly as a complex reaction to the laws, statutes, and legal decisions that were aimed at restricting journalism. Therefore, novels may be seen as tangible forms of highly encoded and profoundly reflexive defenses against authority and power. The novel embodies the contradictory qualities of rebellion and conformity, of criminality and morality, of criticism and approbation of society, and so on. Ideology, on the other hand, serves to eliminate contradictions of this nature. It functions as a counterforce to criticism, rebellion, analysis, and knowledge. Ideology is the rationalization that serves to justify the power and authority of the state, of culture, and of the actual relations between people. This difference is crucial. Novels cannot simply be equated with ideology, but rather must be seen as both embodying and counteracting ideology. That is, novels require the existence of the shared signifying system of ideology to "make sense" to readers, but they oppose that system in order to reveal sense. This seemingly impossible double function has allowed the novel to have a continuing force in the history of discourse.

As I have attempted to show, the novel has come into being as a form of defense against censorship, power, and authority. At the same time, it is equally possible to say that novels also support and establish those power relations, as those who have read Gramsci will of course know. This contradiction is not an easy one to escape; to understand the ambivalence of the novelistic experience is by no means to be freed from that ambivalence. In a sense, the modern reader is no freer from the inherent confusion in any factual fiction than a reader of *Robinson Crusoe* would have been. The modern reader is merely more acculturated to the habit of accepting the ground rules of ambivalence as part of a discourse of reading that has made the contradictions of factual fictions so self-evident as to be commonplace, hence invisible. As a culture, we might better understand the way we tell each other stories, report news events, or record histories if we stepped back to consider that lost moment in history when these powerful contradictions were reconciled. In that lost moment, one might observe the unity of news, novels, ideology, history, fact, and fiction. One might also observe the transformation of that unity through the meticulous workings of lived experience and the vagaries of material life. The history of the subsequent division of fact and fiction, news and novel, the movement from untroubled fictionality of Cervantes to the inherent ambivalence of Defoe, Richardson, Fielding, and later writers, the objectification of factual news and the factualizing of fictionality— all can tell us much about the way we now consider the social and political role of narrative, journalism, and history. Thus, the moment of ambivalence can lead to a moment of reconciliation, but only through the most complicated dialectical wanderings from windmills to desert islands, from country to city, from revolt to resolution, and back again.

NOTES

Introduction: TOWARD A METHODOLOGY OF BEGINNINGS

1. Michel Foucault, *The Archaeology of Knowledge* (New York: Harper and Row, 1972), p. 12.

2. Edward W. Said, *Beginnings: Intention and Method* (New York: Basic Books, 1975), p. 5. For the purposes of this discussion, I will not be using Said's distinction between origins and beginnings. While such a distinction has been extremely useful in other contexts, I am following the road of simplicity here by using the terms interchangeably.

3. Robert Scholes and Robert Kellogg, *The Nature of Narrative* (New York: Oxford University Press, 1966), pp. 4, 17.

4. *Ibid.*, p. 10.

5. Ernest A. Baker, *The History of the English Novel* (London: H. F. G. Witherby, 1924), pp. 12, 49.

6. *Ibid.* p. 12.

7. English Showalter, *The Evolution of the French Novel, 1641–1782* (Princeton: Princeton University Press, 1972), pp. 5–6.

8. Foucault, *Archaeology*, p. 22.

9. Ian Watt, *The Rise of the Novel* (Berkeley: University of California Press, 1964), pp. 24, 15.

10. Philip Stevick, ed., *The Theory of the Novel* (New York: Macmillan, 1967), p. 2.

11. "Questions à Michel Foucault sur la géographie," *Hérodote* (January–March 1976), p. 85.

12. Edward W. Said, "The Problem of Textuality: Two Exemplary Positions," *Critical Inquiry* (Summer 1978), 4(4):709.

13. Northrop Frye, *The Secular Scripture* (Cambridge: Harvard University Press, 1976), p. 17.

I. FRAME, CONTEXT, PRESTRUCTURE

1. Miguel de Cervantes Saavedra, *The Adventures of Don Quixote*, trans. J. M. Cohen (Baltimore, Md.: Penguin, 1950), p. 26.

2. Daniel Defoe, *Roxana, The Fortunate Mistress* (London: Oxford University Press, 1964), p. 1.

3. Cervantes, *Don Quixote*, p. 27.

4. Maximillian Novak's book, *Defoe and the Nature of Man* (Oxford: Oxford University Press, 1963), and G. A. Starr's *Defoe and Casuistry* (Princeton: Princeton University Press, 1971) have done much to place Defoe in the role of consistent moral critic—Novak maintains that Defoe's works reflect Pufendorf's ideas about natural philosophy; Starr feels that Defoe

created novelistic situations which conflicted with conventional morality and that therefore such situations had to be scrutinized and judged with the aid of casuistry's hair-splitting apparatus. Both books, along with J. Paul Hunter's *The Reluctant Pilgrim* (Baltimore, Md.: Johns Hopkins University Press, 1966), stress the extent to which Defoe had intended his works to be morally edifying to his readers.

5. Cervantes, *Don Quixote*, p. 36.

6. *Ibid.*, p. 147.

7. *Ibid.*, p. 139.

8. *Ibid.*, p. 490.

9. Michel Foucault, *The Order of Things* (New York: Pantheon, 1970), p. 48.

10. Defoe, *Roxana*, pp. 167–71.

11. Erving Goffman, *Frame Analysis: An Essay on the Organization of Experience* (New York: Harper and Row, 1974).

12. Yet another modern reader could be added to this list—one who believes that, although "fictional," Defoe's works may be based on historical or autobiographical material. Professor Sutherland in his *Daniel Defoe: A Critical Study* (Boston: Houghton Mifflin, 1971) suggests many biographical details which he asserts may have transmuted themselves into Defoe's various plots. Such a reader as Sutherland is somewhat analogous to the hypothetical eighteenth-century reader who is uncertain whether or not the novel he is reading is true. Farther along the continuum is Arthur Gold who maintains that *Robinson Crusoe* is the disguised biography of Defoe (see "The Origins of *Robinson Crusoe* in the Mind of Daniel Defoe," [Ph.D. diss., Harvard University, 1964]). Gold's stance is a problem since he acknowledges that Crusoe is a fictional creation but believes that his story represents a true account. One might say that such a reading is prenovelistic since it harks back to an allegorical reading.

13. I will discuss this subject in greater detail in chapter 10. See also the first chapter of John Richetti's *Defoe's Narratives: Situations and Structures* (Oxford: Oxford University Press, 1975).

II. THE ROMANCE: LIMINALITY AND INFLUENCE

1. Such books would include Arthur Heiserman, *The Novel Before the Novel* (Chicago: University of Chicago Press, 1977); Ernest A. Baker, *The History of the English Novel* (London: H. F. G. Witherby, 1924); J. J. Juserand, *The English Novel in the Time of Shakespeare* (New York: AMS Press, 1965), among others.

2. In the past few years there has been an attempt to broaden the range of reference to previous nonfictional forebears of the novel. See Susan Staves, "Studies in Eighteenth-Century Fiction, 1979," *Philological Quarterly* (1980), 59:465–514. See also J. Paul Hunter's works, "Biography and the Novel," *Modern Language Studies*, 9:68–84 and "The Insistent 'I,'" *Novel*, 13:19–37.

3. Mlle. de Scudéry, *Ibrahim ou L'illustre Bassa* (Paris: Antoine de Sommaville, 1661), unnumbered preface: ". . . premiers maistres . . . ces fameux romans de l'antiquité." The translation given here is my own. I will provide both English and French for all quotations I have translated.

4. Arped Steiner, "A French Poetics of the Novel in 1683," *Romanic Review*, 30:233.

5. Northrop Frye, *Anatomy of Criticism* (Princeton: Princeton University Press, 1957).

6. Although the illustration is taken from a work entitled *Nouvelles galantes, comiques, et tragiques* by Donneau de Visé (Paris: Claude Barbin, 1669), the audience for these *nouvelles* was not radically different from the readers of romance at this early stage. In fact, one could argue that by and large *nouvelle* had not taken on its later meaning in 1669.

7. George May, "L'histoire a-t-elle engendré le roman?" *Revue d'Histoire Litteraire de la France* (June 1955), 55(2):157.

8. Mlle. de Scudéry, *Ibrahim ou L'illustre Bassa*, trans. Henry Cogen (1674), reprinted in *Augustan Reprint Society* (Los Angeles: William Andrews Clark Memorial Library, 1952), vol. 32.

9. Mlle. de Scudéry, *Artamene ou Le Grand Cyrus* (Paris: August Courbe, 1664), un-numbered preface: "Le heros que vous allez voir n'est pas un de ces heros imaginaires, qui ne sont que le beau songe d'un homme esueillé, et qui n'ont jamais esté en l'estre des choses. C'est un hero effectif: mais un des plus grande dont l'Histoire conserve le souvenir. . . . "

10. Charlotte Morgan, *The Rise of the Novel of Manners: A Study of English Prose Fiction Between 1600 and 1740* (New York: Columbia University Press, 1911), p. 38.

11. Sterling Haig, *Madame de Lafayette* (New York: Twayne, 1970), p. 60.

12. Charles Sorel, *De la connaissance des bons livres* (Paris: André Pralard, 1671), p. 172: "N'est-ce pas comme si l'on comparoit un singe à un homme? Quelle satisfaction pouvons-nous esperer d'un recit, qui n'estant que pure fiction, ne nous donne point d'asseurance que les évenemens qu'il rapporte s'accordent aux loix de la prudence souveraine? Et quel profit y a-t-il d'aprendre des choses qui ne doivent jamais estre alleguées pour authorité, ny pour exemple, puisque ce qui est imaginaire et controuvé à plaisir n'a aucune force dans le discours."

13. Scudéry, *Artamene*, unnumbered preface: " . . . une fable ne soit pas une histoire, et qu'il suffice à celuy qui la compose de s'attacher au vray-semblable, sans s'attacher toujours au vray."

14. *Ibid.*: " . . . tantost l'un et tantost l'autre, selon qu'ils ont esté plus ou moins propres à mon dessein . . . j'ay dit ce qu'ils n'ont dit ny l'un ny l'autre: car apres tout, c'est une fable que je compose, et non pas une histoire que j'écris."

15. George May has shown how a shift in the definition and methodology of history in the late seventeenth century led to a concomitant shift in the development of the novel in his article "L'histoire a-t-elle engendré le roman?"

16. Mlle. de Scudéry, *Clélie*, cited in Haig, *Madame de Lafayette*, pp. 134–35.

17. Moses Ratner, *Theory and Criticism of the Novel in France From L'Astrée to 1750* (New York: Russell and Russell, 1938), p. 12n.

18. Donneau de Visé, *Les nouvelles galantes, comiques, et tragiques* (Paris: Claude Barbin, 1669), unnumbered preface. (Translation by Sterling Haig in *Madame de Lafayette*, p. 64.)

19. As I will demonstrate in the ensuing chapters, writers in England also saw them-selves as making a break with past literary forms. For reasons of organization, however, this chapter will only focus on the French phenomenon and may therefore seem incomplete.

20. English Showalter, *The Evolution of the French Novel, 1641–1782* (Princeton: Princeton University Press), p. 36.

21. Jean Regnould de Segrais, *Les Nouvelles Francoise*, quoted in Showalter, *Evolution*

of the French Novel, p. 23: " . . . nous avons entrepris de raconter les choses comme elles sont, et non pas comme elles doivent être: Qu'au reste il me semble que c'est la différence qu'il y a entre le roman et la nouvelle; que le roman écrit ces choses comme la bienseance le veut, et à la maniere du poète; mais que la nouvelle doit un peu davantage tenir de l'histoire, et s'attacher plûtôt à donner les images des choses comme d'ordinaire nous les voyons arriver, que comme notre imagination se les figures."

22. May, "L'histoire a-t-elle engendré le roman?" pp. 168–69.

23. Charles Sorel, *De la connoissance des bons livres* (Paris: André Pralard, 1671), pp. 165–66; *idem, La bibliothèque Francoise* (Paris: Compaigne des Libraires du Palais, 1664), pp. 161–62. " . . . de soulager l'impatience des personnes . . . des choses arrivées depuis peu, autrement il n'y auroit pas de raison de les appeler des Nouvelles?"

24. Scudéry, *Artamene*, unnumbered preface: "Que si cette raison ne satisfait pas pleinement les scrupuleux, ils n'ont qu'à s'imaginer pour se mettre l'espirit en repos, que mon ouvrage est tiré d'un vieux manuscrit Grec d'Egesippe, qui est dans la Bibliotheque Vaticane, si precieux et si rare, qu'il n'a jamais esté imprimé, et ne se sera jamais."

25. Isaac Claude, *Le Comte de Soisson*, cited in Haig, *Madame de Lafayette*, p. 74, and Abbé Terrasson, *Sethos* (Paris, 1667): "Histoire ou vie tirée des monuments anecdotes de l'ancienne Egypt, traduit d'un manuscrit grec."

26. Abbé Prevost, *Le philosophe anglois ou histoire de Monsieur Cleveland* (London: Paul Vaillant, 1778), pp. iii, v: "L'histoire de M. Cleveland m'est venue d'une bonne source. Je la tiens de son fils, qui porte le même nom, et qui vit actuellement à Londres . . . j'ai employé ce que des occupations plus importantes m'ont laissé liberté pour lui donner la forme sous laquelle elle peut paroître aujourdhui."

27. Showalter, *Evolution of the French Novel*, p. 59.

28. Pierre Bayle, *Dictionaire Historique et Critique* (Rotterdam: Renier Leers, 1697). See entry under "Nidhard": " . . . l'on n'ose croire ce qui au fond est croiable. . . . L'on n'a point d'autre voye de discerner ce qui est fiction d'avec les fait veritables, que de savoir par d'autres livres si ce qu'elle narre est vrai."

29. Sorel, *Connoissance des bons livres*, p. 173: " . . . l'action feintes qu'l'on introduire avec les veritable seront soupçonner les autres de mensonge, des mesme qu'ayant trouve quelque piece fausse en des affaires d'importance, tout le reste est revoque en doute."

30. Bayle, *Dictionaire*. See entry under "Nidhard": " . . . ou qu'au moins ils se servent de crochets pour separer l'une de l'autre, la verité et la fausseté."

31. Edme Boursault, *Prince de Condé* (Paris, 1675) cited in Haig, *Madame de Lafayette*, p. 63.

32. Abbé Prevost, *Le Pour et Contre*, 6:340, cited in May, "L'histoire a-t-elle engendré le roman?" p. 162.

33. Bayle, *Dictionaire*. See entry under "Nidhard": "De là vient que l'on s'éloigne autant que l'on peut de l'air romanesque dans les nouveaux Romans."

34. Pierre Daniel Huet, *Traité de l'origine des romans* (Paris, 1670); rpt. Stuttgart: Metzler, 1966).

35. Viviene Mylne, *The Eighteenth-Century French Novel: Technique and Illusion* (Manchester: University of Manchester Press, 1965), p. 24.

36. Sorel, *Bibliothèque Francoise*, p. 159.

37. Madame de Lafayette, *La Princesse de Montpensier* (Paris: Louis Billaine, 1662), un-numbered preface: " . . . des aventures inventées à plaisir."

38. Haig, *Madame de Lafayette*, p. 65.

39. See George May, *Le dilemme du roman au XVIIIe siècle* (Paris: Presse Universitaire de France, 1963).

40. Silas Paul Jones in *A List of French Prose Fiction from 1700 to 1740* (New York: H. W. Wilson, 1939) lists 200 novels written in the first person out of a total of 946.

41. Clara Reeve, *The Progress of Romance* (London, 1785), I:iii.

42. Harold Bloom's view of literary influence as expressed in *The Anxiety of Influence* (New York: Oxford University Press, 1973) and other works suffers from this logic as well, although to the credit of his system Bloom has developed some powerful arguments based on Freudian premises to support his contentions. In general, though, literary historians have by and large based the justification for their assumptions about literary change on shared beliefs, common sense, and unspoken ideological affinities. To my knowledge, there has been no book that has fully developed a convincing and documented theory to account for literary change and the rise of genres.

III. News/Novels: The Undifferentiated Matrix

1. See George May, *Le dilemme du roman au XVIIIe siècle* (Paris: Presse Universitaire de France, 1963), pp. 162–69 for his assessment of the fact that social realism, as he calls it, was developed in the English novel first and only later emerged in the French novel.

2. See a discussion of Glen Gould's adaptation of Beethoven's Fifth Symphony in the Liszt piano transcription, and the peculiar problems inherent in Gould's use of electronic recording as opposed to stage performance in Edward W. Said, "The Text, the World, the Critic," in Josué V. Harari, ed., *Textual Strategies: Perspectives in Post-Structuralist Criticism* (Ithaca, N.Y.: Cornell University Press, 1979), pp. 161–67.

3. Louis Dudek, *Literature and the Press: A History of Printing, Printed Media and Their Relation to Literature* (Toronto: Ryerson, 1960), pp. 19, 296.

4. Hyder Rollins, ed., *A Pepysian Garland: Black Letter Broadside Ballads of the Years 1595–1639* (Cambridge: Harvard University Press, 1971), p. xi.

5. *Ibid.*

6. Vivian De Sola Pinto and Allan Rodway, *The Common Muse: An Anthology of Popular British Ballad Poetry* (London: Chatto and Windus, 1957), p. 17.

7. This can be found in *The Euing Collection of English Ballads* (Glascow: University of Glascow Publications, 1971), p. 179.

8. A. H. Bullen, ed., *The Works of Thomas Middleton* (New York: AMS Press, 1964), 7:154.

9. Hyder Rollins, "The Black-Letter Broadside Ballad," *PMLA* (1919), 34:258. Of course, since ballads were only printed on one page, one could argue that in sheer volume of pages books outweighed ballads. However, the figures themselves still reveal the tremendous distribution and impact of ballads in the general sphere of printed matter.

10. Charles Knight, *The Old Printer and the Modern Press* (London: J. Murray, 1854), p. 253.

11. Rollins, "Black-Letter Ballad," p. 269.

12. Hyder Rollins, "An Analytical Index to the Ballad Entries in the Stationers' Register, 1557–1709," *Studies in Philology* (1924), 21:165; Hyder Rollins, *The Pack of Autolycus* (1927; rpt. Cambridge: Harvard University Press, 1969.) p. 3.

13. William Chappell and J. W. Ebsworth, eds., *Roxburghe Ballads* (Hertford, England: Ballad Society, 1871–1895), 4:605.

14. Rollins, "Black-Letter Ballad," p. 308.

15. *Ibid.*, p. 315.

16. J. Payne Collier, *Broadside Black-Letter Ballads* (London, 1868), p. 138.

17. William Painter, *The Palace of Pleasure* (London: Robert Triphook, 1817), p. viii.

18. J. Payne Collier, ed., *Extracts from the Registers of the Stationers' Company* (London, 1849), 2:19.

19. H. R. Fox Bourne, *English Newspapers: Chapters in the History of Journalism* (New York: Russel and Russel, 1966) 1:2.

20. *Ibid.* See also Joseph Frank, *The Beginnings of the English Newspaper* (Cambridge: Harvard University Press, 1961), p. 3.

21. Edward Arber, *A Transcript of the Registers of the Company of Stationers of London, 1554–1640* (London, 1875), 3:91.

22. Mathais A. Shaaber, *Some Forerunners of the Newspaper in England, 1476–1622* (Philadelphia: University of Pennsylvania Press, 1929), p. 146n.

23. Rollins, *Pack of Autolycus*, p. 22.

24. Collier, *Broadside Ballads*, p. viii.

25. Rollins, "Black-Letter Ballad," p. 263n.

26. Rollins, *Pack of Autolycus*, pp. 145, 86.

27. *Ibid.*, pp. 97–100.

28. Rollins, *A Pepysian Garland*, p. 217.

29. Arber, *Transcript*, 2:663.

30. Rollins, "Black-Letter Ballad," p. 337.

31. Shaaber, *Forerunners of the Newspaper*, p. 144.

32. Rollins, *A Pepysian Garland*, p. 254.

33. *Ibid.*, p. 431.

34. *Ibid.*, p. 287.

35. *Ibid.*, p. 292.

36. Herbert Collman, ed., *Ballads and Broadsides* (Oxford: Oxford University Press, 1912), p. 144.

37. Rollins, *A Pepysian Garland*, p. 317.

38. *The Euing Collection*, p. 78.

39. *Ibid.*, p. 224.

40. Rollins, *A Pepysian Garland*, p. 327.

41. William K. Nelson, *Fact or Fiction: The Dilemma of the Renaissance Storyteller* (Cambridge: Harvard University Press, 1973), pp. 5, 41.

42. Sir Walter Raleigh, *The History of the World*, quoted in Nelson, *Fact or Fiction*, p. 43.

IV. PROSE NEWS 1

3. Sir Philip Sidney, *An Apology for Poetry; or, the Defence of Poetry*, ed. Geoffrey Shepherd (1965; rpt. Manchester, England: Manchester University Press, 1973), p. 110.

44. Aristotle, *On Poetry and Style*, trans. G. M. A. Grube (New York: Bobbs-Merrill, 1958), p. 180.

45. Michel Foucault, *The Order of Things: An Archaeology of the Human Sciences* (New York: Pantheon, 1970), p. 40.

IV. PROSE NEWS: CONTINUITY, SERIALITY, AND IDEOLOGY

1. *The Continuation* (August 21, 1623), no. 44.

2. Ben Jonson, *Works*, ed. C. H. Hereford Percy and Evelyn Simpson (1938; rpt. Oxford: Oxford University Press, Clarendon Press, 1966), 6:325.

3. Abraham Holland, *A Continu'd Just Inquisition of Paper Persecutors* (London, 1625), p. 10.

4. John Fletcher, *The Fair Maid of the Inn*, in Alexander Dyce, ed., *The Works of Beaumont and Fletcher* (London: E. Moxon, 1843–46).

5. Richard Braithewaite, *Whimzies: or a New Cast of Characters* (London, 1631), pp. 15, 20.

6. Joseph Frank, *The Beginnings of the English Newspaper* (Cambridge: Harvard University Press, 1961), p. 277.

7. Frederick S. Siebert, *Freedom of the Press in England, 1476–1776: The Rise and Decline of Government Controls* (Urbana: University of Illinois Press, 1952), p. 191*n*.

8. G. M. Trevelyan, *England Under the Stuarts* (London: Methuen, 1961), p. 163.

9. Samuel Hartlib, *A Description of the Famous Kingdom of Macaria* (London, 1641), p. 1.

10. *Mercurius Britanicus* (November 2–9, 1643).

11. Wilbur Samuel Howell, *Eighteenth-Century British Logic and Rhetoric* (Princeton: Princeton University Press, 1971), p. 385.

12. Perry Miller, "The New England Mind: The Seventeenth Century," in Stanley Fish, ed., *Seventeenth-Century Prose: Modern Essays in Criticism* (New York: Oxford University Press, 1958), pp. 38–39.

13. Christopher Hill, *Reformation to Industrial Revolution* (Middlesex, England: Penguin, 1969), p. 118.

14. Thomas Hobbes, *Leviathan* (New York: Bobbs-Merrill, 1958), p. 4.

15. *Ibid.*, pp. 10, 11.

16. *Ibid.*, p. 49.

17. *Ibid.*, pp. 38–39.

18. Michel Foucault, *The Order of Things: An Archaeology of the Human Sciences* (New York: Patheon, 1970), p. 79.

19. Alvin Gouldner, *The Dialectic of Ideology and Technology: The Origins, Grammar, and Future of Ideology* (New York: Seabury, 1976), p. 91.

20. *Ibid.*, p. 104. For a further discussion of ideology and news/novels see chapter 12.

V. THE LAW AND THE PRESS: SPLITTING THE DISCOURSE

1. Michel Foucault's entire opus is devoted to this idea. Perhaps the more recent and best exposition of these theories can be found in his book *Discipline and Punish: The Birth of the Prison* (New York: Pantheon, 1977).

2. Lawrence Hanson, *Government and the Press, 1695–1763* (London: Oxford University Press, 1936), p. 33; Francis Holt, *The Law of Libel* (New York, 1818), pp. 92–163.

3. 3 Edward I, c. 34.

4. Richard II, Stat. 1, c. 5 (1387).

5. Frederick S. Siebert, *Freedom of the Press in England 1476–1776: The Rise and Decline of Government Controls* (Urbana: University of Illinois Press, 1952), p. 118.

6. James Godwin, ed., *Six Ballads With Burdens* (London: Percy Society, 1844), p. 4.

7. Siebert, *Freedom of the Press*, p. 25; Marjorie Plant, *The English Booktrade: An Economic History of the Making and Sale of Books* (London: Allen and Unwin, 1965), p. 28.

8. 14 and 15 Henry VIII, c. 2.

9. Edward Arber, *Transcripts of the Stationers' Company, 1554–1640* (London, 1875), 1:xxviii, xxxi; Plant, *English Booktrade*, p. 126.

10. Siebert, *Freedom of the Press*, p. 119.

11. E. Neville Williams, *The Eighteenth-Century Constitution 1688–1815* (Cambridge: Cambridge University Press, 1960), pp. 397, 400.

12. *Ibid.*, p. 399.

13. Siebert, *Freedom of the Press*, p. 296.

14. Williams, *The Eighteenth-Century Constitution*, p. 402.

15. Hanson, *Government and the Press*, p. 33.

16. Williams, *The Eighteenth-Century Constitution*, p. 402.

17. Siebert, *Freedom of the Press*, p. 365.

18. Leonard Levy, *Legacy of Suppression: Freedom of Speech and Press in Early American History* (Cambridge, Harvard University Press, 1960), p. 11n.

19. Jonathan Swift, *Political Tracts, 1713–1719*, ed. Herbert Davis and Irvin Ehrenpreis (Oxford: Basil Blackwell, 1953), pp. 14–15.

20. Holt, *Law of Libel*, p. 243.

21. Sir Richard Steele, *Mr. Steele's Apology for Himself and His Writings Occasioned by his Expulsion from the House of Commons* (London, 1714), p. 54.

22. 10 Anne, c. 12.

23. Siebert, *Freedom of the Press*, p. 315.

24. 11 George I, c. 8.

25. R. M. Wiles, *Serial Publication in England Before 1700* (Cambridge: Cambridge University Press, 1937), pp. 36–37.

26. *London Magazine* (May 1733), p. 262.

27. *Ibid.*, p. 263.

28. Siebert, *Freedom of the Press*, p. 347.

29. *Complete Statutes of England* (London: Butterworth and Company, 1930) 13:510.

30. Robert Mayo, *The English Novel in the Magazines, 1740–1815* (Evanston: University of Illinois Press, 1962), p. 62.

VI. THEORIES OF FICTION IN EARLY ENGLISH NOVELS

1. See John Richetti, *Popular Fiction Before Richardson* (New York: Oxford University Press, 1969), one of the few books on the subject.

2. Charlotte Morgan, *The Rise of the Novel of Manners: A Study of English Prose Fiction Between 1600 and 1740* (New York: Columbia University Press, 1911), p. 2.

3. Ian Watt, *The Rise of the Novel* (Berkeley: University of California Press, 1964), p. 42.

4. Samuel Johnson, *Works*, ed. W. J. Bate and Albrecht B. Strauss (New Haven: Yale University Press, 1969), 3:19.

5. Morgan, *Rise of the Novel of Manners*, p. 35.

6. William Congreve, *Incognita: or Love and Duty Reconciled. A Novel*, ed. H. F. B. Brett-Smith (Oxford: Basil Blackwell, 1922), pp. 5–6.

7. Lord Chesterfield, *Letters* (London, 1800), 1:197–98.

8. Clara Reeve, *The Progress of Romance* (London, 1785), 1:iii.

9. John Bunyan, *The Pilgrim's Progress From This World to That Which Is to Come* (New York: Grosset and Dunlap, n.d.), p. 12.

10. *Ibid.*

11. John Bunyan, *The Life and Death of Mr. Badman and The Holy War*, ed. John Brown (Cambridge: Cambridge University Press, 1905), p. 3.

12. *Ibid.*, p. 6.

13. *Ibid.*, p. 74.

14. *Ibid.*, p. 21.

15. *Ibid.*, p. 23.

16. Aphra Behn, *The Works of Aphra Behn*, ed. Montague Summers (1915; rpt. New York: Phaeton Press, 1967), p. 129. Ernest Bernbaum has proven that Behn is indeed lying about the truth of her encounters with Oroonoko in an article entitled "Mrs. Behn's Biography a Fiction," *PMLA* (1913), 28:432–53.

17. Behn, *Works*, p. 129.

18. *Ibid.*, p. 70.

19. *Ibid.*, p. 131.

20. *Ibid.*, p. 132.

21. *Ibid.*, p. 206.

22. *Ibid.*, p. 182.

23. Mary de la Rivière Manley, *The Novels of Mary de la Rivière Manley*, ed. Patricia Koster (Gainesville: Scholar's Facsimile and Reprint, 1971), unnumbered preface to *The Secret History of Queen Zarah*.

24. *Ibid.*

25. *Ibid.*

26. *Ibid.*

27. John Dennis, *The Critical Works of John Dennis*, ed. Edward N. Hooker (Baltimore, Md.: Johns Hopkins University Press, 1943), 2:6.

28. *Ibid.*

29. Manley, *Novels*, p. 109. The identification key is on p. 263.

30. *Ibid.*, pp. 123–24.

31. *Ibid.*, p. 568.

32. Eliza Haywood, *Love in Excess: or the Fatal Inquiry*, in *Secret Histories* (London: R. Ware, 1742), 1:84.

33. Manley, *Novels*, p. 89.

34. Criticisms of Manley appear in *Tatler*, nos. 6, 35, 63, 92, 177, 229, and 243.

35. Manley, *Novels*, 529.

36. See David Foxon, *Libertine Literature in England 1660–1745* (New Hyde Park, N.Y.: University Books, 1966).

37. See John Berger, *Ways of Seeing* (Harmondsworth, England: Penquin, 1972), for an excellent description of the pornographization of art.

38. Manley, *Novels*, unnumbered preface to *Queen Zarah*.

39. Dennis, *Works*, 2:49.

40. See Lawrence Stone, *The Family, Sex, and Marriage in England 1500–1800* (New York: Harper and Row, 1977), chapter 7.

41. Manley, *Novels*, 2:740.

42. *Ibid.*, p. 744.

43. *Ibid.*, pp. 745, 746.

44. *Ibid.*, p. 855.

45. *Ibid.*, p. 856.

46. *Ibid.*, p. 765.

47. *Ibid.*, pp. 845, 849, 853.

48. Eliza Haywood, *The Injured Husband or the Mistaken Resentment: A Novel* in *Secret Histories*, 1:2.

49. Mary Davys, *The Accomplished Rake or Modern Fine Gentleman* in *Four Before Richardson: Selected English Novels 1720–1727*, ed. W. H. McBurney (Lincoln: University of Nebraska Press, 1963), p. 235.

50. *Ibid.*

VII. CRIMINALITY AND THE DOUBLE DISCOURSE

1. James Arbuckle, *A Collection of Letters and Essays . . . Lately Published in the Dublin Journal* (London, 1729), 1:71, in Alan D. McKillop, *The Early Masters of English Fiction* (Lawrence: University of Kansas Press, 1956), p. 44.

2. Richard Head, *The English Rogue* (Boston: New Frontiers, 1961), p. 8.

3. Daniel Defoe, *Moll Flanders* (New York: Norton, 1973), p. 3.

4. *Poor Robin's Memoires with his Life, Travels and Adventures* (London, 1677), 1:1.

5. *The Magazine of Magazines* (April 1751), 1:286–89, in *Henry Fielding: The Critical Heritage*, ed. Ronald Paulson and Thomas Lockwood (New York: Barnes and Noble, 1969), pp. 270–71.

6. Pat Rogers, *Grub Street: Studies in Subculture* (London: Methuen, 1972), p. 291.

7. Spiro Peterson, ed., *The Counterfeit Lady Unveiled and Other Criminal Fiction of Seventeenth-Century England* (Garden City, N. Y.: Archer, 1961), p. 98; John Dunton, *The Night*

Walker: or Evening Rambles in Search After Lewd Women (October 1696) no. 1; John Bunyan, *The Life and Death of Mr. Badman and The Holy War* (Cambridge: Cambridge University Press, 1905), p. 23.

8. Daniel Defoe, *The Fortunate Mistress or . . . Roxana* (Oxford: Blackwell, publishers to the Shakespeare head press of Stratford-upon-Avon, 1928), p. x.

9. Defoe, *Moll Flanders*, pp. 214, 226.

10. Michel Foucault, *Discipline and Punish: The Birth of the Prison* (New York: Pantheon, 1977), p. 43.

11. Béat de Muralt, *Letters Describing the Character and Customs of the English and French Nations* (London: Thomas Edlin, 1726), p. 43.

12. Daniel Defoe, *An Essay Upon Literature or an Inquiry into the Antiquity and Original Letters* (London: Thomas Bowles, 1726), p. 108.

13. Christopher Hill, *The World Turned Upside Down: Radical Ideas During the English Revolution* (New York: Viking, 1972), pp. 32–45.

14. Douglas Hay, Peter Linebaugh, John G. Rule, E. P. Thompson, and Cal Winslow, *Albion's Fatal Tree: Crime and Society in Eighteenth-Century England* (New York: Pantheon, 1975) p. 13.

15. *Ibid.*, p. 14.

16. Foucault, *Discipline and Punish*, p. 67.

17. Hay et al., *Albion's Fatal Tree*, p. 82.

18. *Ibid.*, pp. 102–3.

19. *Ibid.*, pp. 109–10, 112.

20. Hill, *The World Turned Upside Down*, p. 31.

21. *Ibid.*, p. 58.

22. Defoe, *Roxana*, p. x.

23. Defoe, *Moll Flanders*, p. 3.

24. Peterson, *Counterfeit Lady*, pp. 21, 85.

25. Pierre Daniel Huet, *Traité de l'origine des romans* (Paris, 1670; rpt. Stuttgart: Metzler, 1966), p. 87. English translation from Huet, *History of Romances, An Inquiry Into Their Origin . . .*, trans. Stephen Lewis (London, 1715), in Ioan Williams, ed., *Novel and Romance: 1700–1800* (London: Routledge and Kegan Paul, 1970), p. 50.

26. John Bunyan, *Pilgrim's Progress* (New York: Grosset and Dunlap, n.d.), p. 12.

27. Charles Gildon, *An Epistle to Daniel Defoe* (London, 1719; rpt. London: J. M. Dent, 1928), p. 128.

28. *The Newgate Calendar or Malefactors' Bloody Register* (New York: Putnam, 1932), p. 20.

VIII. THE LANGUAGE OF PRINT: EMBODIMENT, LEGITIMATION, SIGNIFICATION

1. Louis Dudek, *Literature and the Press: A History of Printing, Printed Media and Their Relation to Literature* (Toronto, Canada: Ryerson, 1960), p. 18.

2. From a facsimile of the First Folio reprinted in William Shakespeare, *The Complete Works*, ed. Alfred Harbage (London: Penguin, 1969), p. xvii.

3. *Ibid.*

4. Joseph Glanville, *Scepsis Scientifica* (London: Henry Eversden, 1665), unnumbered preface.

5. Michel Foucault, *The Archaeology of Knowledge* (New York: Harper and Row, 1972), p. 130.

6. Jacob Burkhardt, *The Civilization of the Renaissance in Italy* (New York: Harper and Row, 1958), 1:196–204.

7. The modern concept of the library has a considerable prehistory. See for example Raymond Irwin, *The Origins of the English Library* (London: G. Allen, 1958).

8. Raymond Irwin, *The Heritage of the English Library* (New York: Hafner, 1964), p. 226; see also Burnett Hillman Streeter, *The Chained Library: A Survey of Four Centuries in the Evolution of the English Library* (London: Macmillan, 1931), p. xiii ff.

9. Streeter, *The Chained Library*, p. xiii.

10. Irwin, *Origins of the English Library*, p. 138.

11. Paul Kaufman, *Libraries and Their Users: Collected Papers in Library History* (London: Library Association, 1969), p. 19.

12. *Ibid.*

13. See Paul Delaney, *British Autobiography in the Seventeenth Century* (London: Routledge and Kegan Paul, 1969).

14. Madame de Motteville, *Memoirs for the History of Anne of Austria* (London, 1725), 1:xiii–xiv.

15. The Houghton Library at Harvard University has a collection of some of these seventeenth-century *Proceedings.*

16. Raymond Williams, *Marxism and Literature* (Oxford: Oxford University Press, 1977), pp. 154–64.

17. Christopher Hill, *The World Turned Upside Down: Radical Ideas During the English Revolution* (New York: Viking, 1972), pp. 32–45.

18. Spiro Peterson, ed., *The Counterfeit Lady Unveiled and Other Criminal Fiction of Seventeenth-Century England* (Garden City, N.Y.: Archer, 1961), p. 14.

19. *Ibid.*, pp. 21–22.

20. *Ibid.*, p. 85.

21. *Ibid.*, p. 98.

22. *Ibid.*, p. 23.

23. Richard Steele, *The Lucubrations of Isaac Bickerstaff, Esq.* (London, 1713), 2:254.

24. Donald Stauffer, *The Art of Biography in Eighteenth-Century England* (Princeton: Princeton University Press, 1941) p. 208n.

25. James Boswell, *Life of Johnson* (New York: Oxford University Press, 1965), p. 84.

26. Jonathan Swift, *Gulliver's Travels*, ed. Herbert Davis (Oxford: Blackwell, publishers to the Shakespeare Head press of Stratford-upon-Avon, 1941) pp. 175–76.

27. Jonathan Swift, *A Tale of a Tub*, ed. Herbert Davis (Oxford: Blackwell, publishers to the Shakespeare head press of Stratford-upon-Avon, 1939), p. 24.

28. Lawrence Hanson, *Government and the Press, 1695–1763* (London: Oxford University Press, 1936), p. 25.

29. Tobias Smollett, *Roderick Random*, ed. G. H. Maynadier (New York: Spraul, 1902), p. xxxvii.

IX. Daniel Defoe: Lies as Truth

1. Daniel Defoe, *The Life and Strange Surprising Adventures of Robinson Crusoe* (Oxford: Blackwell, publishers to the Shakespeare head press of Stratford-upon-Avon, 1928), p. ix. Defoe's theory of fact and fiction is treated to a certain extent in the appendix, "Fiction and Mendacity," to G. A. Starr, *Defoe and Casuistry* (Princeton: Princeton University Press, 1971), although the conclusions Professor Starr draws are quite different from my own. Maximillian Novak explores some aspects of Defoe's theory of fiction in his article "Defoe's Theory of Fiction," *Studies in Philology* (1964), vol. 61.

2. Charles Gildon, *An Epistle to Daniel Defoe* (London, 1719; rpt. London: J. M. Dent, 1923).

3. Defoe, *Robinson Crusoe*, p. x.

4. Daniel Defoe, *Serious Reflections . . . of Robinson Crusoe*, ed. G. H. Maynadier (New York: G. D. Sproul, 1903), p. 107.

5. Gildon, *Epistle*, pp. 113–14.

6. Defoe, *Serious Reflections*, p. ix.

7. *Ibid.*

8. Even if, as J. Paul Hunter suggests in his book *The Reluctant Pilgrim* (Baltimore, Md.: Johns Hopkins University Press, 1966), Defoe was relying on a readership which would perceive his book as a series of spiritual emblems, the claim made here seems a little too all-encompassing. Arthur Gold goes even further than Hunter and takes Defoe at his word. Gold sees *Robinson Crusoe* as actually being an autobiographical allegory. He pursues this exegetical chimera and comes up with such ingenious correspondences as the equation of Crusoe's shipwreck with Defoe's bankruptcy. ("The Origins of Robinson Crusoe in the Mind of Daniel Defoe," [Ph.D. diss., Harvard University, 1964, p. 54].)

9. Defoe, *Serious Reflections*, pp. ix–x, xii, xiii.

10. *Ibid.*, p. x.

11. *Ibid.*, p. xi.

12. *Ibid.*, p. xii.

13. *Ibid.*

14. Daniel Defoe, *Colonel Jack* (Oxford: Blackwell, publishers to the Shakespeare head press of Stratford-upon-Avon, 1927), p. viii.

15. Daniel Defoe, *Moll Flanders* (Oxford: Blackwell, publishers to the Shakespeare head press of Stratford-upon-Avon, 1928), p. viii.

16. *Ibid.*

17. *Ibid.*

18. *Ibid.*, pp. ix–xi.

19. Daniel Defoe, *The Fortunate Mistress or . . . Roxana* (Oxford: Blackwell, publishers to the Shakespeare head press of Stratford-upon-Avon, 1928), p. ix.

20. *Ibid.*

21. *Ibid.*, p. x.

22. James Sutherland attempts to link Defoe's biographical history with his literary— and particularly journalistic—writings in *Daniel Defoe: A Critical Study* (Boston: Houghton Mifflin, 1971).

23. James Sutherland, *Defoe* (Boston: Houghton Mifflin, 1937), p. 86.

24. Sutherland, *Defoe*, pp. 106, 113*n*.

25. George Harris Healey, ed., *The Letters of Daniel Defoe* (Oxford: Oxford University Press, Clarendon Press, 1955), p. 69.

26. Sutherland, *Defoe*, p. 148.

27. Healey, *Letters of Defoe*, p. 211. Aphra Behn was also a secret agent for the government—and one wonders if there is any further relationship in this context between novel-writing and political disguise. See Ernst Bernbaum, "Mrs. Behn's Biography a Fiction," *PMLA* (1913) 28:443.

28. Arthur Secord, ed., *Defoe's Review* (New York: Columbia University Press, 1938) 4:377.

29. Healey, *Letters of Defoe*, pp. 379–80.

30. Maximillian Novak in *Defoe and the Nature of Man* (London: Oxford Univerity Press, 1963), J. Paul Hunter in *The Reluctant Pilgrim*, and G. A. Starr in *Defoe and Casuistry* have all tried to justify Defoe's seeming lack of moral consistency by placing him within various traditions—natural law, emblematic narratives, and casuistical practice. However, none of these scholars has fully dealt with the idea that even if Defoe had held consistently to the precepts of any of these traditions, he still was immoral to the extent that he sought to find emblems, rules of natural law, or moral instruction in what are essentially fabricated stories. Morals and lessons drawn from such fictions cannot claim to tell us about God's world—only about Defoe's.

31. Daniel Defoe, *An Appeal to Honor and Justice* (London, 1715), in George Chalmers, *The Life of Daniel Defoe* (Oxford: D. A. Talboys, 1841), p. 41.

32. Healey, *Letters of Defoe*, p. 441.

33. Sutherland, *Defoe*, p. 201.

34. Healey, *Letters of Defoe*, p. 446.

35. *Ibid.*, pp. 451–52.

36. *Ibid.*, p. 452.

37. Sutherland, *Defoe*, p. 216.

38. Defoe, *Serious Reflections*, p. 108.

X. SAMUEL RICHARDSON: DISAVOWAL AND SPONTANEITY

1. Samuel Richardson, *Selected Letters*, ed. John Carroll (Oxford: Oxford University Press, Clarendon Press, 1964), p. 85.

2. Daniel Defoe, *Serious Reflections . . . of Robinson Crusoe*, ed. G. H. Maynadier (New York: Sproul, 1903), p. 106.

3. Wayne C. Booth, *The Rhetoric of Fiction* (Chicago: University of Chicago Press, 1966), pp. 155–59.

4. Ian Watt, *The Rise of the Novel* (Berkeley: University of California Press, 1964), pp. 31–34.

5. Henry Fielding, *Joseph Andrews*, ed. Martin Battestin (Boston: Houghton Mifflin, 1961), p. 7.

6. Harry Levin, *The Gates of Horn* (New York: Oxford University Press, 1963), p. 51.

7. *Pamela Censured* (Los Angeles: William Andrew Clark Memorial Library, 1976), p. 7.

8. Samuel Richardson, *Introduction to Pamela*, ed. Sheridan W. Baker, Jr. (Los Angeles: William Andrew Clark Memorial Library, 1954), p. xiii.

9. Richardson, *Selected Letters*, p. 223.

10. *Pamela Censured*, p. ix.

11. *Daily Advertiser*, May 11, 1741; *London Evening Post*, May 14–16, 1741, in Alan Dugald McKillop, *Samuel Richardson: Printer and Novelist* (Hamden, Conn.: Shoe String Press, 1960), p. 54.

12. *London Daily Mail and General Advertiser*, May 30, 1741.

13. *Pamela's Conduct in High Life* (London: Ward and Chandler, 1741), pp. iii–iv.

14. Richardson, *Selected Letters*, p. 173n.

15. *Ibid.*, pp. 53, 127.

16. Samuel Richardson, *Clarissa: Preface, Hints of Prefaces and Postscript* (Los Angeles: William Andrew Clark Memorial Library, 1964), p. 368.

17. Richardson, *Selected Letters*, p. 41.

18. Katherine Gee Hornbeak, *The Complete Letter Writer in England, 1568–1800: Smith College Studies in Modern Languages* (April–July 1934) 15:3–4.

19. Richardson, *Clarissa: Preface, Hints of Prefaces*, p. 366.

20. Richardson, *Selected Letters*, p. 41.

21. Richardson, *Clarissa; Preface, Hints of Prefaces*, p. 7.

22. Samuel Richardson, *Clarissa* (Oxford: Blackwell, publishers to the Shakespeare head press of Stratford-upon-Avon, 1930), 5:312.

23. Samuel Richardson, *Sir Charles Grandison* (Oxford: Blackwell, publishers to the Shakespeare head press of Stratford-upon-Avon, 1931), 2:414.

24. Samuel Richardson, *Pamela* (Oxford: Blackwell, publishers of the Shakespeare head press of Stratford-upon-Avon, 1929), 1:242, 243, 251.

25. *Ibid.*, p. 482.

26. *Ibid.*, p. 166.

27. *Ibid.*, p. 83.

28. *Ibid.*, p. 245.

29. Richardson, *Clarissa*, 4:52.

30. Richardson, *Pamela*, p. 144.

31. *Ibid.*, 2:65.

32. Richardson, *Clarissa*, ed. John Burrell (New York: Random House, 1950), p. x.

33. Richardson, *Clarissa*, 7:233.

34. Richardson, *Selected Letters*, p. 77n

35. Richardson, *Clarissa*, 7:73, 7:232–33.

36. *Ibid.*, 7:328.

37. *Ibid.*, 8:87.

38. Richardson, *Clarissa*, 1:29.

39. Lawrence Stone points to the increase in privacy in the eighteenth century in *The Family, Sex, and Marriage in England, 1500–1800* (New York: Harper and Row, 1979); one could speculate that increased privacy created the fantasy need for the opposite—exhibitionism and publicity—which function was answered in part by Richardson's work and the novel in general.

40. *Pamela's Conduct in High Life*, p. xiii.
41. *Ibid.*, p. xv.
42. Richardson, *Selected Letters*, pp. 70–71.
43. *Ibid.*, p. 242.
44. *Ibid.*, pp. 305–6.
45. *Ibid.*, p. 28.
46. Michel Foucault, *The Order of Things* (New York: Pantheon, 1970).
47. Raymond Williams, *Marxism and Literature* (Oxford: Oxford University Press, 1977), pp. 151–64.
48. Ian Watt, *The Rise of the Novel*, pp. 186, 191.
49. McKillop, *Samuel Richardson*, p. 15.

XI. HENRY FIELDING: POLITICS AND FACT

1. *The Daily Gazeteer*, May 7, 1737.
2. *The Gentleman's Magazine* (July 1737), p. 409.
3. F. Holmes Dudden, *Henry Fielding: His Life, Works, and Times* (Oxford: Oxford University Press, Clarendon Press, 1952), p. 327.
4. Arthur Murphy, ed., *The Works of Henry Fielding, esq.* (London: Bickers and Son, 1903), p. 91.
5. Henry Fielding, *Joseph Andrews*, ed. Martin C. Battestin (Oxford: Oxford University Press, Clarendon Press, 1967), p. 3.
6. Henry Fielding, *The History of Tom Jones: A Foundling* (Middletown, Conn.: Wesleyan University Press, 1975), Book II, chapter i. I have used this edition of *Tom Jones* throughout this chapter. Citations of book and chapter number will be indicated after quotations in my text. For example, II, i refers to book two, chapter i.
7. Fielding, *Joseph Andrews*, p. 10.
8. *Ibid.*, p. 40.
9. Ronald Paulson and Thomas Lockwood, eds., *Henry Fielding: The Critical Heritage* (London: Routledge and Kegan Paul, 1969), p. 7.
10. Fielding, *Joseph Andrews*, p. 12.
11. *Ibid.*, p. 3.
12. Dudden seems to have been drawing on F. S. Dickson's articles in *Notes and Queries* (May 30, 1914), 11th ser., vol. 9, and *The Library* (1917), 3:viii and his conclusions are disputed by Fredson Bowers in the Wesleyan *Tom Jones* (p. 435n).
13. Fielding, *Tom Jones*, p. 436n.
14. Peter H. Hemingson, "Fielding and the '45: A Critical Edition of Fielding's Anti-Jacobite Pamphlets," (Ph. D. diss., Columbia University, 1973), p. 274.
15. *The True Patriot*, November 19, 1745; *The True Patriot*, January 7, 1746.
16. Fielding, *Tom Jones*, p. xxxviii. Martin Battestin makes this interpretation in his introduction to the Wesleyan *Tom Jones*.
17. Fielding, *Tom Jones*, p. xxxix.
18. Fielding, *Tom Jones*, p. 1036 (appendix 4).
19. Hemingson, "Fielding and the '45," p. 246.

20. *Ibid.*, p. 241.

21. Hyder Rollins, ed., *A Pepysian Garland: Black Letter Broadside Ballads of the Years 1595–1639* (Cambridge: Harvard University Press, 1971), p. 288.

22. Francis Coventry, *An Essay on the New Species of Writing* (London, 1751; rpt. Los Angeles: William Andrew Clark Memorial Library, 1962), pp. 26–27.

23. Paulson and Lockwood, *Henry Fielding*, p. 361.

24. Dr. John Hill, *The History of a Woman of Quality* (London, 1751), p. 3.

25. Samuel Richardson, *Selected Letters*, ed. John Carroll (Oxford: Oxford University Press, Clarendon Press, 1964), p. 198.

26. Paulson and Lockwood, *Henry Fielding*, p. 160.

27. J. P. Feil, "Fielding's Character of Mrs. Whitefield," *Philological Quarterly* (1960), 39:510.

28. *The Rambler* (March 31, 1750), no. 4.

29. Paulson and Lockwood, *Henry Fielding*, pp. 173–74.

XII. CONCLUSION: IDEOLOGY AND THE NOVEL

1. Louis Althusser, *For Marx* (London: New Left Books, 1977), p. 252.

2. Terry Eagleton, "Ideology, Fiction, Narrative," *Social Text* (1979), 2:64.

3. The following history of ideology relies on Raymond Williams, *Marxism and Literature* (Oxford: Oxford University Press, 1977) and *Keywords* (New York: Oxford University Press, 1976). For a discussion of recent left criticism see Edward W. Said, "Reflections on Recent American 'Left' Literary Criticism," *Boundary 2* (Fall 1979) 8:1.

4. Williams, *Marxism and Literature*, p. 57.

5. *Ibid.*, p. 58.

6. Williams, *Keywords*, p. 127.

7. *Ibid.*

8. Althusser, *For Marx*, pp. 231, 233.

9. *Ibid.*, p. 234.

10. Eagleton, "Ideology, Fiction, Narrative," pp. 70, 79.

11. Pierre Macherey, *A Theory of Literary Production* (London: Routledge and Kegan Paul, 1978), p. 131.

12. Eagleton, "Ideology, Fiction, Narrative," p. 63.

13. Terry Eagleton, *Criticism and Ideology* (London: Verso, 1978), p. 64.

14. Alvin Gouldner, *The Dialectic of Ideology and Technology* (New York: Seabury, 1976), p. 91.

15. Althusser, *For Marx*, pp. 233–34.

16. Eagleton, "Ideology, Fiction, Narrative," p. 63.

17. Williams, *Marxism and Literature*, p. 68.

18. *Ibid.*, p. 65.

19. Pierre Macherey gets caught in the sticky web of fact and fiction as well. In the following quotation, he might be expressing the confusion of an eighteenth-century reader: "Fiction is not *truer* than illusion; indeed, it cannot usurp the place of knowledge. But it can set illusion in motion by penetrating its insufficiency, by transforming our relationship to

ideology. . . . Fiction deceives us in so far as it is feigned; but this is not a primary act of deception, because it is aimed at one even more profound, exposing it, helping to release us from it" (*A Theory of Literary Production*, p. 64).

20. Eagleton, *Criticism and Ideology*, p. 165.
21. Althusser, *For Marx*, p. 234.
22. Eagleton, "Ideology, Fiction, Narrative," p. 64.
23. Eagleton, *Criticism and Ideology*, p. 174.

INDEX

Hill, Christopher, 128
History, 36, 68–69, 143, 196, 198
Hobbes, Thomas, 80–82, 151
Hornbeak, Katherine, 182
Huet, Pierre Daniel, 38, 107, 132
Hunter, J. Paul, 226*n*4, 237*n*8, 238*n*30

Ideology, 8, 77, 83, 145, 197, 202, 213–23; definition of, 214–16

Jacobitism, 202
James I, 72
Johnson, Samuel, 4, 103, 149, 164, 209–10
Jonson, Ben, 74–75
Journalism, 7, 15, 46, 66, 69, 72, 192, 193, 195, 197, 202, 212; and *newes*, 49, 50, 54; and median past tense, 73, 184, 212; and Stamp Act, 96; definition of, 99; and criminality, 134

Kellogg, Robert, 2
Kirkman, Francis, 125, 131, 146–47

La Calprenède, Gautier de Costes de, 27, 30
Lafayette, Comtesse de, 39, 114
Le Sage, Alain René, 103
Licensing Act, 92
Locke, John, 92

Macherey, Pierre, 216, 241*n*19
MacKenzie, Sir George, 103
Manley, Mary de la Rivière, 103, 110–121, 131, 132, 165, 175, 196
Marx, Karl, 215, 219
Mary Tudor, Queen, 90
May, George, 227*n*15
Mayo, Robert, 100
Median past tense, *see* Journalism
Middleton, Thomas, 47
Morgan, Charlotte, 102

Nelson, William, 67, 68
News/novels discourse, 44, 51, 53–56, 58, 61, 66, 67, 70, 74; breakdown of, 152, 197

Newsbooks, *see* Journalism
Newspapers, *see* Journalism
Nouvelle, 27*n*, 33–34, 42, 50, 227*n*6
Novak, Maximillian, 225*n*4, 238*n*30
Novel: definition of, 11, 26, 34, 148, 197–98; and romance, 25, 35, 38, 40; and recentness, 48; as a double or reflexive discourse, 70, 108, 112, 213; theory of, 104–122; simulacrum theory of, 113, 136, 212

Paine, Thomas, 221
Pepys, Samuel, 7, 70
Plain style, 82, 144
Plato, 69, 213
Prestructure, 12, 17, 19, 35, 212
Prevost, Abbé, 35, 37
Printing, 45, 46–48; as guarantor of truth, 55, 138, 140; and the law, 86, 89, 101
Pufendorf, Friedrich, 225*n*40

Raleigh, Sir Walter, 68
Reeve, Clara, 41, 104
Richardson, Samuel, 11, 32, 67, 161, 174–91; *Pamela*, 57, 155, 179–86; and spontaneous writing, 182–83, 190; *Clarissa*, 186–87; assessment of Fielding, 208–10
Roman, 27*n*, 33
Romance, 25, 41, 43, 103

Said, Edward, 1, 9, 103
Scarron, Paul, 34, 39, 103
Scholes, Robert, 2
Scudéry, Madeleine de, 27–32, 35, 43, 113
Selkirk, Alexander, 155
Serial publication, 75
Shakespeare, William, 48, 54, 139–40
Showalter, English, 3, 33
Sidney, Sir Philip, 68–69, 139, 199
Smith, Alexander, 135
Smollett, Tobias, 152
Sorel, Charles, 30, 34, 39, 103
Spectator, 7, 208
Stamp Act, 92, 96
Star Chamber, 91